Security of
BANKS & CASH
in Transit

Editor

R K Sinha

Vitasta

Let Knowledge Spread

Published by
Renu Kaul Verma for
Vitasta Publishing Pvt. Ltd.
2/15, Ansari Road, Daryaganj,
New Delhi - 110 002
info@vitastapublishing.com

ISBN: 978-93-80828-60-2

First Edition 2012
Second Reprint 2023
MRP ₹ 850

Layout and Cover Design by Vitasta Publishing Pvt. Ltd.
Printed by Vits Press, New Delhi

Acknowledgement

I acknowledge the valuable contribution of Ms Jyoti Sinha, Mr Praveen Kumar and Ms Seema Sharma in collecting suitable articles for this book from amongst various papers presented in IISSM annual seminars, workshops and various short term training courses in the past 20 years.

I am thankful to Alka Choudhury for her editorial assistance. Thanks is also due to Ms Ratna Sinha, joint secretary, IISSM for monitoring and administrating this project, on a day-to-day basis. I also acknowledge support of Lt Gen (Retd) Prem Sagar, director general, IISSM and Brig (Retd) S Sreeramulu, deputy director general (Academic Services), IISSM, without whose cooperation completion of this project in record time was not possible.

Editor & Executive Chairman, IISSM

Content

Foreword

In past three decades banking industry has become one of the fastest growing service industries in India. With emergence of ATMs and e-banking, online banking and services like RTGS and multi city cheque book, this industry has really become consumer friendly and available to the masses.

However, with increased facilities, networking and door step banking services, the risk factors in security of banks and cash-in-transit has also tremendously increased and so is the role of a security manager assigned to protect a bank. In today's situation one cannot even imagine of a security manager in banks, who is not computer savvy or unfamiliar with possible threats of frauds and embezzlements or problems of transportation of currency and bullions!

Till 1990, the security of banks was mostly limited to the security of bank branch or regional/tonal office premises and currency chest. Almost all currency chests were guarded by police and para-military forces till recently or even today. Therefore, the role of bank security manager was limited mostly to the security of bank premises, residential colonies and periodical inspections of currency chests as per RBI regulations. Cash transportation from one currency chest to another or currency chest to the bank branches and vice - versa was the entire responsibility of the state armed police force. But, due to liberalisation of economy and also due to increased pressure on police and paramilitary forces, cash-in-transit business has developed in the country as a full fledged business and has grown exponentially. An estimated number of 5000+ cash vans are running on the roads on 24 x 7 basis which are owned by 3rd party private security agencies, whose selection hiring, preparation of SOP, training, inspection and monitoring of the services has also become additional responsibility of the bank security managers. CIT has several threats, not only from organised criminal gangs, extremist and terrorist group, but; also from novice, stray and strange youngsters who are aspirant to become gangsters by trying their luck on a cash van moving on a deserted road.

All these problems, threat and challenges has made the position of security manager of a bank as the most valuable and responsible. Now, require of the banks is of a young active and always vigilant security manager who has to not only to do the strategic planning, recruitment and training, but; also monitoring of ongoing operation on 24 × 7 basis. In the current book, we have included presentation papers on issues related to banks, ATMs and CIT. These papers have been presented in various annual seminars, training programmes and short terms courses organised by IISSM.

With the advent of technology, the way people bank their assets and the role of banks have changed. Various kinds of security instruments are now required to protect a bank and its services. This aspect has been addressed in this book. Shilpan Patel's contributions on fake currency and history of the Indian rupee make for compelling reading. How to detect fake notes is always useful knowledge for not only the bank staff but also for the common man, who becomes the first victim of fake notes.

The American Special Risk group's analysis of what are the top loss risk locations, and how software can alert and at times even prevent loss of cash thefts from ATM machines, too make an interesting reading. The physical vulnerability of the ATM is also often an issue. With telecommunication, the use of banks, transaction volumes, delivery mode of banking services changed dramatically.

However, as John E. Venn points out in his articles on fraud, the basic principle of fraud remains the same. It's the idea of duping the gullible. Technology only changed the way the fraud is perpetrated -like the telephone billing, coin box frauds etc. happened regularly until the technology was changed. Theft of calling cards to computer hacking, all depend on identity thefts.

Prof Renu Mattoo talks about how to motivate people to go that extra mile required to maintain workstation security and transaction security in banks and allied organisations. Katherin Xin talks of the importance of 'safety managers' and their role in maintaining banking and financial security atmospheres. Famous management Guru Sharu Rangnekar talks of how to manage technology and relationships to get managers who perform, without using the traditional "stick and carrot" model of people management.

We have also given elaborate recommendations of suggested readings and listed a number of books at the end of each chapter. I hope the articles in the book and also the suggested readings only make a useful and interesting reading for the banking security professionals, who are desirous to upgrade and update their knowledge and become an expert in security of banks. We propose to revised this book from time to time and bring out second edition of the book in the couple of years depending on the demand of readers. I will be happy and satisfied if this book has helped you in enhancing your knowledge base in any way and to improve your operational efficiency on the ground.

Ravindra Sinha

Editor & Executive Chairman, IISSM

Contributors

Brig (retd) P. N. Rao, VSM

Brig P. N. Rao has 34 years of distinguished service to his credit. He has taken part in 1965 and 1971 wars and served long stints fighting insurgency in the North East and militancy in J&K. He is the recipient of the Vishista Seva Medal. A computer expert, he heads the security of the State Bank of India.

Brig (retd) Ashok Anand

Brig Anand is Head of Security, the Punjab National Bank. He has served in the Indian army for 35 years, and is an expert in Defence studies and Mass Communication.

Shreedhar Behera

Shreedhar Behera is DGM & officer-in-charge of Urban Banks Department in the office of the Reserve Bank of India. The Department has under its jurisdiction 166 urban cooperative banks. Before taking up this assignment, he was faculty-in-charge of one of the RBI training centers and brings long years of experience in the private banking industry.

James Tappin

James Tappin is a professionally qualified multi-discipline consultant and trainer with long experience in the British government as a Royal Marines Officer. His experience includes six years as security advisor and training coordinator for the International Professional Security Association, where he was awarded a fellowship. He is chairman, IPSA south-west region, a council member of the Association of Security Consultants and a member of the Institute of Personnel and Development and the American Society for Industrial Security.

U K Chaubey

U K Chaubey, lifelong an official in public sector steel companies, is a man management expert. He was president of the National Institute of Personnel Management from 1991-93 and has presented many papers on worker-management relationships in national and international fora.

Prof Sharu S Rangnekar

Sharu S Rangnekar is a chemical engineer and has been a visiting faculty at the Tata Institute of Social Sciences and the Management Institutes of the Bombay University. He has been a popular lecturer and writer on management. His books: "In the Wonderland of Indian Manager" and "In the World of Corporate Managers" have become management classics.

Prof Renu Mattoo

Renu Mattoo is an independent trainer-consultant, offering programmes in leadership and confidence building. She also runs a programme on global etiquette. On the faculty of XLRI,, she has been involved in offering a unique programme on personality development, Personality Plus, to companies all over the country.

Shilpan Patel

Shilpan Patel is the chairman and managing director of Arrow Coated Products Ltd. He is an expert on business development and strategic management. In 1989, he started his own venture, the Patel Paper Products, and developed unique products in the Document Security field. His innovations are patented in USA, Europe, South Africa, Australia and India

Lt Gen Prem Sagar (retd)

With 37 years of service in the Indian army, Lt Gen Prem Sagar is the Director General, International Institute of Security and Safety Management (IISSM), New Delhi. Before that, he was Dean, College of Materials Management, responsible for training of officers and other personnel in management, planning, procurement and warehousing.

Katherin Xin

Katherin Xin is research associate, Graduate School of Management University of California, USA.

Richard P Grassic

Richard Grassic is president, Techmark, Security Integration Services, Hanover Mass, USA.

Maj Gen (retd) N Viswanathan

Dr Pramod Damle

Pramod Damle is a mentor & evangelist on info-security governance, risk and compliance and has been balancing IT practice and higher education for over two decades. He helps top rung of Directors/ VPs/ GMs of reputed companies to achieve their info-tech missions by leveraging his consulting, training and education in info security, systems audit, software quality & projects for benefits spanning across multiple projects/ functions/divisions/ locations of clients. He also devotes part of his time as a 'Distinguished Fellow' in the area of info security at the Institute of Development and Research for Banking Technology (IDRBT).

Swaranjit Singh Duggal

S S Duggal has worked in the pharmaceutical, chemical, export, hospital and security industry for over 40 years. At present, he heads the Cash Services of the SIS group and was earlier, was managing director of G4S - Cash Services India Pvt Ltd.

RBI Vision Statement

Reserve Bank of India

Information Technology (IT) has transformed the conduct of businesses in every sector of the economy. Financial sector is one such area where the touch of the IT has completely overhauled the nature and accelerated the pace of business. IT has been instrumental in improved communication and connectivity across all segments/players of this sector as well as in enhancing the quality, efficiency and speed of the delivery of financial services.

The Reserve Bank has played a pivotal role in this process of transformation of the financial sector with the use of IT. As the central bank, the Reserve Bank has strived to create a conducive environment for promoting technological adoption encompassing the financial sector. Moreover, being an important institution in the financial sector, it too has undergone the process of technological change. Finally, the Reserve Bank has endeavoured to streamline technological change in a manner that would help to enhance the inclusiveness of the financial sector.

While technology has become an integral part of conducting and managing business in the financial sector, it can hardly ever be characterised as static. It has evolved over the years and it is important, therefore, that the financial sector too reviews these developments and adapts itself to the same. It is in this context of review and adaptation to technology that information management requires specific attention.

The Department of Information Technology (DIT) of the Reserve Bank was formed in 1995 to exclusively look after the Reserve Bank's requirements in the field of computerisation and modern communications network and undertake advance planning for technology upgradation in the banking sector. Over a period of fifteen years, DIT has satisfactorily fulfilled most of the objectives set to it at the time of formation. It has been instrumental in designing, developing and implementing IT-based systems, which have helped in the discharge of various functions of the Reserve Bank.

During this period, several developments have taken place in the realm of IT and its adoption in the banking sector. The developments largely relate to improvements in back office management in the form of streamlining Management Information System (MIS), strengthening centralised processing and improving communication networks. As these developments have a bearing on the role, functions and organisation of the Department, it is necessary to review the objectives of DIT in the light of these developments. To steer the financial sector to achieve the desired technological goals, the Reserve Bank has brought out two vision documents encompassing the periods 2005-08 and 2008-10. As the tenure of the previous IT vision document was 2008-10, it was incumbent upon the department to prepare the next version of the vision document for the period 2011-17.

Constitution of the High Level Committee (HLC)

It was in the above background that an HLC was constituted to prepare the IT Vision for 2011-17. The objective was to identify the information needs of the Reserve Bank as also to work on the changes to the organisational structure of DIT. The terms of reference for the Committee were the following:

- Review of the contribution of DIT in establishment of IT infrastructure in the Reserve Bank and banking sector over the period of fifteen years;
- Preparation of Information Technology Vision Document for the period 2011-17, taking into account requirements and expectations of banking system in general and the Reserve Bank in particular;
- Keeping in view the IT Vision Document, redefining the role, functions and organisation of DIT;
- Specifying the role of the department in meeting the information needs of the Reserve Bank and the society at large.

As the terms of reference covered diverse and specialized areas, there was a need to associate experts with varied backgrounds from within and outside the Reserve Bank to conduct the review. Accordingly, the Committee was formed.

Approach of the Committee

The prime focus of the Committee has been on the preparation of the IT Vision Document for the Reserve Bank of India for the period 2011-17. For this purpose, the Committee had taken into consideration the issues, challenges, evolving technology and changing business environment. In addition to preparing the Vision Document, the Committee had also given specific recommendations for its operationalisation. As DIT is responsible for adoption of IT in the Reserve Bank, the Committee reviewed its activities during the past fifteen years. The Committee recognised the need for extensive use of information for decision making, identified the gaps and put forth specific recommendations in terms of systems and structure. Based on the review of its past activities and its evolving role for development of information systems, the Committee has given recommendations on the future role, responsibilities and organization of DIT.

Three sub-groups were formed to concentrate essentially on the terms of reference and recommend the measures to accomplish them, as follows:-

(a) Sub-Group on preparing IT Vision for the Reserve Bank for 2011-2017:
(b) Sub-Group on specifying the role of the department in meeting the information needs of the Reserve Bank in particular and the society in general.
(c) Sub-Group on redefining the role, responsibilities, functions and organization of DIT

Layout of the Report

- Chapter 1 gives the background for the preparation of the IT Vision 2011-17.
- Chapter 2 discusses the context in which the IT Vision Document has been prepared and also gives strategy for achieving the goals set in the document.
- Chapter 3 delineates the review of the contribution of DIT in establishment of IT infrastructure in the Reserve Bank and banking sector over the period of fifteen years.
- Chapter 4 discusses the information needs of the Reserve Bank and the society
- Chapter 5 redefines the role, responsibilities and organization of DIT.

Strategy for implementation of IT Vision 2011-17

Changing Environment and Challenges ahead

Over the years, the functions of the Reserve Bank and its focus have evolved in response to the changing economic environment. While discharging its traditional functions, the Reserve Bank has been in the forefront of adopting new initiatives. These new initiatives required adoption of appropriate technology to deliver optimal solutions and in the process increased the need to plan and implement newer IT strategies.

Simultaneously, there have been changes in the technological environment. The Reserve Bank is committed to creating adoption of newer technologies. In this context, cloud computing, virtualisation and open source technologies can be used for driving efficiencies of operation and reducing costs to customer. By using cloud computing, the service providers can deliver a variety of IT enabled capabilities to the customers.

The adoption of technology has brought in efficiency in the payment systems operated by the Reserve Bank. This can be measured by the increasing use of electronic mode of transmission of money by customers of banks. Adoption of Core Banking Solutions has emerged as a single most significant innovation which has transformed the way banks have managed their businesses. However, these systems have not been fully exploited for information management and decision support. Similarly, the IT governance structures are yet to be fully strengthened.

In the context of (a) increased demand on IT solutions (b) changing technology scene and (c) gaps in adoption of technology to meet the information needs, the Committee has identified the specific areas that need to be addressed during the ensuing years. These issues may be addressed in the short, medium and long term. Some of the important issues are delineated below:

- issues in integration of information and technology
- focused approach in usage of data for MIS and Decision Support System (DSS)
- inadequacies in information needed to take vital decisions
- disparate IT systems at different levels of maturity
- metadata and uniform data reporting standards
- adoption of data mining and business analytics for information refinement
- re-engineered business processes and delivery models
- strategic alignment between business and IT
- information and security policies
- business continuity management
- project management
- vendor management
- Trained manpower for deployment of technology

The Committee has taken into account the above challenges while preparing the IT Vision Document 2011-17.

Implementation Strategy

Keeping in view the goals identified in the Vision Document, and taking into account the steps required to operationalise the same, the HLC has reviewed the activities of DIT during the past 15 years and identified the information needs of the Reserve Bank and society and has recommended certain changes in the present role, responsibilities, functions and organization of the department.

DIT may be entrusted with the responsibility to identify the specific action points and prepare action plans for short, medium and long term implementation. For this purpose, the department may use the recommendations given by the Committee in this report. Further, the department may coordinate with other departments of the Reserve Bank and also external organizations to achieve the goals set in the Vision Document.

A high level standing committee at the top management level may be formed to monitor the progress of implementation of IT Vision Document.

Review of Activities of DIT in the Last 15 Years

Genesis

Following the macroeconomic and structural reforms undertaken from July 1991 onwards, it was important for the Reserve Bank to gear up its internal Information Technology (IT) set up for an effective handling of the new tasks that were devolved on it. The Reserve Bank undertook a number of steps to exploit the rapid strides in the field of computers and communications towards improving efficiency, productivity and customer services not only within its own organisation but also across the banking sector as a whole.

In order to focus on planning and implementation of computerised systems, a department known as the Department of Information Technology (DIT) was set up on January 1, 1995. The department was mandated to service the technology needs of the Reserve Bank and serve as a facilitator in the deployment of IT in banks and the financial sector. It was also entrusted with the responsibility of facilitating reforms in the Payment and Settlement Systems of the country, a role it played till the constitution of a separate department called Department of Payment and Settlement Systems (DPSS) in March 2005.

Functions of DIT

The mission of DIT was to function as the nodal agency for technological improvements and for achieving operational excellence both within the Reserve Bank and in the banking sector, and to implement a safe, secure and efficient integrated payment and settlement system for the country. DIT was carved out of two divisions of the erstwhile Department of Statistical Analysis and Computer Services (DESACS) viz. Computer Operations Division and Systems and Programming Division which were merged with the erstwhile Management Services Department. The functions of DIT went beyond those of its constituent units. The functional areas of DIT were broadly grouped as following:

Computer Technology: This included:

- Development of new software for various departments
- Computerisation of banking departments, such as DADs, PADs, PDOs
- Introduction of cash dispensers for payment of bills
- Procurement of office automation equipment

Communication Technology: This included:

- Setting up of inter-office connectivity using satellite (VSAT)
- Use of terrestrial lines for varied applications
- Facilitation of SWIFT network in banking sector in India

Payment systems and Technology upgradation: Monitoring of upgradation of technology in Public Sector Banks (PSBs) included progress in the development of an integrated and robust Payment and Settlement system and implementation of the decisions of the

Payment System Advisory Committee. It also included:

- Development and operationalisation of Securities Settlement System (SSS), Negotiated Dealing System (NDS) and Real Time Gross Settlement System (RTGS)
- Ensuring optimal use of electronic media for eliminating delays and ensuring adequate security in payment areas through Electronic Clearing System (ECS) and Electronic Funds Transfer (EFT);
- Monitoring National Clearing Cells (NCC) operating from four metros and introducing MICR systems at more centres.

Coordination with banks: Monitoring the progress achieved by public sector banks in computerisation and informing the Government of the same.

The other functions of DIT included:

- Contributions to various Committees/Working Groups using technology as a platform
- Preparation of guidelines for Indian Financial Network (INFINET)- network for the exclusive use of the Closed User Group (CUG) - banks and financial institutions
- Introduction of various channels/products of payment i.e. Centralised Funds Management System (CFMS), Structured Financial Messaging Solution (SFMS), Magnetic Ink Character Recognition (MICR), ECS, EFT and National EFT

Activities during various phases

Initial efforts within the Reserve Bank were aimed at mechanisation of activities in the 1980s, which expanded into computerisation of its critical operations in the 1990s. The next decade marked a phase of consolidation, with renewed thrust towards putting in place comprehensive systems following the generic architecture and providing solutions to enhance the efficiency of the payment and settlement systems in India. The broad approach followed in implementation of IT initiatives centred around the need for having homogenous IT systems catering to varied processing requirements of the Reserve

Bank and providing for seamless integration across the various applications, wherever feasible. Recognising the need for distributed computing across the various locations of the Reserve Bank and taking advantage of the benefits of centralised processing in an IT environment, DIT adopted the approach of 'Centralised Processing with Decentralised Access'. While managing technology implementation was a major activity which had to be handled by DIT, managing and imbibing the rapid developments taking place in the field of technology was a bigger challenge. Though hardware-related technological obsolescence has not greatly impacted the progress achieved, there have been issues related to software obsolescence. Some of the notable developments which have taken place during the last fifteen years of DIT's operation are as follows:

Formative Phase: 1995-2000

In the initial period, DIT brought into focus the need for quick and efficient use of new technologies in the Bank in the areas of:

i. **Payment and Settlement Systems:** One of the major responsibilities entrusted to DIT was the compliance of the Core Principles for Systemically Important Payment Systems (SIPS) as outlined by the Bank for International Settlements, Basle, Switzerland. During this period, the NDS, SSS and the RTGS were introduced. For coordinating the process at the national level, a National Payments Council was formed in 1999 to lay out policy framework for reforms in payment and settlement systems.
ii. **Maintenance of Network:** DIT spearheaded setting up of the INFINET (WAN based satellite communication and terrestrial lines network) using VSAT technology. It was the forerunner of an efficient telecommunication backbone for the banking and financial sector. Hub and network management system was located at IDRBT and also managed by them.
iii. **Setting Standards in IT:** Rapid computerisation across different financial sector entities made it essential for Reserve Bank

to adopt international best practices and standards. In order to ensure this and to facilitate Straight Through Processing (STP), DIT took various steps towards getting International Standards Organisation (ISO) and BS7799 certification in respect of certain critical applications and systems. DIT also took steps towards standardising the operating system, databases and messaging platforms.

iv. **Ensuring delivery channels:** Guidelines relating to IT based delivery channels from the perspective of conforming to critical minimum requirements were issued by the Reserve Bank. At the root of all the new delivery channels was the need for banks to migrate towards the use of core banking solutions, which facilitated all centralised offerings by the banks.

Stabilisation Phase: 2000-2005

During this period, the focus of DIT shifted to stabilising the responsibilities/projects that were entrusted to it. The main areas of work related to the following:

i. **Critical Payment Systems/Applications:** These years saw the commencement of the RTGS system, increasing awareness of its applicability as also setting legal framework of the rights and responsibilities of its participants. The PDO-NDS application was also made operational which resulted in computerising the functioning of the PDO. Further it also saw the integration of the RTGS with the internal accounting system of the Reserve Bank.

ii. **Maintenance of Network:** The Local Area Network (LAN) was operationalised in all offices of the Reserve Bank. This enabled all the desktops in an office to be connected to each other in a LAN environment.

iii. **Availability of infrastructure:** Digital signatures with Public Key Infrastructure (PKI) were used to protect data and image flow over the network and to establish authenticity and non-repudiation.

iv. **Preparedness of the banking sector:** Work dealing with the advent of the Year 2000 and the reforms of payment and settlement systems including drafting Payment Systems Act to take care of legal requirements for payment and settlement systems reforms, was also initiated during this period.

v. **Technology Upgradation in the banking sector was mainly done in the following areas**

- Adoption of international standards in areas of hardware, systems software and security
- Networking of computerised branches
- Data warehousing and data mining
- Implementation of the re-engineering process
- Extensive training and development of human resources
- Computer/Information audit

Maturity Phase: 2005-to date

During this period, the major activities conducted / overseen by DIT were the following:

i. Payment and Settlement Systems:

- Department of Payment and Settlement Systems (DPSS) was carved out of DIT in 2005 for regulation and supervision of payment and settlement systems encompassing cheque based clearing systems, ECS, EFT, interinstitutional government securities clearing as also the RTGS.
- Integration of RTGS with the Integrated Accounting System
- Centralised Public Accounts Department System (CPADS) was made functional

ii. Infrastructure:

- To enable the consolidation of systems and centralised data processing as also for business continuity and disaster recovery in the event of any contingency, it was decided to set up Data Centres in the Reserve Bank. Accordingly, three state-of-the-art data centres were set up followed by migration of all payment and non-payment system applications. The data centres were designed to meet the Tier-IV standard of the Uptime Institute.

- There was migration to Multi-Protocol Label Switching (MPLS) of Indian financial network (INFINET).
- Centralised Data Base Management System (CDBMS) - Data Warehouse of the Reserve Bank was made operational.

iii. Non-Payment Applications i.e. Human Resources Management System (HRMS), Integrated Establishment System (IES), Mail Messaging System (MMS), Enterprise Knowledge Portal (EKP) and Document Management Information System (DMIS) were also implemented thus heralding a new generation of applications for the use by every staff member of the Reserve Bank. This period also saw the introduction of Smart card-based access control system as also connectivity of all Reserve Bank offices by the video conferencing facility. Migration of Secured Internet Website to a centralised system at the data centre was also undertaken.

iv. Miscellaneous: There was an effort towards ensuring constant availability of services by effective and failsafe Business Continuity Plans (BCP) and hence, periodical BCP exercises were undertaken. Information Security policy put in place. There was adoption of Core Banking Solutions (CBS) by almost all the banks.

From the above, it can be seen that DIT has accomplished the tasks entrusted to it, particularly those relating to the building of efficient and secure payment systems. It has also put in place a fairly robust IT infrastructure in the form of data centres, Local Area Network (LAN) and Wide Area Network (WAN). Over the last decade and a half, attention has been focused particularly on operationalising and maintaining the payment systems in a safe, secure and efficient manner.

Consequently, the implementation of distinct information systems to support decision making activities and re-engineering the business processes could not be accorded equal priority.

Reserve Bank and Information Systems

Existing Setup

The existing system of gathering information in the Reserve Bank is based on the functions / roles performed by it. Various departments play a contributory role in collection of information. Information is also collected from external sources.

The present data collection systems in various departments are disparate and are at different levels of automation. The Bank has started a process of bringing all such systems to single interface in the form of On-line Returns Filing System (ORFS). Currently some returns are already under ORFS while efforts are on to bring others in its fold.

There are consistent efforts to set standards for data reporting in the form of Extensible Business Reporting Language (XBRL). XBRL taxonomies have already been developed and implemented for Basel II return.

Most of the information collected or generated in various departments flows into the Reserve Bank's Enterprise Data Warehouse (EDW). The EDW also contains data of 72 countries which are members of the BIS data bank. The process of flow of data from various systems to EDW is getting automated. There are still manual procedures in the data flow from several systems. As an information sharing mechanism, this system, provides consistent time series on broad spectrum of macroeconomic variables. However, departments still rely on their respective systems for meeting regular reports / ad hoc queries. As a result, the facilities provided by dash boards and business analytics are yet to be fully exploited. The Enterprise Knowledge Portal (EKP) is fast emerging as a robust information and collaborative channel for sharing information within the organization.

Information Systems for Society

Market participants/ analysts/ academicians/ other professionals rely heavily on the information provided by the Reserve Bank. In addition to the regular publications in the printed format, Reserve Bank is also providing information to the public through its website.

By providing access to the general public for the publishable part of the data warehouse over the internet through a link Data Base on Indian Economy (DBIE), a beginning has been made towards the real-time dissemination of data to the society. With institution of 'Real Time Hand Book of Statistics on Indian Economy' in 2009, the scope of this work has been further broadened.

Need for review

There have been several changes in the financial sector, both domestically and internationally, necessitating collection of data to meet the new requirements of regulation and policy making. Further there have been changes in the technology for collection of data and dissemination of information. Therefore, there is a need to review the existing systems in the Reserve Bank, based on the principles of information management, information technology and information governance.

Issues and Concerns

After examining the present data and information management systems in the Reserve Bank, the Committee identified following issues and concerns to be addressed:

Information Management: One of the major objectives of information management is to collect, process, compile and analyse data in a timely manner for taking policy decisions. However, at present, a strong linkage in the use and sharing of information for decision making is missing within the Bank. This, to some extent, has bred information illiteracy within the organisation. Hence, in order to make policies based on timely and correct data, the following issues need to be addressed:

i. **Data Quality:** Presently, the data reported to Reserve Bank is not necessarily forwarded from the centralised system or the MIS servers of banks. Manual intervention often leads to incorrect reporting. This raises doubts on the genuineness of data management. Policy decisions based on such data may be erroneous.

ii. **Data Definition:** There is no data available encompassing all the returns received by the Reserve Bank. The EDW has its own metadata and it covers statistics only conforming to this data.

iii. **Timeliness:** While regulatory returns are received well in time due to their statutory nature, statistical returns, which are more granular in nature, are received with considerable time lag limiting their use for policy decisions.

iv. **Availability:** All data in the Reserve Bank is not ported to the EDW. Further, users are not aware of the availability of data. The EDW is not used optimally.

v. **Accountability:** Often there is no accountability for the data submission.

vi. **Coverage:** Though the data captured in the Reserve Bank from primary and secondary sources is satisfactory, there are some data gaps in the coverage and these need to be adequately addressed.

vii. **Data dissemination:** This needs to be strengthened in the areas:
   - high frequency data on financial markets
   - data on progress in financial inclusion and
   - socio-economic data like unemployment rate

Information Technology

- Various departments of the Reserve Bank have their own disjointed data management systems that lack the capability of data analysis.
- Reserve Bank still relies excessively on paper-based documents which are preserved in physical files. There is no fully IT enabled system, wherein internal notes are prepared, authorised electronically, using digital signatures, and stored in a networked server for future retrieval.
- Aggregation and Distribution of information pose a challenge.
- Cyber attacks and newer forms of security threats pose challenges.

Information Governance

The concerns and issues regarding data and information can be addressed by having a proper governance structure in place with respect to the data, information, security and information technology. There is an overarching need for adoption of principles of integrity, accessibility and security for setting the appropriate benchmarks.

Recommendations

After examining the issues and concerns that need to be addressed, the Committee recommended the following:

Information Management

- The quality of data received in Reserve Bank needs to be improved for its use in decision support system. The generation of required data directly from the transaction processing system at the bank's end and automating flow of such data to the Reserve Bank without any manual intervention in a straight through process is recommended.
- While respective departments who have prescribed the return/statement should be from the owner of the received data, the data should reside in the central repository.
- A comprehensive assessment of the Reserve Bank's information architecture needs to be done to help identify potential inefficiencies. A complete list of data items, their definitions, concepts and metadata for all the data collected and maintained by the Reserve Bank should be compiled and prepared.
- All data managed by the Reserve Bank to move to the EDW on a near real time basis.
- In the Reserve Bank, the culture of using data and information for policy making needs to be encouraged.
- Information hubs across departments with built-in safeguards.
- Real time links to be provided between RBI and Financial Institutions to facilitate remote examination.
- Reserve Bank may equip itself to make virtual visits to banks.

Information Technology

- There is a need to adopt efficient IT solutions, which can be enabled to improve methods of data submission, receipt of data for staging purpose, transfer of clean data for appropriate access and analytical capability to the stored data.
- The Reserve Bank needs to encourage use of more technological solutions such as business intelligence tools, business analytics, data mining tools and semantic search for analysis of data.
- Reserve Bank may also implement the second generation intelligent data warehouse.
- The Reserve Bank to move to a fully IT enabled workflow and document management system thus paving the way for a paperless environment.
- Use of DSS for MIS to be encouraged.
- RBI to be constantly remain vigilant to security threats and keep in touch with agencies like CERT-IN etc for prevention of cyber attacks.

Information Governance

- It is suggested to put in place policies/guidelines in the following areas:
    a. Data Governance - covers governance structure with respect to the organisation's data asset which is structured in nature.
    b. Information Governance - covers governance structure with respect to the organisation's information assets which may be structured or unstructured.
    c. Information Security (IS) Governance–deals with the security and risk aspect of information assets of the organisation.
    d. Information Technology (IT) Governance is the overall structural framework which covers entire gamut of IT systems and their performance and risk management.
- Comprehensive guidelines on the data quality and uniform data

reporting standards to be prepared.

- Comprehensive guidelines on the data quality and uniform data reporting standards to be prepared.
- Data dissemination policy may be put in place to ensure that the requisite data is available to the users.
- Management of received data should be with one department with expertise in IT. This will enable harnessing the latest available technology.

Role of DIT, DSIM and other departments

To carry forward the above recommendations, the Committee suggests the following:

- DIT needs to provide technical support to all the information system initiatives and the necessary IT infrastructure.
- Receipt of data from all sources should be consolidated at a common repository at the Reserve Bank.
- An inter-department group to be formed for examining, overseeing and implementing new data requests.
- Each Central Office Department (COD) and Regional Office (RO) of the Reserve Bank need to have a separate unit to cater to their information needs. A nodal officer needs to be posted in each COD/RO for coordinating with the central department which is maintaining the central data repository.
- The nodal officer of the COD unit to have the responsibility of maintaining accuracy, consistency, completeness, and updating of data. The responsibility of the nodal officer may also include:
    a. Coordination with the data suppliers
    b. Supply the data to users
    c. Handle the data related queries
- The nodal officer of the RO units to coordinate with the local bank branches in cases of training and conducting surveys among banks and other financial entities.
- Data supply to any other entity needs to be routed through cen-

tral data repository i.e. EDW. The EDW and its internet portal Database on Indian Economy (DBIE) may be the predominant platform for data dissemination internally as well as outside the Reserve Bank.

Role of DIT
Present structure

Based on the roles, responsibilities and functions of DIT, the department is presently organised into the following divisions:

i. IT Applications – Payment Systems
ii. IT Applications – Non Payment Systems
iii. IT Infrastructure – Networking
iv. IT Infrastructure –Hardware and Software
v. IT Policy
vi. Administration (General and Data Centre) at central office

In addition to the divisions at Central Office, the Department operates and maintains three data centres namely Primary data centre, On-City data centre and Off-City data centre.

Presently the staff in DIT is a complement of the DSIM cadre and general officers. Although there is no separate IT cadre in the Bank, officers with either IT background or aptitude to work in an IT environment are considered to be posted to DIT. There have been some efforts by the Reserve Bank to employ people with IT background through a special recruitment / contract appointment.

The present IT Vision Document 2011-17 provides the genesis for reviewing the functions and consequently the organisation structure of this department.

Issues faced by the department

After examining the present roles, responsibilities and functions as also the organisation structure of DIT, the Committee observed the following issues posing challenges to the department. These issues grouped under related heads are enumerated below:

Policy related

- **Governance:** There are inadequacies in structure in the areas of IT governance, information governance, data governance, information security governance.
- **Policy Formulation:** For ensuring overall efficiency of the IT systems, there is a need for periodical reviews of information and security policies encompassing data and information governance, information security, IT, audit of IT processes and infrastructure.

Process related

- **Business Continuity Management:** With several critical systems brought under IT at different points of time and with different maturity levels, it is becoming exceedingly difficult to plan and implement business continuity activities relating to crisis management, incident management, emergency management, contingency planning as well as alternate planning of all its applications.
- **Internal Process Re-engineering:** Adoption of IT-based solutions is expected to bring in several advantages like faster processing, cost reduction and qualitative change in the working environment. This requires meticulous process reengineering. Although some efforts are made for process re-engineering, there is no focal point for all the activities, thus leaving scope for considerable improvement.
- **IT Infrastructure Management:** This function relates to procurement and maintenance of IT Infrastructure including hardware and software and network management in the Reserve Bank. Currently, there are a multitude of suppliers and service providers performing various IT related functions in the Reserve Bank. Proper co-ordination is becoming a serious concern in ensuring timely delivery of various items.
- **Vendor Management:** This function relates to single vendor lock-in problems, concentration risk and accountability issues.

Dependency on third party service providers for provision of certain services pose limitations on the range and level of services offered. Lack of coordination among vendors also leads to operational problems. This results in reducing the overall efficiency of systems.

- **Project Management:** Managing IT resources, either for achieving the desired objectives or creating new resources for business or functional objectives, has become complex. Therefore, there is an overarching need for professionally managed projects. Absence of formal project management guidelines in the Reserve Bank often results in project overruns in terms of effort, cost and time.

HR related

There is no separate IT cadre in the Reserve Bank. However, the Reserve Bank had earlier recruited a few IT specialists and had also employed a few on contract basis. In view of the transfer and placement policy of the Reserve Bank, it is not possible to keep officers posted to DIT on a permanent basis. The new entrants to the department, particularly those identified to work at data centres or with specific applications take a longer time to acquire the necessary skill sets. Thus, it has been difficult to identify officers with the right aptitude to work in the IT environment in the Reserve Bank. There is an alignment mismatch between IT and HR related issues.

Recommendations

Based on the issues discussed above, the Committee recommended the following:

Policy related

- A high level multi-disciplinary / multi-departmental group may be entrusted with the preparation of various governance framework/structure/prepare appropriate policies as mentioned above for the Reserve Bank. DIT may provide the secretarial services for this high level group.

- RBI may consider constituting a top level body with external technical & domain expertise to address bank-wide IT strategy, plan and standards.
- In order to put in place the above governance frameworks, there is a need to define and assign the following roles in the Reserve Bank:
    a. **Chief Information Officer** (CIO) - Responsible for managing information assets of the organisation including data, and implementing data governance and information governance framework.
    b. **Chief Information Security Officer** (CISO) - Responsible for ensuring the security framework for the information assets of the Reserve Bank. CISO will prepare the information security policy in accordance with the business priorities and risk. CISO will be responsible for implementing the information security governance framework.
    c. **Chief Information Technology Officer** (CITO) - Responsible for providing and maintaining the IT infrastructure of the Reserve Bank.

Process related

- A department/division may be entrusted with the responsibility of BCM which would include Business Impact Analysis (BIA: process of analyzing the effect of interruptions to business operations or processes on all business functions) and preparing Business Continuity Plans (BCP: process of developing prior arrangements and procedures that enable an organization to respond to an event in such a manner that critical business functions can continue within planned levels of disruption).
- A multi-disciplinary group(s) is to be entrusted with the responsibility of process re-engineering. The Group would be responsible for optimizing processes and allocating resources before taking up any new development as outlined under:

a. Creation of an Internal Process Re-engineering (IPR) Cell in DIT.
b. The IPR Cell to consist of a group of experts with domain knowledge and also with knowledge of IT management. The domain knowledge group will change for each project. External experts may also form part of the team.
c. Any computerisation in the Bank must start after certification from IPR Cell that it is process compliant.

HR related

(A) Suggested structure

- Some institutions have attempted to resolve the issues relating to IT Infrastructure Management by setting up a separate subsidiary for providing total IT infrastructure management services. The Reserve Bank could also consider this option. This subsidiary could attract talent with proper market related remuneration package.
- The new subsidiary could relieve IDRBT from network management and other services to enable it to concentrate on research related activities. This would enable IDRBT to become a Centre of Excellence (CoE) by serving as a laboratory for all research and development activities. It would also help the Reserve Bank to focus on policy related issues.
- There could be several operational and legal hurdles that need to be addressed before achieving the above objective. Therefore, until the formation of a subsidiary, DIT may attempt to bring all outsourcing activities relating to procurement and maintenance of hardware and software as also network management to a single vendor.
- In case it is not possible to achieve the above objectives, DIT may recruit specialists on contract basis for IT infrastructure management.
- In order to implement IT projects in a professional manner, specific multidisciplinary groups consisting of officers from

various domains including business, technology and legal may be formed. The groups may be responsible and accountable for the project and be entrusted with necessary powers. The groups may be flat in their structure and may be disbanded at the end of the project.

- Appropriate project management guidelines may be put in place.
- DIT to be solely responsible for providing IT services, systems and technology for maximising value of information and knowledge.

(B) Others

- There should be a talent pool of IT resources in the Reserve Bank. This pool may be formed with the joint concurrence of DAPM, HRDD and DIT. DIT will have to articulate and identify the criteria for IT personnel.
- The awareness about the functions and opportunities of DIT should be highly publicised and the relevance of the department to the overall functioning of the Reserve Bank should be suitably indicated so as to reflect that tenure at DIT would serve as an encouragement for career progression within Reserve Bank.
- The initiative taken by the Reserve Bank for lateral recruitment of officers at the senior level can be further pursued. This will help in strengthening the IT pool.
- A core team of officers who have an aptitude for IT and who have the necessary minimum expertise can be identified and trained in core IT areas for forming the IT pool.
- DIT and HRDD should jointly work towards formulating a policy for providing continuous training to this pool of resources which would help in up-gradation of skills and would also keep the resources abreast with latest technology trends.
- Resources from the IT pool could be deployed to Regional Offices for effective implementation and monitoring of all IT projects.
- A model organisation structure for IT governance on the lines prepared by IDRBT can serve as a reference model (Annex 2).

Study of organisation structures of other Central Banks

Members of the Sub-Group 3 in its first meeting held on July 7, 2010 deliberated upon the IT practices & organization structure followed in Central Banks across the globe. Members desired that a study of the IT Organisation Structure of few central banks could be taken up by DIT, which could facilitate the sub-group in finalising its recommendations. Accordingly, DIT initiated the study of central banks by contacting a few central banks through e-mail, and by also seeking information through websites.

Bank Negara Malaysia

The IT services Department in Bank Negara Malaysia is structured to look after system development and solutions (called sollutioning department) , services and infrastructure management and strategic planning and governance on a broader scale.

The system development and solutioning division looks after the payments and treasury systems, statistical and administrative systems and knowledge management systems. The services and infrastructure management division looks after the DC and RC operations and management, systems and storage management, IT services management, network management and end user computing services.

The strategic planning and governance division looks after the strategic planning, governance security and risk management, project management office and finance administration and training. The IT Department is headed by a Director who reports to the Assistant Governor of the Bank in the organizational hierarchy. The Assistant Governor in turn reports to the Deputy Governor and Governor.

Staffing, Remuneration and Career path of IT personnel in Bank Negara

Nintyone per cent of IT personnel (Executives and Managers) hold bachelor/master degree in ITrelated fields. Basically, three categories of applications/infrastructure services are managed by the IT skilled personnel:

- Enterprise Applications such as email, search, collaboration tools, and document management system
- Business Applications which are developed or procured (off-the-shelf software) to meet the needs of the line departments
- Infrastructure services such as network, server, storage, end-user empowerment tools as well as security monitoring tools

Further, the Bank Negara Malaysia (BNM) offers tangible and intangible reward propositions based on value contributions and continuity in earning potential. It provides common benefits to all staff in the organization and their remuneration package are commensurate with their respective roles and positions. To ensure that its remuneration package remains competitive and relevant, BNM continuously benchmarks with the relevant industries, specialists and job families annually.

Infrastructure (i.e. network, servers, database and security) and application system development skilled IT personnel are recruited mainly for IT Department. However, there are IT personnel who were recruited for some departments to undertake specific roles such as the following:

- IT-related skills for the design and development of multi-media contents and development of websites in Corporate Communication Department.
- IT-related skills to undertake 1st level technical support for software packages such as the treasury and financial systems.
- The IT personnel career path follows the same organization-wide generic career path.
- All responsibilities assigned are related to IT (with the exception of departmental administration staff). This includes the support and maintenance of ICT Infrastructure, Application Development and Planning.

Swiss National Bank

The Swiss National Bank's Information and Technology Management generally deals with the areas of Management Support, Banking Applications, Banking Operations and Infrastructure. The organization of the IT department is structured into banking applications comprising of banking applications, monetary applications, statistical applications and inter-bank interfaces, enterprise applications comprising HR and financial applications, enterprise content management applications, electronic workplace and databases, infrastructure viz client systems, server systems, network and storage and data centre services and IT security and architecture. The CTO at the Swiss National Bank is called "Head of IT" and reports directly to the Governing Board – he is not a member of the board.

The IT Department is fully staffed with IT professionals (exception: Secretary) holding either a degree in computer science, engineering or a similar educational background. A number of them have many years of experience in IT.

Bank of Canada

The Bank of Canada has developed a framework that establishes at a high level, the roles, responsibilities, structure, principles, and process of all management bodies and people involved in IT decision making within the Bank. The Executive Team is very actively and visibly involved in strategic Bank-wide IT and performs the following role:

- Clear alignment of IT strategy with Bank strategy involves balancing trade-offs, building agreement, and resolving conflicting priorities.
- Co-ordinated and efficient use of shared IT solutions and services in pursuit of business value
- Consistent and common standards for processes, tools, and technology more predictability
- Collaboration across IT to improve learning and knowledge-sharing, less reinvention and fewer mistakes

- Improved performance and quality measures demonstrating how well we are doing

At the executive management level there is a Corporate Management Committee which provides oversight on all corporate policies and standards, approves IT strategic direction, priorities and budget and resolves contentious issues. The chiefs of all departments are members of the Information Technology Review Committee which essentially:

- Provides strategic coherence
- Builds consensus, approves exceptions to standards
- Advises CMC on IT investment at the Bank level and the Program level
- Analyzes issues raised by ITRC
- Prioritization of smaller initiatives on an annual basis and advises ITRC
- Proposes standards and principles and advise ITRC of the bank-wide impact

The Directors are the members of the Business Information Technology Council which:

- Run IT operations, deliver IT programs
- Finalises strategy, budget, service agreements and performance metrics

The executive sponsor is the champion and the guide to the program and performs the following role:

- Defines and drives business value
- Ultimate authority for the project
- Approves overall scope, schedule and budget, approves major changes and champions approval at EMC.
- Represents project to the EMC.

Key role of the business leader supported by Steering Committee

- Deliver the Business Value Approve resource allocation and key project people
- Resolves major scope, schedule and budget issues
- Resolves issues escalated by the Program Manager

- Approves key internal and external positioning and communications
- Drives rapid decisions on issues with wider Bank implication

Key role of Program Manager

- Provides program leadership and direction
- Deliver the Program/Project objectives
- Approves detailed project plans, budgets and work products
- Resolves or forwards policy issues requiring action
- Controls project stream resource allocation
- Makes user resources available as required
- Disposes of issues and project scope change requests
- Monitors and reports progress

The Bank of Canada has in its IT governance the Chief at the helm of ITS and is supported by Directors for Operations and Infrastructure, Applications and Data Management Services , Enterprise Portfolio Management ,Project Delivery and IT transformation

Better business value delivered by Information Technology Services

- Clear roles, responsibility and accountability between the business and ITS, with enhanced decision making processes
- Greater focus on the right priorities and allocation of the right expertise at the strategic, tactical, and operational levels
- Improved quality and effectiveness of end-to-end delivery
- Prioritization decisions based on a Bank-wide views
- Joint business and IT planning, focused on longer term projections
- Simplification and leveraging of technologies across businesses
- Collaborative and transparent processes

Federal Reserve Bank New York

The Technology Services Group (TSG) is responsible for the strategic planning and provisioning of automation services to the Federal Reserve Bank New York. These include application development, data architecture, network, communications and data center infrastructure and operations, project management, technology vendor management, and overall information technology and information security. The TSG also provides national information security, incident response, national remote access and enterprise search services for the Federal Reserve System. The TSG reports to the first Vice-President who reports to the Chairman of Federal Reserve Bank. TSG is organized around various business lines that work together to deliver high-quality products and services to Bank and System clients viz. Application Development, Governance, Information Security, Program Management Office and Technical Engineering and Computing Services.

Bank of England

The Information Systems and Technology Division (ISTD) of the Bank of England deals with Security, Communications, Information Strategy, IT Governance, Risk Management, Application Platform Support, Infrastructure Management, Service Operations, Data Centre Operations etc. The Chief Information Officer (CIO) is the Head of the ISTD and is supported by Chief Technology Office; Application Development and Maintenance comprises of analytical IT and financial operations and central services IT; CIO support ; infrastructure; service management and operations. The CIO reports to an Executive Director who is the Central Services

Secretary of the Bank and the Executive Director reports directly to the Governor of the Bank.

IT – Organizational Structures

IT Governance Model

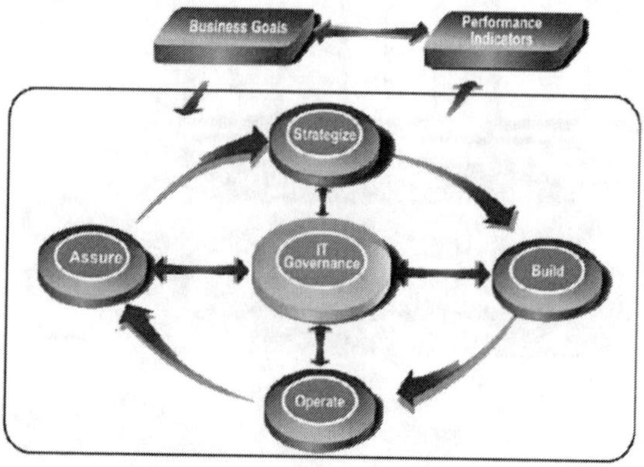

Model Organizational Structure for IT

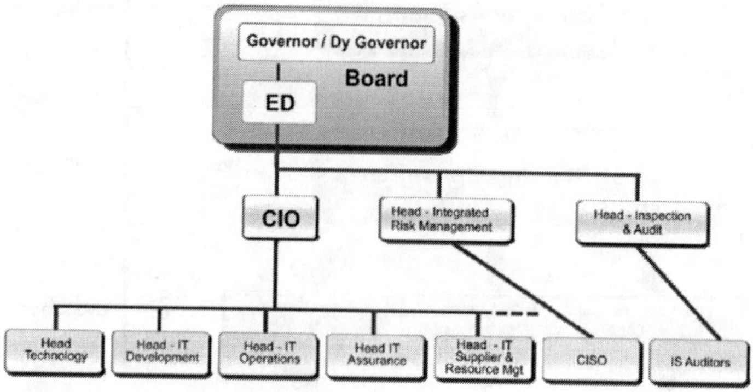

Functional Overview of IT

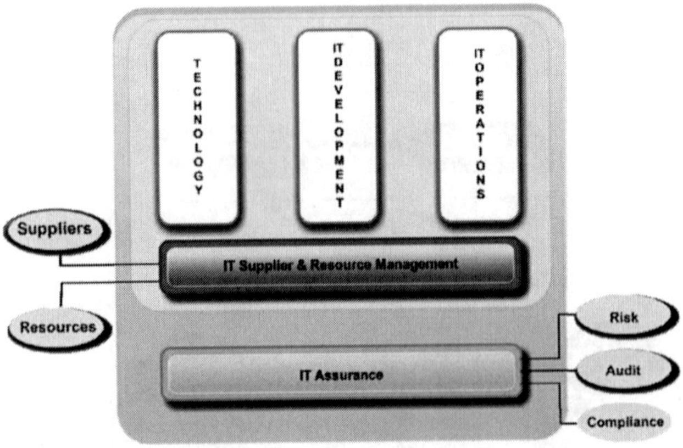

Alignment in Action

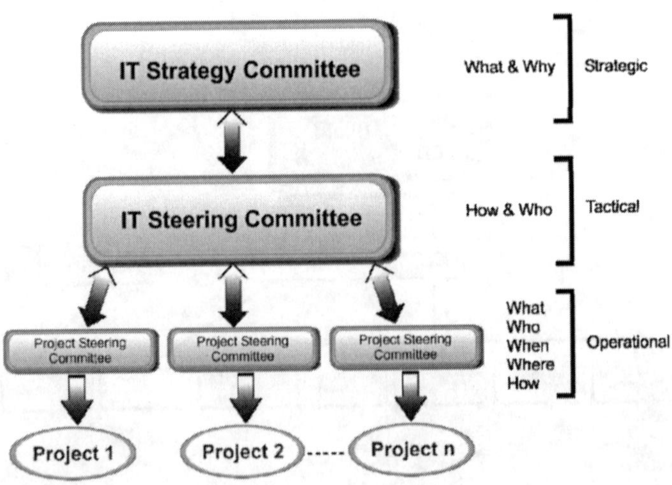

Information Security Function

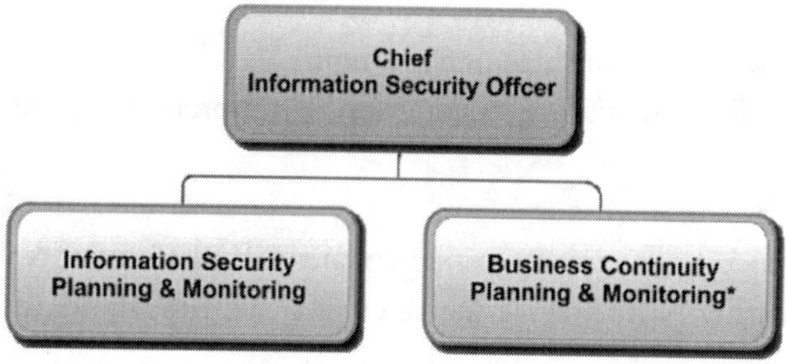

Responsibilities

- Information security strategy and policy for the bank. (applications, data, infrastructure and people related)
- Owning and sponsoring all security programs in the bank.
- Monitoring security logs of applications, operating systems, databases, networks, etc.
- Business continuity and disaster recovery planning and monitoring.
- Facilitating investigations in IT frauds and mitigation measures.

IT Supplier and Resource Management Function

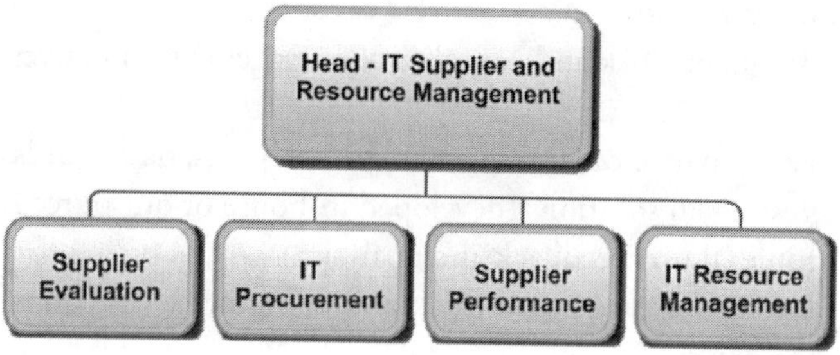

Responsibilities

- All IT sourcing (in-sourcing, outsourcing and co-sourcing) activities
- Supplier relationship management
- Supplier shortlisting, negotiation, selection (through EOI, RFI, RFP etc.)
- IT procurements
- Service-level agreement management: Enforcement & Review
- Supplier performance management (metrics, standards, audits etc.)
- Maintain the IT supplier service catalogue (empanelment)
- Planning, training and development of human resources in IT
- Promoting green IT initiatives like saving energy, cost and other resources

IT Assurance Function

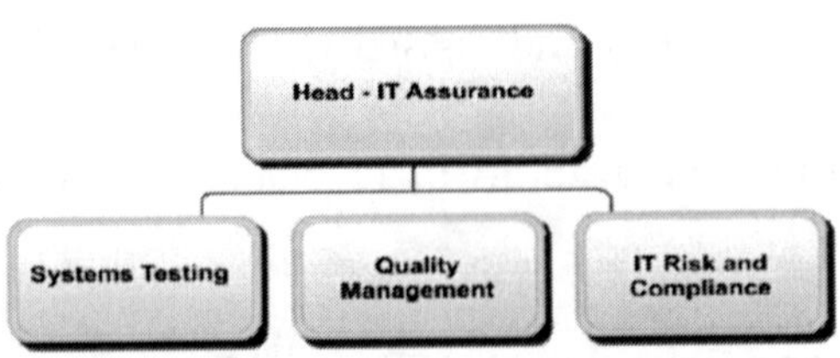

Responsibilities

- All quality, risk and compliance management initiatives within IT
- Performance/conformance metrics, reports, dashboards
- Testing all solutions (developed in-house or outsourced)
- Internal user feedback and analysis
- Interaction with audit, risk and compliance functions within the bank

Memorandum High Level Committee for Information Technology Vision of the Reserve Bank of India

The Department of Information Technology (DIT) at the Reserve Bank of India was formed in 1995 to take care of information technology (IT) deployment within the RBI and to serve as facilitator for adoption of IT in the banks. Over a period of fifteen years the department has satisfactorly fulfilled most of the objectives set to it at the time of formation. During this period, several developments have taken place in the realm of technology and its adoption in the banking sector, which have a bearing on the role, responsibilities, functions and organization of the department. IT environment has undergone substantial transformation over this period and hence there is felt a need to revisit the Department's objectives with an aim of redefining goal, focus and mandate for the department in the changed environment. It has accordingly been decided to set up a high-level committee for this purpose.

The terms of reference for the Committee are:

a. Review of the contribution of DIT in establishment of IT infrastructure in the Reserve Bank and banking sector over the period of fifteen years
b. Preparation of Information Technology Vision Document for the period 2011-17, taking into account requirements and expectations of banking system in general and Reserve Bank in particular.
c. Keeping in view the IT Vision Document, redefining the role, responsibilities, functions and organization of DIT
d. Specifying the role of the department in meeting the information needs of the Reserve Bank in particular and the society in general.

Bank Security In India

N Vishwanathan

> Crime results from the co-existence of the desire to commit the act and the belief that the opportunity to do so exists. When either factor is absent, the criminal act will not be committed. The presence of one factor alone, regardless of how strong it may be, will not result in crime.
>
> — **Wilson & Macharen**

Introduction

When I was young, I would often visit the then Imperial Bank of India branch where my father was the agent. I would look at the gatekeeper or *durwan* with awe. The man was immaculately dressed in liveries and stood his full height of over six feet. He would recognize me, give a board smile and let me enter the premises. At the same time, I noticed that he scrutinizing all the new faces and questioned their identity before allowing them to enter. He was, in fact, exercising access control as we call it today.

Little did I realize then that one day, I would also be playing a part in organizing the security of banks. From the unarmed, liveried *durwan*, bank security in India has come a long way even as about the number of security problems in a bank has multiplied. These problems have been further accentuated after the introduction of computer technology in banks.

You will remember the story of *Alibaba and Forty Thieves.* On learning the code-word, 'open sesame' he gained entry to the robbers cave containing stolen wealth. The cave door recognized the code word but could not differentiate individuals using it. Today, computer criminals can be based in Hamburg, for instance, and steal money from the UK branch via a telephone network in South America. How can this be possible? It has to do with the nature of the communications technology. The criminals have access to computer networks for transfer of the money. Even when the criminals can be identified, prosecutions becomes difficult in such cases due to the international implications of the act because it involves special aspects of security management in the banking industry in different countries.

Before we look into the present utilization of modern technology in banking industry, let us first look into the existing security scenario, especially in our country.

Security Scenario

The rapid growth of India's banks has, in its wake, brought about a number of problems for the banks to tackle. One such problem that cropped up, particularly in the 1980s, was the increasing incidence of burglary, dacoities, holdups related to terrorism and insurgency, resulting even in loss of customers and bank staff, besides the cash and valuables.

The Reserve Bank of India licensing policy was intended to spread the network of banks to rural and unbanked areas in the country. This has resulted in banks opening a large number of branches in the rural and semi-urban areas without adequate planning and trained staff. A number of these centers lack even the basic infrastructures such as transport, post office, rail station etc. Coupled with this rapid expansion of branches is the increasing numbers and variety of customers that a branch has to handle on account of the social banking policies introduced by the government. For instance, banks in rural centres take gold ornaments as security for certain types of lending and a large number of such branches hold as security gold ornaments of substantial value, carrying unimaginable risks.

The banks found it difficult to cope with the increase in the volume and variety of work. Control became inadequate and inefficient and this resulted in the increase in frauds and misappropriation. Enquires show that the rapid growth in the number of frauds and misappropriation was caused by unscrupulous members of the staff and or with their connivance, by resourceful outsiders. Loss to the banks through frauds and misappropriation is dramatically detailed below:

The stock market scams are indicators of the magnitude of loss that can result from collusion. The loss through collusion is difficult to detect. These crimes are not fully reported like external bank crime statistics, as to do so would cause an ever greater loss of public confidence in banks. For bankers, image is a large factor in their reluctance to report all these crimes. I am, however, not including the white collar crimes in banks. In order to reduce, if not avoid, such losses, banks are progressively undertaking mechanization and computerization..

In addition, the following aspects have increased the risks in banks:

- Increase in population.
- Unemployment.
- Effect of movies showing hold-ups etc.

Currency not identifiable in case of a dacoit. Even the decoy money used is often not traceable.

Procedural problems in obtaining licenses for weapons etc.

Casual attitude towards security in the bank hierarchy.

All these factors have brought banks, more than any other organization in our country, to public attention in a pronounced manner and rendered them attractive targets for attacks. The security arrangements in the branches cannot be deemed anywhere adequate, much less ideal.

Incident of bank robberies, dacoities and hold-ups and other forms of crimes have become widespread and are no longer confined to any particular geographic area of the country. However, majority of dacoities due to terrorism happen in the entire northern belt of our country. A state-wise distribution of bank dacoities in the last few years clearly shows that a few states in the north have had majority of dacoities linked to terrorism.

Planning Bank Security

The urgent need for proper planning and designing of security measures in banks has assumed great significance. The availability of ready money and values have emboldened the criminals and made them resort to even daylight dacoities. Banks are no longer perceived as impregnable bastions but have come to be regarded as easy targets for attacks.

Bank security and risk management involves a careful management of existing and anticipated threats arising from external or internal sources or a combination of both.

The cardinals principle of bank security is to create deterrents and if this is adequate, crime can be minimized, if not completely prevented. The initial stage of planning security can be an early-warning system, which can be achieved by proper 'access control'. If the criminal is able to overcome the initial defence like access control, there must be a second line of defence which may be called as the 'detection and prevention' line. The final stage would have to be the 'deny the target' stage, which in the case of banks is the vault/ strong room.

Security Designing

The security measures that are required to protect assets vary from branch to branch and hence need individual profiles. Four major factors viz. Location, operational and economic, Psychological, Structure and Layout have been listed for risk assessment. Each factor has under it a group of sub factors. Having measured the security risks of each branch and converting the points into percentage, a bank can be categorized as:

High risk	70% to 100% points
Normal risk	50% to 69%
Low risk	1% to 49% points.

There is another way of looking at this problem. The method is to match the threat, target and environment with the anticipated degree of dangers / loss on the threat perspective. The marketability or liquidity factor depends upon the attractiveness of the threat to a potential offender. While cash is fully convertible and cannot be easily traced, jewels pose not only difficulty in conversion but may also lead investigators to the robber. Therefore, normally, jewels are not that attractive to a robber or a burglar. This also must be taken into considerations while designing a security system.

The layout of a branch itself is very important. Apart from the physical barriers, psychological barriers are also to be created to achieve the required deterrents. Staff vigilance plays an important part. The layout and grouping of the departments should be with a progressively increasing security control, as one proceeds from one zone to the other, The principle is shown diagrammatically below:

The main entrance and the customer lounge form the 'Surveillance Zone' where everyone present is under the observation of the security personnel and bank staff.

The next zone, the 'Detection Zone' should be the area which consists only the staff and customers who are permitted inside and any other outsider is easily spotted. The next zone is the 'Secure Zone' which consists of the cash departments. No one can access this area without permission. An additional barrier in the form of wooden partitions, with wire mesh, can be created between the detection and the secure zone if required. The target could be further protected with an additional grill.

Traditional and Modern Methods Of Countering Threats:

A wind of change is blowing throughout the world as more and more countries orient their economy towards the world market. In this customer-centered economy, industries are competing to meet the changing needs of the customers.

Banking is a service-oriented organization and banks are now bringing about changes to serve the customers at his/her convenience in terms of time and place. Customer, in this sense, includes not only the depositors but also the borrowers.

You may have seen a television advertisement for an international bank, which says, 'There are still some places where you cannot reach your bank'. Yet, global access with thousands of 24x7 ATMs is today available. A bank account holder at a branch can withdraw money anytime at anyone of the ATMs. Transfer of large amounts of money can be made across international borders through the Electronic Fund Transfer system. There is hardly any delay in these transactions, funds are positioned at the point of need end at the time of need. This has been made possible due to technological advances.

The two main areas of advanced technology involved are: Computer technology and the Telecommunications Technology.

A host computer at a central location maintains all the data. This computer is accessed by other distributed computers, after identifying the operator. The host computer then, depending on the data source, authorizes or denies the payment. The operation is illustrated in a simplified manner below:

In traditional transactions the customer had to go to the bank for withdrawal of cash. On the other hand, with an ATM, he can be at any location and yet can draw from his accounts, have access to the account, establish authenticity.

There is a significant difference in the process. In the traditional way, there is the physical presence of the individual at the branch. In an ATM transaction, not only there is geographical distance involved, but also the anonymity of the individual except through a card, claiming a particular identity. With minor changes for our understanding, EFT also operates in a similar fashion

Conceptually the threats and countermeasures remain the same in both cases. The threats that banks face are :

- Fraud
- Theft Robbery/Dacoit
- Fire
- Terrorism (bomb threats etc.)

Since banks are threatened in both traditional and modern methods, the security manager has to draw a profile of the bank and design its protection accordingly.

First let us discuss the traditional way of countering threats. The security measures can be generally divided into physical, procedural and motivational.

Physical

The physical measures can be categorized as defensive and offensive. Some of the measures taken by the banks are:

- Security guards
- Structural safety and electronic fencing
- Alarm systems
- Surveillance by staff
- CCTV
- Training of the bank Staff

State level committees organized by the Reserve Bank of India to review the various security measures periodically

- Police patrolling
- Weapon system
- Time delay locks

Procedural

These could be categorized as operational safety and emergency measures like:

- Timing of opening and closing of our branches

- Liaison with various authorities
- Custody of keys and documents
- Fire safety
- Cash in transit
- Action during hold-ups

Motivational

This involves motivating the staff members, thereby creating a sense of security consciousness amongst them. Training is one of the most effective means of doing this. It can be undertaken to make certain that personnel understand the reasons for security procedures and policies. A recent study on training in banks, carried out by a working group nominated by the Reserve Bank of India revealed that there are serious shortcomings in so far as security training is concerned. The working group has suggested regular security training programmes to be conducted for various levels. With proper training in addition to improvement in the awareness, knowledge skills and attitude of bank personnel, the vulnerability of banks as perceived by the miscreants at present would also decrease. Security consciousness on the part of the banks is bound to act as a deterrent leading to minimization, if not elimination, of dacoities, robberies, burglaries etc.

Modern transaction can be visualized as

Transmitter authorized — Communications lines — Received disbursed beneficiary

In such a situation the vulnerable points are:

Pint of authorization — unauthorized access and knowledge of passwords.

Authorizing authenticity at a low level in hierarchy.

Hacker

Logic manipulator

Communications lines interception (EMI)

Action addressee — No confirmation of signatures

Now let us have a look at a few security aids available:

Personnel Access Control Systems

Access control technology has undergone a sea change from the Hollerith coded card circuit, capacitance cards to electronic smart card, RF proximity card and even cordless biometric system. There are very high security cards, offering high resistance to counterfeiting and duplication along with a self destruction facility. Owing to increased cost of security, these systems are becoming cost effective and banks should be able to introduce them to strengthen their security measures.

Intrusion Detection System

IDS detects a perpetrator's action before he seeks entry to a protected area. Basically, it consists of three major elements – sensor, alarm assessment and alarm annunciation or reporting system. Most commonly used interior intrusion detectors are micro-wave infrared, ultrasonic detectors, vibrations sensors glass break sensors, photo electric beam sensors etc. These detectors and sensors could be used in banks effectively providing depth to the security system.

Far and Nar

One of the fundamental considerations of an effective intrusion detection system is its false alarm rate (FAR) and nuisance alarm rate (NAR) FAR and NAR are expected to improve greatly, using techniques of digital signal processing, e.g., the microwave intrusion detector will be intelligent enough to differentiate most of the times a stray dog or bird movements or even swaying of grass. New cable and fiber optic intrusion detectors are cost effective and provide good performance.

Explosive Detectors

Today, one half of a kilo of high performance explosives is enough to blow up a bank. The deadly plastic can be shaped into almost any configurations, including thin sheets that might look like a lining of a suitcase. Moreover the preferred bombs are made of hydrogen, oxygen, nitrogen and carbon, the same elements that makes up most clothing and plastic. I understand that in the UK,, a small gadgets has been effectively tested to identify such plastic materials. This identifies the materials through the vapors emanating from it.

Metal Detectors

Future metal detectors may be available which may combine both the principle of detection (i.e. detection of a particular metal at a particular frequency) and also provide information about the type and shape of metal.

CCTV Surveillance

All the three subsystems of CCTV the camera, the transmission media and the display unit are undergoing rapid modifications. In India, we have utilized this system only in selected bank branches.

ATM Surveillance

A new ATM surveillance system which captures a set of digital images of each user, via a pinhole camera, which can be cancelled or mounted outside the machine as a visible deterrent. The images, together with details of time, account and branch are loaded to a tape streamer for archiving. Each surveillance unit can monitor three ATMs and hold 8,000 transactions on memory. If an act of vandalism occurs an anti-tamper device is triggered

Remote Monitoring of Alarms

As I have emphasized before, the rural and semi- urban branches in our country find it difficult to mobilize an effective reaction force in time of any threat.

Silent Communicator

This is a small communications unit, interfaced with a telephone line and to various sensors and detectors. In case of a potential threat, the sensors or detectors activate an alarm. The salient communicator is automatically activated which dials up to ten numbers and communicates a pre-recorded threat massage. The lacuna in this system is that it fails, once the telephone communications is dead.

Integrated Monitoring System

There are various kinds of integrated alarms and sensors available which monitor the signals received from the sensors into telephonic communication signals and carry these through telephones to a signal processor unit which identifies and classifies the nature of the threatened alarms, and alerts the reaction forces accordingly.

The security arrangements in the banks have to withstand growing pressure form terrorists/saboteurs etc., who will have access to upgraded technology. However, even a security man with little technical knowledge will be able to operate the equipment efficiently and meet the threat response effectively

From the reports available, It is expected that India will be able to produce the requirements of electronic-based security systems indigenously. We are self- sufficient in the IT sector and able to offer computer-based systems to others also in future. Infrared intravenous dictators, CLIPS for the making tamper- proof identity-catch video image retrieval systems, armoured vehicles for transportation of the cash and valuables, alarm reporting systems, central controller with data-based for excess control system have already been developed by us.

We should be in a position to develop completely integrated security systems, which will incorporate all the functions using indigenous resources for all of India's needs.

Recommendations

We should remember that whatever benefit technology confers on law abiding citizen is also available to criminally minded person. He utilizes this opportunity and consequently, detection as well as prosecution becomes difficult. Therefore, first and foremost, laws relating to such crimes need to be revised. Secondly, since different locales can be involved in such crimes, international agreements on prosecuting such criminals must be uniform and mutually supportive.

Coming to measures within the industry, the following can be considered:

Principle of complicity to be introduced in all transactions. Transactions of instructions or authorization to be done only after positive identification of the receiver or action addressee.

- Introduction of modern systems at both ends.
- Fiber optic linkages wherever possible.
- Messages in codes – encoded and decoded by two different personnel.

Introduction of tiger teams

A national laboratory be installed to undertake design, development, evaluation and introduction of reliable integrated security systems for industries, including banks.

There is a need to educate the higher echelons, middle level and the working staff regarding the advancement and utilization of the modern security system. For the banking industry, Reserve Bank Of India/ the Indians Banks Association should organize the same.

Banks should allot a budget for the development of the security systems in the banking industry. The IBA, in conjunction with the RBI, should be able to coordinate this.

The follow-up action in respect of the recommendations made by various committees as also in pursuance of the instructions issued by the authorities from time to time, which has been tardy and slow in implementation and should be speeded up.

Cash remittances by banks need urgent co-ordination. A grid system of movements should be planned and implemented. This involves the existing branches being grouped together geographically and attached to currency chests close by. This will help in reducing crisscross movements of cash over long distances.

Legal provisions relating to crimes against banks need to be changed. Also, the trial proceedings must be short without denying principles of natural justice. The guilty must be punished severely, so that potential perpetrators abandon their idea.

Conclusion

Security measures and devices will have to be constantly improved and updated in the light of the experience gained and new strategies adopted to prevent and detect crimes involving ever new modus operandi. There is no ready-made recipe to achieve effective security, nor can one achieve total security which is unachievable for any continuous period of time. The requirement for taking concerted steps to improve bank security need not be over emphasized if the environmental factors in the country as regards law and order situation and the threats to the country from the neighboring countries are viewed in proper perspective. The scenario and the level of concern for adherence to law and order by the public are likely to continue to be none too encouraging.

In the final analysis, the severity of threats from external perpetrators depends on the sate of the country's law and order climate.

Bank Security Vision & Response in the New Millennium

P N Rao

Security is vital for efficient and profit oriented operations of all commercial and industrial setups, whether government or private. Essential customer oriented activities of banking and those of the commercial establishments cannot function effectively in an environment of lawlessness, crime and fear of personal safety. The socio-economic factors of rising population, rapid industrialisation, urbanisation and un-satiated aspirations of large segments of populace, coupled with impact of rapidly spreading terrorism, bomb threats and diminishing social and ethical values have vitiated the security scenario.

The information technology and media proliferation have firmed very strongly in India in a very short time, thanks to the liberalisation of our economy. The largely positive results of this have also given an impetus to crime, with new dimensions, growing rapidly. This can be attributed to security deficiencies hither to prevailing. The banking sector, which has undertaken computerisation in a massive scale, to outdo each other in the quality of service promised to be provided, is un-willingly becoming target of unscrupulous elements, from outside as well as from within.

New Millennium Banking

The banking sector, like all others, has undertaken computerisation in a big way, not only to streamline the functioning, as also to provide quality customer services, with speed accuracy.

The availability of technology has led to innovation of various new products, both to retain the customer loyalty and also to enhance profits. New products like ATMs, electronic banking, home banking and the like have gradually led us to the concept of 'paperless banking'. This form of banking, which is prevalent in the developed world, is gradually coming into being in the developing countries, like ours.

While automation of the banking sectors is on hand, the banks are making effort to upgrade and provide value added services to the customers. This is where a threat to the customers, employees and to the assets is increasing as most banks try to maintain customer friendly relations for furtherance of business. It is imperative that the security managers and the management are aware of the lurking threats, so that effective steps can be initiated to minimize, if not neutralize, these security threats.

Threats

The threats to bank security could be broadly classified as physical and electronic. Some of the more serious threats in both forms are highlighted here and some measures to guard against these are suggested.

Physical Threats

Besides commonly practiced forms of hitherto followed crimes, like theft, burglary, dacoities, and looting of cash in transit, more serious and life threatening forms of physical crimes may be adopted by the bank criminals. This could be due to enforcing security norms rigidly to reduce or prevent the crime by the banks, which may lead to a situation of desperation by the criminals, who may adopt more severe nature of physical crimes.

Hostage Taking

The criminals may resort to holding the staff and customers as hostages in bid to get either safe passage or to force ransom. The need of protecting the lives of innocent customers and the staff need not be overemphasized. The staff should be educated about facing such a situation and the security personnel should be trained to handle such situations tactfully, so as to protect the lives. There is a necessity to impose strict access control measures in the event such a threat is anticipated, on selective basis.

Blasts

To spread panic among the staff and customers, the criminals may resort to use of explosives to ensure success in their effort. With easy availability of various types of explosives, this may be widely resorted to in the days to come. Access control and checking of articles being carried by those seeking entry into the premises, by using scanning equipment can reduce this threat to some extent.

Mugging & Tallgating

This threat is more to the customers using ATMs, especially at nights. Use of CCTV, outside the location of ATM covering the approach will, to a large extent assist in apprehending criminals. All customers should be educated by displaying sign boards inside the ATM of such a danger and precautions to be taken, to avoid becoming victims. To avoid tall-gating, customers should be instructed to ensure locking of the entry door immediately on entry and exit. All ATMs, as a rule, must have an in built camera to record the customer transactions.

Adequate security precautions are required to be adopted while handling large amounts of cash by those banks which have introduced home banking, to ensure security of staff and cash.

Larceny

Larceny is the theft of assets. This term is being commonly used to hardware related crimes. Like any other item in the bank premises, computers and computer components are also subject to theft or burglary. Point to remember in such thefts is the value of the data stored in them rather the cost of the lost component. The precautions to be adopted for safe guarding assets inside the premises should be ensured, to prevent thefts.

Sabotage

This means deliberately destroying computers and related resources. This could also include malicious reprogramming or destruction of computer resources. Access denial to unauthorized persons must be strictly ensured into the places where sensitive hard ware is positioned. Installation of integrated alarm systems and CCTV in the overall security management of banking premises will prove invaluable in prevention and detection of physical crimes.

Electronics Threats

The perpetuators of electronic crime generally target the software to manipulate it to carry out the crime. These persons are highly intelligent and do not have any criminal background. There are no geographical limits for carrying out computer crimes. A terminal with a modern and internet connection can be used to carry out crime in an on-line computer anywhere in the world. Tackling electronic crime is not easy since every new security ring created by any organisation appears to induce criminals to discover new methods to break them. Tackling electronic threats is normally vested with the technical experts to create sufficient checks and lay down stringent procedures and with system administrators to ensure strict implementation of laid down procedures. Though security managers are responsible for providing physical security to the hardware, it is essential that they keep themselves updated with software related crimes. Some of the more serious software related crimes are addressed here.

Scanning

This is a process of presenting sequentially changing information to an automated system to identify those items that receive a positive response. A potential intruder can try out many combinations generated by an automated system to break the authorized passwords, IDs, PIN or telephone numbers to access computers. Credit card numbers can be discovered by scanning and them illegally used.

Hacking

By altering a computer system software to achieve tasks for which it was not originally designed, like obtaining unauthorized access to a networked computer system, to utilize the system for any criminal activity.

Superzapping

The misuses of universal emergency access program, which will bypass all controls to modify, disclose any of the contents, in case of emergency, to carry out electronic crimes. Although super zap is a powerful utility, it is dangerous tool in wrong hands. This is similar to using a master key when all other keys are lost.

The security of super zap should be ensured by safekeeping it in program libraries and its use is restricted to authorized persons only. The use of super zap program leaves no evidence of any changes in data files. Hence it is highly impossible to detect this crime.

Salami Technique

This involves in modifying the program or executing an unauthorized program which debits small amounts, like rounded off fractions, from a large number of accounts, to the credit of a specified account. This way, no controls are violated as no amounts are removed from the system of accounting. Only small amounts are rearranged. Loss to the customers is so small that it goes un-noticed.

Trap Doors

While writing the application programs, software writers use debugging aids or escape routines to bypass all security checks, such as unauthorized access, data entry, modifications and the like. This is adopted as it saves a lot of time at the time of testing or to debug. Normally these trapdoors are deleted while implementing the package, but at times they may get overlooked or left intentionally for future access or modifying the program. Unscrupulous elements may target to locate these trap doors, and can modify the application.

Logic Bombs / Time Bombs

This involves execution of previously programmed instructions, which get activated when given conditions are fulfilled. This allows execution of unauthorized act at a predetermined condition / time.

Other commonly known acts of software piracy and viruses are not discussed as their impact is well evident. What is required to be ensured is the periodic verification of all personnel involved in programming, handling and operations for their commitment, integrity, loyalty and dedication? A discreet watch may be kept over any one found to be suspicious. Crimes related to plastic currency is not discussed, as the crime and security aspects related to cards is a different subject by itself.

Conclusion

A large number of crimes are generally found to be a result of the opportunity created by the victim. "Disasters, it is believed, happen to other unfortunate ones and not to us." The biggest threat to security is the belief that there is no threat. There is a total need to draw an integrated security perspective, involving staff, management, technology and systems, manned by security professional, to prepare for a pro-active security environment. Before creating a paperless banking world, we need to create a matching professional security environment for minimizing loss, as there is nothing known as 'fool-proof security'.

Bank Security – A Paradigm Shift

Ashok Anand

The need for security, perhaps, was first felt when human beings started fixing doors in their houses and shops. As individual and state property increased and threat of theft or looting increased, need for security also increased. (A village on the road between Shirdi and Aurangabad in Maharashtra (India) still has houses without doors. This is an exception perhaps only for preservation of our ancient values and heritage.) From locked doors the human race slowly graduated to highly trained security forces with advanced gadgets and weapons. But is that all that security means – guarding our property? This paper will address this question in due course.

What is Security?

The Oxford English Dictionary assigns four main meanings to the word 'security'. These are 'protection', 'feeling happy or safe', 'security for a loan' or 'shares in company'. The relevant meaning in our context is obviously 'protection'. 'Protection', according to the OED, implies 'activities involved in protecting a country, a building or a person against attack or danger'.

Linkage with Law and Order

It is the National Security (security of the country) which should be of paramount importance. It implies the protection of a nation's assets and interests. The subject of Bank Security along with other similar subjects like Aviation Security, Industrial Security, Economic Security and Individual Security, are only smaller disciplines of one of the requirements for effective National Security viz. internal stability or good law and order situation.

The Paradigm Shift

Until a few years ago security in banks implied just watch and ward duties. Security officers supervised opening and closing of office buildings, reception duties and performed protocol duties and other odd jobs. Guards were mostly used as peons. But deteriorating law and order situation and current internal security scenario are slowly changing the approach of bankers to the requirement of security. There is a paradigm shift.

Full fledged security departments have been created in all nationalized banks. This process started around 1986, during the insurgency-like situation in Punjab. Security officers are now posted in Circle, Zonal and Regional Offices. Detailed procedures and guidelines have been laid down for various types of security checks, inspections and banking activities. Modern gadgets like sensors, close circuit TVs and alarms have been installed. The process is still on. Security consciousness is an important subject during various forms of training of bankers. Feedback, evaluation of equipment and analysis of incidents are important tools for security officers for continued refinement of procedures and systems.

Scope

How is security organized in banks? What is the peculiar nature of threat to banks? What resources are available? How are these employed? Are there any checks and balances? How is cash stored? How about inter branch/city move of cash?

Nature of Threat

Cash is the most attractive object for miscreants. Gold and jewellery (only in selected branches), lockers of clients, security documents (drafts, bankers' cheques etc and bank property like fire arms and computers are the other likely targets. There have been cases of kidnapping of bank managers also. These miscreants are not only robbers, dacoits and petty criminals but also some bank staff. More money is lost by banks through frauds (as also through non- re-coverable loans) than through looting/robbery /dacoity. However, prevention of frauds is not strictly in the charter of duties of the security department.

Other Types of Threat to Banks

These types are common to all citizens as also other institutions. Some of these are area specific or equipment specific. Banks make and practise contingency plans to prevent or minimize their effect. I am referring to the following:

Calamities and Accidents: Natural or man-made calamities like cyclone, earthquake, gas leakage or chemical attack, landslides, fire, air accidents or war

Terrorist Actions: Like letter bombs, anthrax, explosive filled cars or scooters in parking lots

Cyber Crimes: Information technology-related crimes against hardware and communication media like introduction of bugs and virus, hacking and jamming of satellite channels

Storage and Movement of Cash

i. When you deposit cash in a bank, where does it go? And, when you want cash, where does it come from? Cash deposited by customers and cash withdrawn by the customers is seldom the same. In fact, there are some branches where cash deposits are very heavy. These are normally close to bazaars and markets. On the other hand in some branch offices, payments are very heavy. These branches are normally located close to office complexes and they mostly service salaried employees.

ii. Left over cash is stored in a bank's strong room immediately after business hours. Strong rooms are constructed as per specifications given by the Reserve Bank of India (RBI). The security department has laid down the type of gadgets to be used for safety of the strong room.

iii. Cash Retention Limit (CRL) is laid down for each branch, based on past experience and normal cash requirement. Cash over and above this limit has to be deposited in a currency chest.

iv. Currency chest is a bigger and safer vault maintained by nationalized banks on behalf of the RBI. Whereas a strong room may store cash in lakhs, the currency chest may have money in crores. But for a few exceptions, a currency chest is guarded by the police, has hot lines to the nearest police station, close circuit TV system and sensor-based alarm.

v. Each bank can afford to maintain only a few such currency chests. For example, the Punjab National (PNB) has 154 currency chests whereas it has approximately 4,000 branch offices.

vi. Similarly, when a branch office needs cash, it collects either from the currency chest or a neighbouring branch with surplus cash.

vii. Cash is most vulnerable when on the move. Specially built cash vans, along with armed escort, are utilized for the purpose. Small amounts can be moved by bank managers and cash officers themselves, using cash bags or boxes fitted with suitable alarms.

Resources Employed for Bank Security

Prevention of crimes against banks is one of the prime tasks of the state police. Nationalised banks not only hold public money, but they also hold government currency in their currency chests on behalf of the RBI. However, the police have multifarious duties to perform and in some states, the police have little resources for law and order. Bihar and UP are two examples of lawlessness. Therefore, banks have to employ their own guards as also depend on technology.

Branch officers are classified into high-risk, low-risk and normal-risk based on detailed parameters laid down by the Security Department. Number of guards and gadgets to be employed are dictated by these parameters. Some branch offices may not even have a single guard. Most banks have strong rooms, which are almost impregnable. In small branches, and remote and rural areas where there are no strong rooms, proper safes duly embedded in the floor are utilized. Services of community *chowkidars* are also utilized. In addition to all these security measures, complete cash, contents of lockers and bank property are also insured against all possible threats.

Organisation of Security Department of a Nationalised Bank

The security department of a nationalised bank comprises a Chief Security Officer at the Head Office, Zonal Security Officers, Regional Security Officers and Guards. The Chief Security Officer evaluates current threats and visualizes future scenarios. He keeps in touch with the RBI and also coordinates the functioning of Zonal Security Officers. He issues policies and monitors their implementation. He also visits all currency chests and selected branches at random. Punjab National Bank (PNB), for example, has 17 Zonal Offices, 65 Regional Offices and 4,229 Branch Offices (including Extension Counters). A Zonal Security Officer not only monitors and coordinates the activities of the Regional Security Officers but he even performs the duties of a RSO since there are large-scale deficiencies of security officers. Security of the branch office is the responsibility of the branch manager. He is given technical advice by ZSO or RSO through periodical detailed security checks and inspection by a team of bankers from the inspection and control department of the Zonal Office or Head Office.

How Safe are the Banks?

As far as the customers are concerned, they have nothing to fear. They will always get their cash. As regards their items in their individual lockers are concerned, only insurance companies will pay up if the contents were insured by the client.

As far as the bank is concerned, all its assets are insured. It will re-coup bulk of its loss from the insurance company, provided all laid down precautions were taken. However, the Cash in Currency Chests held on behalf of the RBI is not insured. Any loss has to be borne by the bank.

Modus Operandi of Miscreants

An analysis of crimes against the PNB over a period of last ten years indicates the following:

i. Most crimes are in the nature of dacoities committed on the premises. Loss of cash in transit accounts for about 30% cases, and particularly when cash is moved on two-wheelers or rick-shaws.

ii. Bulk of the incidents take place during banking hours i.e., between 10.30 am to 2 pm.

iii. In 90% of the cases, the cash loss was less than Rs 5 lakh.

iv. There has been only one attempt on a currency chest in the last ten years. This was at Ludhiana in Punjab during 1987, when insurgency in Punjab was at its peak.

vi. In villages, locals get hold of dacoits, if the alarm is raised in time. In towns, society only provides onlookers.

vii. Wherever there has been a guard, there has been stiff resistance. Reactions of bank staff are mostly poor. In many cases, even the alarm was not raised. Nobody comes to the rescue of the security guard.

Conclusion

Law and order situation in the country has been thoroughly complicated by terrorists and anti-national elements of various shades. This phenomenon is expected to continue in the foreseeable future. Banks, however law abiding and polite, cannot afford and disregard this reality. We need to make up our manpower shortage and rely more and more on technology to further enhance our security arrangements.

Information Security in Bank

Pramod Damle

Prophecy 25 years back…Comes true

"I believe that the information security will become an even bigger problem, as we move into next century, especially as new smaller computers will operate at blinding speed, making millions of computations in seconds"

– Akio Morito, Sony Corpn., 1986

Info. Attacks and Accidents
an unending list

IIMs' entrance exam
CAT derailed

Accident-turned-Attack
2600@Bell Labs

Attacks – a real concern
Chinese Ghost Net

- **2001 Steel rolling mill burnt**
- **2002 Disks with SSN Stolen**
- **2003 Prisoners' e-Escape**
- **2004 Child Helpline Down**
- **2005 Tokyo Bourse glitch**
- **2006 Cheque cashed at gunpoint**
- **2007 T J Max Cr Card Fraud**
- **2008 Chinese Ghost Net**
- **2009 IIM CAT Exam derailed**
- **2010 Spanish Govt Site Defaced**
- **2011 'Malaysiakini' forced shut**

Why the Web has been a green pasture

Technology	Spread to 50 Million users
Radio	38
PC	16
TV	13
Wireless	12
Internet	4

(Economist'98)

I'm a layman, Why to worry for IT Security?

- 2001 World Economic Summit in New Delhi
  devoted a full session to IT security
- IT Act, 2000 (as amended on 27 Oct 2009)
  Nobody can plead ignorant
- Distant Relation with IT
  ATM, Credit Card, Property deals, ...

Special Features of Cyber Crime
IT Goodies, a double-edged sword
Trans-border Nature
No V
Little
Precis
Weak/
Extrem
Surveys & Research
Cyber Crime Boom
In 2005, Cyber crime overtook
Drug traffic by crossing 100 bn.
... http://www.theregister.co.uk/
2005/11/29/cybercrime/

Security is a function of vigilant mind,
Not just delegated to dumb devices
First Noted Robbery
Bank in Delhi, 1982

Of all the links in Security Chain,
The Weakest one is the Human Link.
. . . Social Engineering focuses right there

Dumpster Diving

Fool . . .

- **Carry all the dust-bin contents to get chunks of husk & an ounce of gold**

Cool . . .

- **Contract with your contracted cleaners or somebody down in the disposal line**

Rule . . .

- **Never throw away the papers, unless they are shredded**

Shoulder Surfing

Fool . . .

- Simply Read your Password / PIN while you're keying it in

Cool . . .

- Just keep an eye on your key-strokes even one char. at a time & then sum up

Rule . . .

- Ensure that there's nobody around, Also try to hinder view with palms

Key Logger/ Key-Ghost

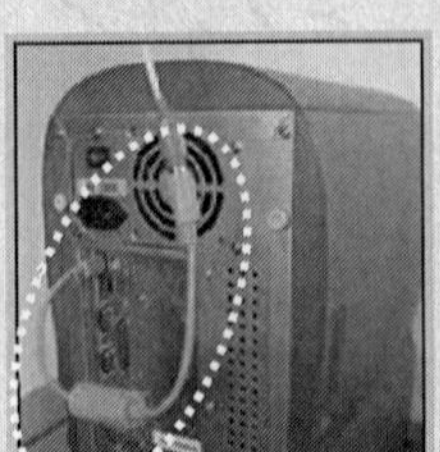

Records each keystroke

Trace & Misuse of

- Password anywhere
- PIN on ATM
- Details of Internet Banking Transaction

Easy Availability

Software & Hardware, too

World is full of Attacks/ Accidents
A – Z of the Exploits

- *0-day Attack*
- *Access Control*
- *Buffer Overrun*
- *Cookies*
- *DOS*
- *Enhanced Rights*
- *Fake Mails*
- *Granularity Issues*
- *Homograph*
- *Identity Theft*
- *Jacking (Blue)*
- *Key Loggers*
- *Log Insertion*
- *Man-in-Middle*
- *Null Dereference*
- *Object Reuse*
- *Phishing*
- *Queued Printing*
- *Race Conditions*
- *SQL Injection*
- *Trap Doors*
- *Unicode Attacks*
- *Virus*
- *Web Applets*
- *XSS*
- *Y2K*
- *Zombies*

... What is the arsenal with us to fight it out?

Reasons for Growing Security Attacks

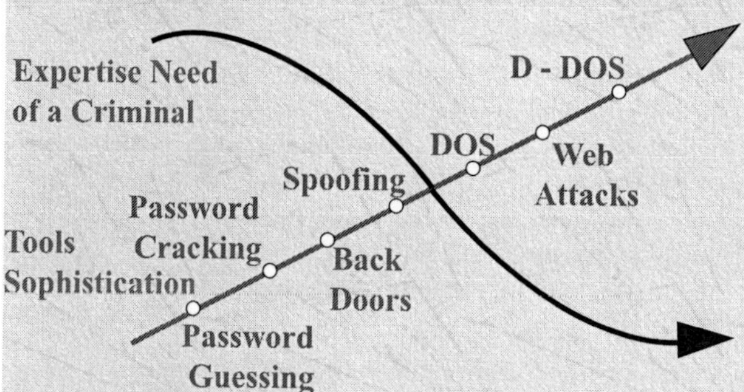

Info security therefore needs a fresh look

Software Blunders: War and Peace

Gulf War 1991 : Patriot missile failed due to clock-drift; effectiveness dropped from 95% to 13%, killing 29 and injuring 97

Peace 1982 : Radiation Therapy device called 'Therac-25', faulty software caused massive radiation overdose to 6 patients, killing 4 of them

- Security not to be bolted on,
  but to be built in the Software
  across all stages of Development

Networks – Some Practical Realities

Message to be transmitted has to be split into several packets

Packets take different paths, and pass thru several network devices, So sniffing possible

Networking systems are highly intricate, and involve many sub-systems

These sub-systems are designed/ deployed by many vendors/ service providers/ nations,
hence the possibility of snooping is high

Thorough security testing is impossible,
as the Internet is a gargantuan phenomenon

Networking Threats
Passive Attacks
Just keeping a watch
Spadework fo
Active A
Inser
Duplic
Deletic
Modific
Change
Spurious Association
Denial of Service
Surveys & Research
Post-26/11 Findings
Less than 10% of the Mumbai Corporate World uses the most rugged network Wi-Fi encryption
... Post-26/11 Survey
STOP

Phishing
• You receive a spoofed mail (from criminals) seemingly sent by your Bank, ISP, ...
• Mail claims that To continue your service It needs Password, PIN, Credit Card No, ...
• Mail gives a link to help you
apparent link of
• Link seems to le
It actually leads
• Your private / co
It might be misus
Surveys & Research
Phishing on Increase ...
Drug lords now prefer phish rings as it's more lucrative & easier than logistics & sale of cocaine
... Gartner Group

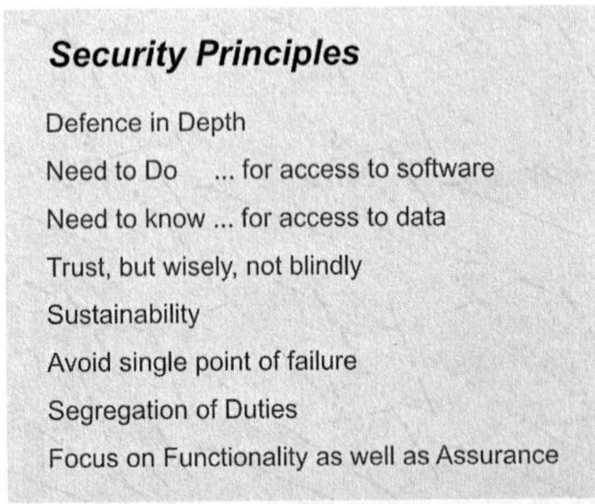
Security Principles
Defence in Depth
Need to Do ... for access to software
Need to know ... for access to data
Trust, but wisely, not blindly
Sustainability
Avoid single point of failure
Segregation of Duties
Focus on Functionality as well as Assurance

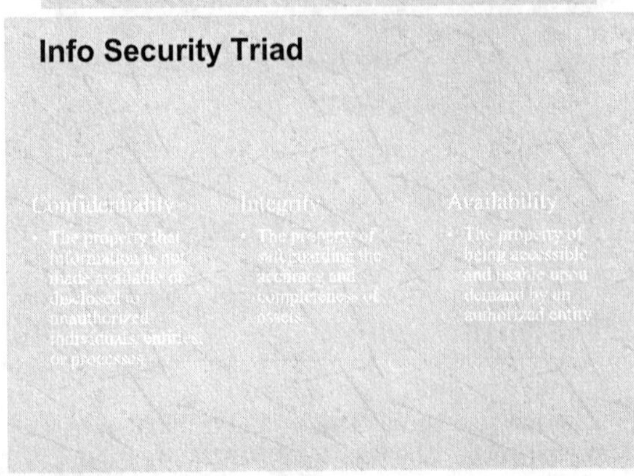
Info Security Triad
Confidentiality
The property that information is not made available or disclosed to unauthorized individuals, entities, or processes
Integrity
The property of safeguarding the accuracy and completeness of assets
Availability
The property of being accessible and usable upon demand by an authorized entity

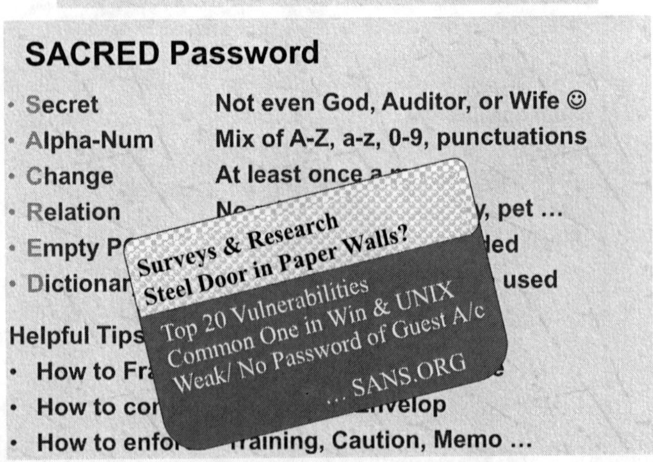
SACRED Password
Secret
Not even God, Auditor, or Wife ☺
Alpha-Num
Mix of A-Z, a-z, 0-9, punctuations
Change
At least once a
Relation
, pet ...
Empty P
led
Dictionar
used
Helpful Tips
How to Fr
How to co
nvelop
How to enfo
raining, Caution, Memo ...
Surveys & Research
Steel Door in Paper Walls?
Top 20 Vulnerabilities
Common One in Win & UNIX
Weak/ No Password of Guest A/c
... SANS.ORG

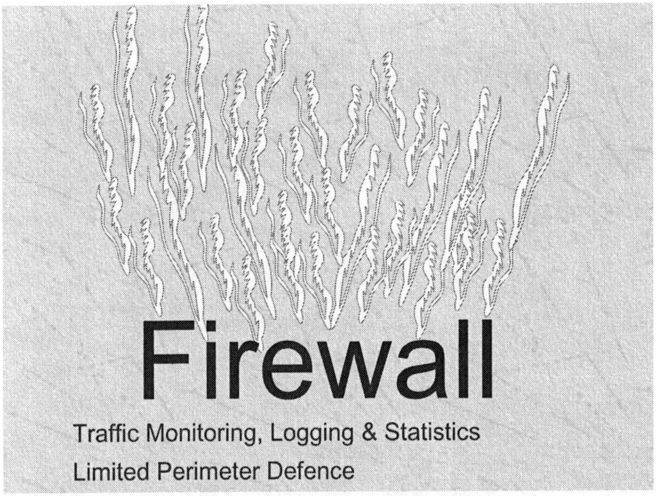
Firewall
Traffic Monitoring, Logging & Statistics
Limited Perimeter Defence

Encryption
keys
Enables Secrecy, Authentication, Integrity
Symmetric Keys & Asymmetric Keys

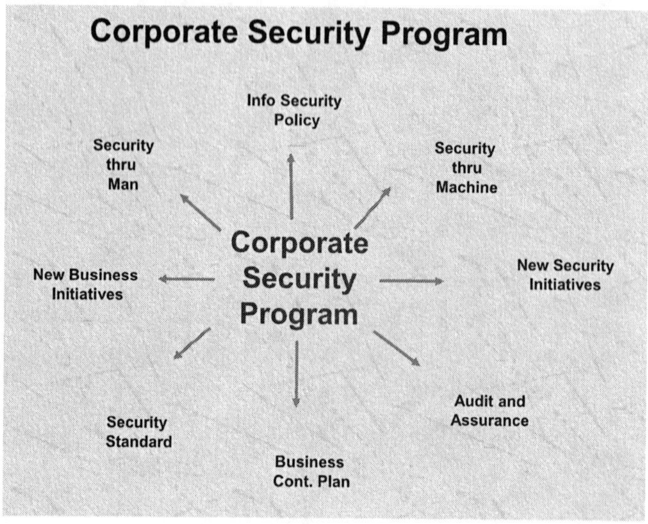

Security Policy Contents

Chapters → *Layers ↓*	*Password*	*Physical*	*Email*	*….*	*….*
Policy	….	….	….	….	….
Procedures	….	….	….	….	….
Guidelines	….	….	….	….	….
….	….	….	….	….	….

When the world was enjoying X'mas 2009,
Barack Obama was signing
Information Classification Order at White House

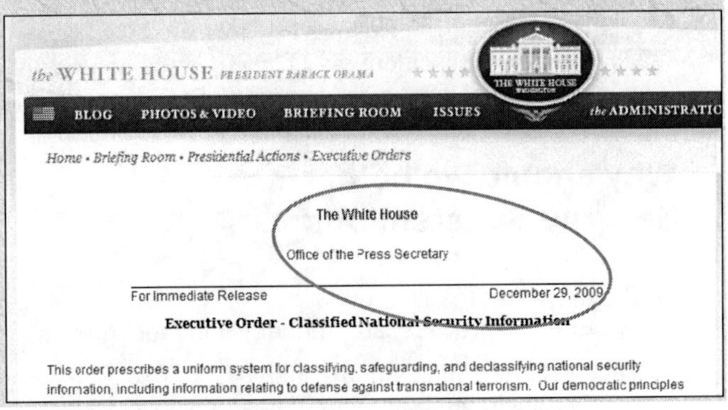

Business Continuity Plan (BCP)

- A plan defined before hand to ensure business continuity even in odd circumstances
- Events like Y2K & 911 have stressed the need, So, now most of companies have BCP in place
- Scope much wider than mere IT function
- Tackles all the critical business processes and their dependence on IT & other resources
- Visualizes various threats and prescribes respective actions commensurate with context

Incident Handling

- Process predefined with templates, workflow and reporting structure
- General incidents: To be reported to general administration
- IT incidents: To be reported to system administrator
- Follow your corporate policy & procedures
- Occasionally, the incident may blow up and become an issue of business continuity, triggering BCP processes

Why should we bother ? Security Superstitions

X Security is a One-time event ?
  ✓ Endless process, so Frequent Hammering !

X Tackle it in 'Formulated' manner ?
  ✓ Needs to be thought from first principles !

X Treated as IT / IS Dept's baby ?
  ✓ Everyone's job : from Sentry to Seniors !

X Ends up in Gadgets / Devices / Systems ?
  ✓ Should Start in Human Mind !

X Firewall will take care of Network ?
  ✓ Preach & Practice 'Defence in Depth' !

Key Points for Users

Lack of password disciplines
Terminals kept logged on
Lax physical access controls
Ignored environmental controls
Careless disposal of printouts
No proper, periodic backup
Improper storage of disks & floppies
Stale/ No Antivirus
Secret data sent in plain text over email
Unlicensed software, games & screensavers
Casual use of Social networking sites

a r e !

Safety First … Cell Phone

- **Cell Phone** ⇨
- ATM

GSM – International Mobile Equipment ID (IMEI)															
Origin & Model Code								Mode Serial Seq.					C	Ver	
A	A	B	B	B	B	B	B	C	C	C	C	C	C	D	E	E

CDMA – Mobile Equipment ID (MEID)														
Manufacturer Code								Serial Number						C
R	R	X	X	X	X	X	X	Z	Z	Z	Z	Z	Z	D

IMSI : 310150312146265		
Country #	310	USA
Company #	150	AT & T
Subscriber #	312146265	Pramod Damle

- •Beware of talking in public place
- •Bluetooth: Safe mate? ↓ after use
- •M-Banking: Caution! Rogue Apps.
- •Caution! Cloning! C…
- •N…
- •… g
- •U… l
- •N… Handset
- •Note IMSI of the SIM card

Surveys & Research
Spoofing equipments let loose

Product called 'Spoof Card' from TelTech Inc. helps change caller's ID & voice at $10/ hour (Feb 2010 … blogs.wsj.com)

Safety First … ATM

- Cell Phone
- **ATM** ⇨

- •Use familiar, well-lit, crowded ATM
- •Caution: Skimmer, Loop, mini-cam
- •Be alert; Don't entertain a stranger
- •Shoulder surf? Shield the keypad!
- •PIN & Card are bad neighbours
- •All cards in wallet? Split them up!
- •Check the A/c; Report shady entry
- •Secure disposal of mini-statement
- •Handy Cust-care no. for hot-listing
- •Memorize PIN, Change it often

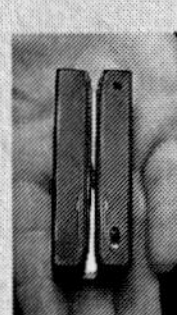

ATM Threats

- Physical Threats
- Shoulder Surfing
- Social Engineering
- Lebanese Loop
- Add-on Devices
- Software Issues
- Data Link down
- Cryptography Factors

ATM Security Solutions

- Wholesome Approach
- Sensors & Alarms
- Cash Management
- Random Checks
- Tab on Outsourcing
- Network Audit
- Software Testing
- Checking of Reports

Tips for Bank Customers

Keep an eye on ATM environ.
In the Booth – Add-On's planted by criminals
Outside – Lurking threats in vicinity
Ensure the Cr/ Dr Card is not out-of-sight
Record CVV of Card elsewhere, deface it from the Card
Enable various SMS alerts for transactions
Intimate your banker, if the mobile no. is changed
Routinely check the statement of account
Don't fall prey to the phishing, smishing, et. al.
Don't put all eggs in one basket
Keep the customer care phone number handy

I have a dream, I have a dream, ...

Everyone is using password neatly
Every surfer has installed a firewall
Digital signatures outnumber traditional ones
Data transmitted in plain is as rare as a ghost
Papers are found only in files & shredders
A CD is either in a drive or in drawers
Nobody is violating any e-mail netiquettes

Let's fulfill the dream
... or else it may turn out to be a nightmare!

Info with Care!

Is it a fantasy ... like cubical watermelons?

Cubical Watermelons Designed & Developed in Japan

Ref. Times of India 17th June, 2001

Our <u>ATTITUDES</u> also could be remoulded with patient & perseverant efforts !!!

Arms Act, Arms Rules, Guns and Ammunition

S Sreeramulu

The Arms Act, 1959

Section 3

- No person shall acquire, have in his possession, carry any fire arms or ammunition unless be holds in this behalf a license issue in accordance with this Act.
- A person may carry a fire arm without holding a license under the written authority of the licensee for repair or for renewal of the license.
- In the presence of the licensee another person may carry fire arms on behalf of the licensee for his use.

The Arms Rules, 1962

Rule 2 (f)

i. "District Magistrate" includes any district or post there of, an additional district magistrate or any other office specially empowered in this behalf by the government of the state concerned.
ii. In relation to a Union Territory, any officer specially empowered by the central government in this behalf.

iii. In relation to the tribal areas of Assam, specified in part B or the table appended to Para 29 of Sixth Schedule to the Constitution, a political officer.

iv. In West Bengal (Kolkota) commissioner of police and deputy commissioner of police.

v. "District Magistrate" in relation to any area for which a commissioner of police has been appointed means the commissioner of police there of and includes any such deputy Commissioner of Police, exercising Jurisdiction over the whole or any part of such area, as may be specified by the state government in this behalf in relation to such area or parts.

Rule 51: Application for license

Every application for the grant of a license under these rules

(a) Shall be submitted in form 'A'.

(b) May be presented by the applicant in person or send through the medium of post office or otherwise, to the licensing authority, as far as possible, showing jurisdiction in respect of the place, where he ordinarily resides or has in his occupation.

Section 13: Provisions relating to licenses

Application form 'A' under Rule 51 of the Arms Rule 1952 is submitted to licensing authority. The licensing authority after following the procedure shall grant a license under Section 3 of the Act for the following requirement.

1. For having gun not less than 22 inches barrel in length
2. For protection, (b) Sport, (c) Display or (d) Muzzle loading gun to be used for bona fide crop protection .

- No person shall acquire, have in his possession or carry at any time, more than three fire arms,
- Except dealer of fire arms,
- Rifle club or Rifle association.
- Licensed by the government of India

Section 14: Refusal to Grant License

- It depends upon the report of the police officer.
- If a person has criminal record though a case ended in an acquittal.

Section 15: Duration of license

- Three years.
- For renewal also the procedure Sections. 13 and 14 apply.
- No time limit is prescribed in the statute for submitting an application by the licensee requesting for renewal.
- Reasonable delay may be granted.
- Renewal shall not be refused on the ground of delay.
- Ramkirpal Vs. State of UP
- 1987 ALJ 1209 Allahabad High Court.

The Arms Rules, 1962

Rule 54: Renewal of Licenses

54 (1) Every license may, at its expiration and subject to the same condition (if any) as to the grant there of, be renewed by the authority mentioned in schedule II as renewing authority.
54 (4) The licensing authority may consider an application renewal of a license, if the period between the date of its expiry and the date of application with due regard to the circumstances of the case, and all renewal fee for the intervening period are paid; otherwise the application may be treated as one for grant of a fresh license.

Section 17: Revocation of licenses

Grounds

- Conviction, unsound mind, prohibited by this Act, suppression of material information, contravention of conditions of license.
- It is necessary for the security of the public peace or for public safety to suspend or revoke the license or on the request of the holder of license the central government by order in the Gazette.

- Section 17 (2)
- The licensing authority may on application of the holder of a license vary the conditions of the license.
- Rule 53 (2) on application from a company holding a license in form No II or form No III for a change in the name of retainer, the necessary amendment may be made by the licensing authority.

Rule 13: Of Retainer

A license in Form III granted to a company for the protection of its premises or property shall be in the name of a member, agent or other representative of the company, who shall be responsible for the custody of weapon. The name of a servant or any other employee entrusted with weapon for guarding the premises or property of the company shall be entered as a retainer in the appropriate column of the license. The licensing authority shall issue to the licensee a permit in Form III – B for each of such retainers shown in the license.

- The permit shall remain in the personal custody of the representative of the company and shall be made over to the retainers when they are entrusted with the weapon covered by the license.
- (Provided that the licensing authority shall obtain a report from the police about the antecedents of the retainer and take into consideration such report before admitting him as retainer) As per Amendment Dt. 15.7.1981.

Section 45

Exempts a public servant from the operation of the provisions contained in the Arms Act, since a forest guard is a public servant and provisions contained in Clause (ii) of Section 45 (b) will apply. According to Section 45, the provisions of Arms Act 1959 shall not apply to a public servant under Clause ii of Section 45 (b) in the course of his duty of such public servant.

Extract of Arms Act 1959, Section 3

no person, other than a person referred to in sub-section (3), shall acquire, have in his possession to carry, at any time, more than three firearms:

(3) Nothing contained in sub-section (2) shall apply to any dealer in firearms or to any member of a rifle club or rifle association licensed or recognised by the Central Government using a point 22 bore rifle or an air rifle for target practice.

(1) No person shall acquire, have in his possession, or carry any firearm or ammunition unless he holds in this behalf a license issued in accordance with the provisions of this Act and the rules made there under:

Provided that a person may, without himself holding a licence carry any firearms or ammunition in the presence, or under the written authority, of the holder of the licence for repair or for renewal of the licence or for use by such holder.

- This notification is the means by which Banks and some Private Security Organizations could purchase arms against the designations and issue the same to the armed guard (an employee of the Bank) for performance of duty at the Branch/with the cash van. ('Retainer' System)
- Recently RBI has allowed banks to outsource the operations of cash vans.
- As a consequence, the need for Security Service Providers to buy weapons in the name of the Branch Manager running the operations becomes justified.
- We need to get the PSAR Act extended to cover this aspect
- Or else, a clarification to be issued by the MHA (to all State Governments) that the said Notification applies mutatis mutandis to well established national level security agencies, will do.

Bomb Threat Training

S B Tyagi

Most bomb threats are hoaxes and are primarily made to disrupt business operations. Authenticity will be gauged by management for the safety of people and property. But we must have a plan in place before a threat is received.

Notification

After creating a response plan tailored to the unit, specifically, taking into account the unique operations of the unit and its size, in the event of a threat, notify police or security for your campus immediately. The respective department will notify the Campus Crisis Decision Team and the local police.

Bomb Threat Response

The campus police will respond to the site to determine if any occupants are present and evacuate the building. Bomb threats can be received in different forms such as by phone, email, mail or observation and should be taken seriously. These threats can be specific or non-specific.

Immediate Actions

If a bomb threat is received it is important to know what to do:

Individual Action

- Remember details of conversation
- Accent, if foreign?
- Gender
- Innuendos as to bomb location
- Respond in a matter-of-fact manner, asking the caller to repeat what they said
- Immediately report the incident to your supervisor
- See bomb threat checklist

Supervisor Action

- Immediately report the incident to the police or security department
- Start building evacuation, and be sure each person is out of building
- Direct an orderly evacuation, if appropriate
- Protect official records, if possible
- Arrange to have members of staff to accompany emergency services on inspection
- If a suspicious object is found, do not touch!
- Keep a running log of conditions as they occur

Receiving a Bomb Threat

Upon receipt of a bomb threat remain calm. Listen carefully about what's being said for background noise or voices and for an accent or other voice characteristics. Always take the call seriously and do not interrupt the caller. Ask the caller to repeat any part of the conversation you did not understand. Obtain as much information as possible and write it down using the Bomb Threat Report Form. Attempt to alert others to contact police while remaining on line with the caller. Inform the caller that detonation can cause injury or death to others. Note the time of the call.

Developing a Response Plan

Each unit within the organization must create a response plan, which MPD is happy to assist with. The response plan should include:

- Formation of a Threat Response Team
- Assigned and defined team functions
- Establish an emergency team communications system
- Know available resources
- Have an understanding of emergency responders procedures
- On a consistent basis conduct a plan review and continually update
- Conduct training as needed
- Coordinate with neighboring units/departments
- It is important to follow and familiarize yourself with the organization's Bomb Threat Procedures.

Security Situation in the Country

D C Nath

In November 2004, a United Nations Secretary General report described terrorism as any act "intended to cause death or serious bodily harm to civilians or non-combatants with the purpose of intimidating a population or compelling a government or an international organization to do or abstain from doing any act." The origin of terrorism: Latin word terrere meaning "to frighten."

Distinguishing terrorism and other types of crimes

- Terrorism is political in aim and motive
- Violent or, equally important, threats
- Designed to have far-reaching psychological repercussions beyond the immediate victim or target
- Conducted by an organization with an identifiable chain of command or conspiratorial cell structure and
- Perpetrated by a sub national group or non-state entity

Sources of Threats to Internal Security

- Foreign sponsored terrorist groups
- Naxalite (LWE) groups

- Separatist groups
- Criminal syndicates and mafias

Forms of Terrorism

- Physical Terrorism
- Cyber Terrorism (Virtual)
- Bio-Terrorism
- Psychological Terrorism
  The terms "terrorism" and "terrorist" (someone who engages in terrorism) carry strong negative connotations.
- Those labelled as terrorists use terms specific to their situation, such as separatist, freedom fighter, liberator, revolutionary, militant, guerrilla, rebel, patriot, or any similar-meaning word in other languages and cultures. Jihadi, mujaheddin, and fedayeen are similar Arabic words

Major Terrorist / Fundamental Entities

- Lashkar-e-Tayyabah
- Al Badr
- Harkat-ul-Jehad-e-Islami (Huji)
- Deendar Anjuman
- SIMI
- LWE (Left wing extremism)

Objectives of Terrorists

- To cause political instability
- To cause social insecurity
- To create fear psychosis
- To cause economic disruption
- To establish Dar-ul-Islam (Land of Islam)
- To escalate drug trafficking/organized crimes
- To establish links with hostile countries

Strategy of Terrorists

- Indoctrination of gullible youths

- Exploiting security lapses
- Availing latest technology/weapons/IED
- Indulging in subversive/disruptive activities
- Targeting Vital installations & prominent persons
- Making use of 'Fidayeen' (Sharp shooters) and 'Suicide squads' as operatives.
- Attract maximum publicity

Indicators

- Plans to carry out sensational acts of violence in India
- Target IT/BT companies
- Mafia and other criminal syndicates extend their support to terrorists/radicals

Major International Terrorist Attacks

11 September 2001:
World Trade Tower:
Death toll over 6000

11 March 2004:
Madrid Train Bombing:
191 dead, 3000 hurt

30 June 2007: Blazing car crashes into Glasgow International Airport

27 December 2007: Pakistan Prime Minister Benazir Bhutto was assassinated in a terrorist attack. More than 20 killed

Terrorist Attacks In India

28 December 2005:

Firing at delegates assembled at Tata Auditorium, IISc, Bangalore, which killed a professor and injured four others.

11 July 2006: Mumbai train bombings:

209 killed and over 700 injured.

25 August 2007: Blasts at Lumbini Amusement Park

and Gokul Chat Bhandar, Hyderabad: Killed 42.

1 January 2008: Seven CRPF Jawns were killed and five injured

in a terrorist attack at Rampur, Uttar Pradesh

26 November 2008: Mumbai attack, over 200 killed

Targets of Terrorism

- Strategic infrastructure
- Defence establishments
- Vital installations
- Public Infrastructure
- Important Places
- Economic Infrastructure
- Historical Monuments

Left wing Extremism (Naxalism)

- Armed agitation at Naxalbari, Silligurhi, West Bengal in 1967.
- 182 districts, 12 states
- Worst affected: Chattisghad, Jharkhand, AP, Orissa
- Partially affected: Madhya Pradesh, Bihar, Maharashtra, UP & Karnataka.
- Collect Rs 500 to 700 crore annually from corporates, big companies, merchants, businessman and the government officials.

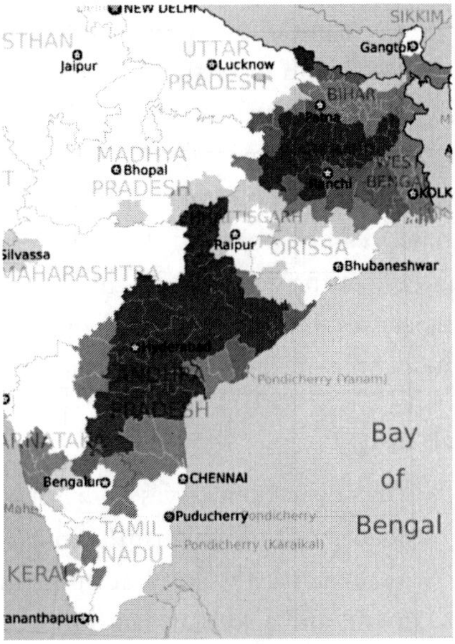

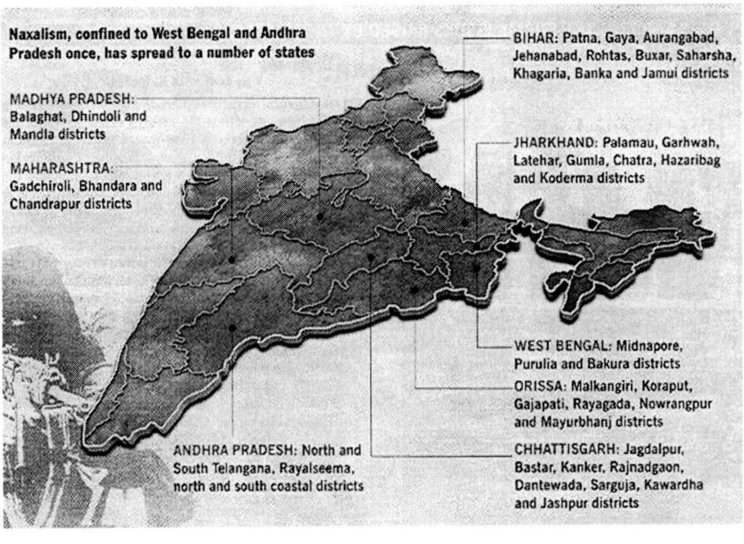

Ideology of Naxals

- Anti-democratic and against the Constitution of India
- To bring about social and economic change through armed resolution to establish revolutionary democracy

Ramakrishna, then general secretary, CPML–PWG announced in 2004: Talks are with a purpose to force the Government to address the pressing problems of the people, we do not believe that suffering masses can be liberated through negotiations and Capturing power and liberating people from the clutches of exploitative capitalists ruling classes. Using the Dandakaranya region as a lever we will liberate the people of this country to establish people's rule.

Strategy

- To project themselves as saviours of tribals / poorer section and champions of socialism/communism;
- To overawe the local administration, including forest department, and also local landlords & tribals.
- Extort money and snatch arms from the rich landlords.
- Attack police & forest officials to take away weapons and to demoralise them.
- Jana Adalats to speedy disposal of local matters.

Composition

- Central Committee
- Politburo
- Regional Bureau
- Zonal Committees
- Divisions
- Dalams - Sangams
- 39 LWE Groups
- PWG and MCC account for 35 per cent of violence.
- 15 October 2004 - PWG & MCC merged as Communist Party of India – CPI (Maoist)
- Overall strength

- 20000 UGs
- 50000 OGs
- More than 1 lakh in Frontal Organizations.

Weapons

- 900 AK 47 Rifles
- 200 LMGs
- Hundreds Grenade Firing Rifles
- Thousands other weapons
- Huge quantity of explosives

Dandakaranya Area

- Claimed as liberated zone
- Spread over Chattisgarh, Andhra Pradesh, Maharashtra.
- 10,000 Sq Kms 237 villages, 20,000 Tribal families.
- More than a dozen Training Camps.
- Nerve Center of Naxalism has used for Central Committee and Poling Bureau meetings.

1980 Resolution of PWG Central Committee

Homogenous contiguous forested area around Bastar Division, Chattisgarh and adjoining areas of Adilabad, Karimnagar, Khammam, East Godavari Districts of AP, Chandrapur and Garchehiroli district of Maharastra, Balaghat districts of MP, Malkagiri and Koraput districts of Orissa would comprise the area of Dandakarnaya which would be liberated and used as base for spreading peoples democratic revolution.

Deaths related to violence

The Silda camp attack killed 24 paramilitary personnel of the Eastern Frontier Rifles in an operation the guerillas stated was the beginning of "Operation Peace Hunt", the Maoist answer to the government "Operation Green Hunt" that was recently launched against them.

Period	Civilians	Security forces	Naxals	Total per period
1996	N/A	N/A	N/A	156[6
1997	202	44	102	348
1998	118	202	110	270
1999	115	36	212	363
2000	N/A	N/A	N/A	50
2001	N/A	N/A	N/A	564
1989-2001	**1,610**	**432**	**1,007**	**3,049**
2002	382	100	141	623
2003	410	105	216	731
2004	466	100	87	653
2005	524	153	225	902
2006	521	157	274	952
2007	460	236	141	837
2008	399	221	214	834
2009	586	317	217	1,120
2010	713	285	171	1,169
Total	**5,982**	**2,097**	**2,796**	**10,875**

On 6 April, Naxalite rebels killed 76, consisting of 74 paramilitary personnel of the CPRF and two policemen. Fifty others were wounded in the series of attacks on security convoys in Dantewada district in the central Indian state of Chattisgarh. The attack resulted in the biggest loss of life security forces have suffered since launching a large-scale offensive against the rebels.

On 17 May, a Naxalite landmine destroyed a bus in Dantewada district, killing up to 44 people including several Special Police Officers (SPOs) and civilians.

On 28 May the derailment of a Kolkata–Mumbai night train killed at least 150 persons. Maoists were responsible for the sabotage which caused the disaster. On 29 June, at least 26 policemen are killed in a Maoist attack in the central Indian state of Chhattisgarh.

On 29 August, a joint team of BSF and district police was attacked by the rebels in Bhuski village (Chhattisgarh) under Durg Kondal police station in the district while they were conducting routine search operations in the wee hours. Following the attack, the forces retaliated and in the action they lost five security personnel, including three BSF jawans.

On 29 and 30 August, rebels ambushed a joint paramilitary-police team in Bihar, killing 10, wounding 10 more, taking 4 prisoners and robbing more than 35 automatic rifles from the state forces. The Naxalites later freed 3 of the policemen after Naxal leader Kishenji met with worried family members.

On 12 September, Naxalites killed three policemen and took 4 more hostage in an ambush in Chhattisgarh. The 4 policemen were later released without conditions after Naxal leaders listened to the appeals of family members. The freed policemen also promised the Naxals to never take up arms against the insurgency again.

On 5 October, rebels killed 4 Special Forces officers as they were on their way to a market in Maharashtra.

On 7 October, Naxalites attempted derailment of Triveni express, a train of Singrauli-Bareilly route, by removing 4 fishplates and 42 sleeper clips.

On 8 October, Naxalites triggered a landmine in the border area between Chhattisgarh and Maharashtra. The attack killed 3 special forces officers, wounded 2 more and destroyed a military jeep.

According to the BBC, more than 6,000 people have died during the rebels' 20-year fight between 1980 and 2000.

Based on the above displayed statistics, it can be determined that more than 14,300 people have been killed since the start of the insurgency in 1980, of which more than half died in the last ten years.

International Cooperation

- Given the external imperatives of terrorist violence in J&K, North-East and certain other parts of the country, bilateral and multilateral cooperation is vital.
- Bilateral talks are held at PM and Foreign Minister levels as well as during calls on the Home Minister by Foreign dignitaries.
- Home Secretary level talks/ Joint Working Groups meetings are held at least once a year with Pakistan, Nepal, Bangladesh, Myanmar and Bhutan to discuss bilateral transborder security and crime related issues.
- Joint Working Groups (JWGs) on Counter Terrorism exist with 27 countries and two regional groups viz. EU and BIMSTEC.
- Mutual Legal Assistance Treaties (MLATs) in criminal matters are in force with 22 countries and ratification process with 5 other countries is in progress.
- Bilateral institutional mechanisms in preventing illicit trafficking in drugs matters have been signed with 27 countries.
- Extradition Treaties with 26 countries are in force and ratification process with 6 other countries is in process.
- A Memorandum of Understanding on Cooperation is signed with China and Vietnam.
- India is an active member of the global coalition against terrorism.
- India has been supportive of all UN measures to combat the menace of global terrorism.

- SAARC provides regional forum to fight terrorism and drug trafficking.

Initiatives Proposed to Strengthen Internal Security Systems

- Well co-ordinated and efficient intelligence machinery at the Centre and in the States is critical.
- Need to strengthen new mechanisms like MAC, SMACs, JTFI and ISISTs to improve collection and dissemination of counter intelligence.
- The States have been asked to earmark upto 5% of their annual allocations under the Scheme for Modernization of State Police Forces for strengthening Special Branches of State Police and also revive the Beat constable system, to improve skills for actionable intelligence gathering.
- Need for greater alertness and regular surveillance on the part of intelligence agencies and local police to identify and pre-empt terrorist modules or sleeper cells in some parts of the country.
- Strengthening of community policing systems to enable improved understanding between the police and the people and collection of local intelligence.
- A low cost proxy-war situation is to be managed over a longer term. Therefore, the Central Government needs to provide more resources for maintenance of internal security including in the 11th Five Year Plan.
- The States also need to allocate more funds in their budgets and State Plans for augmenting their police strength, number of police stations, and improving overall policing, particularly in the areas prone to, and affected by, terrorism/extremism.
- The States will need to improve the existing police population ratio of 1:699.
- Need for enhanced physical security of vital installations, important buildings, places of congregations, market places, etc.

- Need for upgradation of security of railway infrastructure and trains including Metro Rail systems.
- Need for including specific security requirements of various infrastructure projects in naxal/terrorism affected areas, into project costs.

Area, Population Density and Incidence of Crime per 1 lakh Population in different Countries

S. No.	Country	Area (in sq.miles)	Population density (per sq. Mile)	Incidence of crime per 1 lakh population
1.	Argentina	10753514	36	3541.50
2.	Australia	2988888	7	4440.70
3.	Austria	32378	256	7404.20
4.	Bulgaria	42822	180	1775.50
5.	Canada	3849670	8	8512.60
6.	England and Wales*	94548	640	9312.36
7.	Finland	130560	40	1525.00
8.	Germany	137830	598	7747.40
9.	India	1269340	884	455.80
10.	Israel	8131	890	6001.70
11.	Japan	145869	876	1488.32
12.	Malaysia	127317	211	672.34
16.	New Zealand	104452	40	10116.58
17.	Pakistan	307375	539	286.99
18.	South Africa	471444	100	4171.10
19.	Sri Lanka	25332	784	213.00
20.	Sweden	173730	52	13753.00
21.	Thailand	198116	329	576.22
22.	USA	3717796	80	7797.80

* Area and population density pertain to England and Wales; Incidence of crime pertains to UK, N.B. Compiled by National Crime Records Bureau.

Incidence of Crime under various Crime-heads in different Countries

Country	Murder	Robberyand Voilent theft	Breaking and Entering	Other Thefts	Fraud	Counterfiet Currency	Total
Argentina	3130	386916	792889	-	12218	2197	1349654
Australia	769	16789	284188	599866	89198	-	902733
Canada	1430	28669	259521	658205	94468	163323	2747053
England and Wales	-	98200	645200	721500	233000	-	5556500
Germany	2396	54841	889883	1786804	1102261	7873	6391715
India	32719	22814	90108	187402	67197	2383	5026337
Israel	177	3105	60061	34529	12130	364	419339
Japan	1392	1725072	34518	-	85596	3765	1902113
Pakistan	9631	12863	14594	36677	-	-	453264
Sri Lanka	1221	13976	18656	-	4009	35	42548
USA	16692	417122	6776807	-	-	-	23113708

- A mechanism for co-ordination and support on security related issues among Delhi and the adjoining States within the NCR.
- Effective enforcement of the Unlawful Activities (Prevention) Act, 1967 and National Security Act, 1980 and other relevant laws.
- It may be necessary to consider concurrent jurisdiction by a Central Agency to investigate and prosecute select cases of terrorism and other related crimes, with support of, and in coordination with, the concerned State police.
- Participation of local community leaders to be enlisted to help prevent terrorist activities. No particular community is to be held responsible for anti-national activities of a few fringe individuals.
- The Central Government will continue to coordinate with the States and closely monitor the internal security situation in the country and provide all possible assistance to supplement their efforts and resources in successfully managing the challenges and threats to internal security and law and order situation in the country.

Trends in Banking crimes

- Change in services provided
  # Banks ready to take risk
- Crime trend in society
- Legislations and relevant regulations

Types of Crimes

- (a) Burglary, (b)Theft, (c) Extortion, (d)Robbery, (e)Dacoity, (f)Cash Snatching, etc.,
- Frauds and Embezzlement
- e-crimes
- ATMs
- Cards

Theft/Robbery

- Predictable and standardized layout
- Un-armed bank staff
- Tellers young and predominantly females
- Staff compliant, efficient and facilitate quick and efficient transaction

Fraud & Embezzlement

- Product management acceptance of risk
  * Probability of failure
  * Staff services become costlier and increase in automation
  * POS concept
- Banking services through electronic system
  * Verification of identity
  * Correct identification through biometrics
  * Requisite no of staff with IT knowledge
  * Use electronics for earlier deduction crimes
- Data loss
  * No restriction on removable devices
  * Rely on staff loyalty alone

ATM Crimes

Types of ATM Frauds?

- Card fraud
- Operational frauds
- Equipment fraud

Types of ATM Security

- Digital Security
- Physical Security
- Transactional Integrity & Security
- Device Operation & Security
- Customer Identity Security
- Consumer Safety at ATM

ATM Fraud Techniques

- Card Theft
- Card skimming
- Shoulder surfing
- Fake PIN Pad Overlays & Other Fake Equipment
- PIN Interception
- Accessing Cash with False Presenters
- Transactional Reversal
- Burglaries
- Operational Fraud

Are ATMs Really Secure?

- Rs 4.5 lakh was looted from the ATM of a well known bank in Hyderabad
- The fact that the criminal was able to get inside the ATM enclosure through a ventilator and that he knew the combination number for the ATM cash vault speaks a lot about the present state of security awareness in banks.
- ATM users in Chennai were recently swindled to the tune of Rs 7.5. lakh by the use of forged cards.
- A businessman in Pune, a shopkeeper & a film personality in Chennai were kidnapped and forced to withdraw money from ATMs.
- A customer's card was swallowed by the ATM after a time out operation in Hyderabad. The next day an unauthorised withdrawal of Rs 5,100 was made from her account.
- Still, what has happened so far in India is peanuts compared with what is happening the world over. Crimes are taking place all over the globe on a large scale and the police are battling organised gangs which capture PIN codes and magnetic stripe data, inflicting losses running to millions of dollars on banks and their customers.
- Criminals use several ways of stealing from ATMs. Take, for example, Phantom Withdrawals

- ATM debit entries that baffle both bank officials and detectives.
- Large sums of money vanish from accounts in spite of the customer not using the ATM, keeping the card secure and keeping the PIN confidential.
- How does the money vanish? By capturing the ATM card through a Lebonese loop inserted into the card slot or through the 'skimming' method where criminals fix tiny spy cameras and magnetic devices on the ATM, which transmit the magnetic stripe data and the PIN information to recording equipment placed in a car nearby.
- In the 'social engineering' method, the criminal presents himself as a police officer, bank employee or some other responsible person and coaxes the card details out of the victim through one tale or another.
- A variant of this method is to send email messages to ATM users in a format that exactly resembles the bank's letterhead convincing them that they should send their credit card numbers and PIN codes to a web site. Customers of Citibank, ANZ, Barclays Bank and America Online were targets of this scam.
- Criminals ambush the ATM user while he is withdrawing money or kidnap him while he stops the car near an ATM. Sometimes, they burgle a house and then take the owner to an ATM and force him to withdraw cash.
- Those who do not have the patience for clever and cunning methods opt for a direct attack on the ATM. They use drills, heavy hammers or welding equipment for opening a hole in the ATM and reach out for the cash.
- Strongly built ATMs are pulled out with a lorry or heavy construction equipment and taken away.

Role of Security Head

- To be highly involved in protection & Investigation
- Manage specialized and technically proficient persons.

- Make management aware of crime and security and translate importance of security within organization
- Integrate problems of loss exposure and product performance, monitor evidence of fraud
- Use of security expertise and technical competence security professionals can become valued business partners

Loss prevention

- Preventing frauds and embezzlement should be primary focus
- As security rarely performs a function not performed by others it should ensured that internal specialist are not assigned from within business unit

- What he really is doing is placing a trap in the ATM machine to "capture" the next user card.

- Altering the ATMs is a risky business, these individuals work in teams. The lookout warns of any possible eye witnesses / or of the next potential victim.

- Here we see the next client using the ATM, after the trap has been set. He inserts his card and begins his transaction.

- The ATM card is confiscated, and the customer is confused, asking himself, Why has my card been confiscated? However, here we see the cavalry coming to help, (HELP!!!).

- The good Samaritan convinces the "Customer" He can recover the card, if he presses his PIN at the same time the Samaritan press "cancel" and "enter".

- After several attempts the "customer" is convinced his card has been confiscated. The "customer" and the Samaritan leave the ATM.

- Satisfied the area is clear, the thief
- returns to recover the confiscated card from his trap. He not only has the card, he also has the PIN the "customer" provided unknowingly.

- The trap is made up of XRAY film, which is the preferred material by thieves; Simply because of the black color which is similar in appearance to the slot on the card reader.

- The trap is then inserted into the ATM slot. Care is taken not to insert the entire film into the slot, the ends are folded and contain glue strips for better adhesion to the inner and outer surface of the slots.

- Once the ends are firmly glued and fixed to the slot, it is almost impossible to detect by unsuspecting clients.

- Slits are cut into both sides of the trap, This prevents your card being returned prior to completing your transaction.

- As soon as the "Customer" has gone, and they have your PIN , The thief can remove the glued trap, by grasping the folded tips, he simply pulls the trap out that has retained your card..

- 1.-Once your card has been confiscated, observe the ATM slot and the card reader for any signs of tampering. Should you see the film tips glued to the slot, unglue, pull the trap out and recover your card.
- 2.- Report IMMEDIATELY to the BanK.

HRD Role in Security

Prem Sagar

The safety, honour and welfare of the country comes first, the honour, welfare and comfort of the men you command come next and your own ease, comfort and safety comes the last. Always and every time.

What is Security?

Security means:

- without care or anxiety
- Free from danger
- Safe, confident and over confident
- Assured
- Stable
- Firmly fixed or held
- To make secure the possession

Who is responsible for security?

Security is for the people, by the people and of the people. Every human being has the right to full growth. He has the right to demand from humanity all that can confirm its development. He has the right to work, to produce, to create without any category of human being submitting his work to Usury or to a yoke. So all of us are in a way responsible for security or insecurity. More specifically, it is:

- You and I create wealth – you and I steal it.
- You and I create computers and information technology for betterment of mankind. You and I commit cyber crimes, steal credit cards and encash them.
- You and I bring about advancement in pharmaceuticals and medical care. You and I become doctors to heal mankind. You and I steal kidneys and other body parts and trade them for money.
- You and I create nuclear energy to power our industry and to make as much comfortable by use of electricity. You and I use this technology to make nuclear weapons for our own destruction. Now we are worried as to how to secure ourselves form such weapons. Similar is the situation with chemical and biological weapons.
- It is you and I who are moles within and it is you and I who are the unfaithful. We have reached a stage where we suspect each other.
- It means you have to secure yourself from me and I have to secure myself for you.
- It means the only cause of insecurity is you and me.
- It is you and me who are good and it is you and me who are evil.
- Therefore, HR means banishment of evil from you and me, the only cause of insecurity.
- Therefore, HR means development of you and me, i.e. education of you and I. Education to banish evil from us.

What is education?

- Bringing up of a child – Training of a Child
- Strengthening of the powers of body and mind

- Refined understanding and appreciation of art and literature.
- Napoleon said, give me good mothers. I will give you a great nation
- Mark Twain said, I do not allow my schooling to influence my education

Development of Human being

Development of human being commences right in his childhood. If we can develop a person who is:

- Caring
- Un-selfish
- Co-operating
- Helpful in others' needs. Hold hand while some one is in distress.
- God fearing
- Noble
- Honest
- Dependable
- Upright
- Man of honour, man of character, man with high morals
- Man who shares sorrows and happiness with others equally

People – Development

- Are they well-fed – Availability of good nutrition during various phases of growth.
- Average Life Expectancy, The infant mortality Rate.
- The availability of living space.
- Availability of Drinking Water and its quality.
- Availability of sanitation.
- Lower incidence of various diseases – Availability of Health Centres medicines and Hospitals – Access to medical facilities.
- Literacy – Availability of schools and educational facilities.
- Impart various levels of skills to cope with fast changing economic and social demands.

- Can be and will be many more as per the needs of economic dynamics.

What kind of a human being should be developed?

A human being should have the following virtues to be secured

- Right beliefs
- Right aspirations
- Right conduct
- Right mode of livelihood
- Right mindedness
- Right Rapture (extreme delight)

Empowerment of People

- Empowerment will only come when national political consensus reigns – Mr Subir Raha, Chairman, ONGC.
- Empowerment is in seeking and speaking without fear or favour. It is the ability to achieve what we want – Army Chief Gen JJ Singh.
- There can be no economic freedom, indeed no freedom at all, without employment – Kamal Nath, Union Minister for Urban Dvelopment.
- India will be fully empowered when service and technology become crucial to all developmental processes, fields, as diverse as health education, transportation, housing, rural electrification, sanitation, drinking water and desalination require intensive employment of new technology and this could go a long way in empowering the country – Kapil Sibal, Union Minister of Science and Technology.
- The day I can provide the same healthcare to a poor farmer that the President receives, that will be "India Empowered" to me – Dr Anbumani Ramdass, Ex-Union Minister for Health and Family Welfare.
- A Citizen who pursues a legal avenue can bring peace and prosperity to himself, his family and surroundings. In the larger

sphere of a nation, due care takes that thought further. Until we are internally at peace our strides in the international arena will always be unsure. This is why we need good people making good decision for us. Empowerment will lie in ensuring that those good people are brought to the fore and given the chance – Shiv Khera, Motivation Speaker.

- Empowerment will mean most when a sense of power fills each of us and that ability is used for the good of all. Thankfully, sports is looked at as a source of positive inspiration and that perhaps is the contribution to nation building – Anjum Chopra, Former Women's Cricket Captain.
- India will become empowered when politics matter less and good will and good intentions matter more – Jaya Panda, MP (Biju Janta Dal).
- Equality, spirituality and modernity are critical to true improvement. We need to think beyond the bare basics of *Roti, Kapda* and *Makan* – Nalini Singh, Media Person.
- For me an empowered India would be a nation where no body goes to sleep on an empty stomach, where there is social justice and where human dignity is of prime interest – Romesh Sharma, Television personality.
- India can be empowered through its youth power. Our country has the youngest working population and that is where we should direct our energy. Specialised education and employment assurance can help take the nation a long way – Vijay Shanker, CBI.
- As a country, we are at the threshold of an economic explosion and hence, at this moment, empowerment means most those who hold the key to future. I talk of the younger generation. Sound economic and strategic planning will bring about this change. Unfortunately, since our prosperity comes in bursts, good governance, in the form of dedicated politicians and bureaucrats, is essential to usher any changes – Lt Gen JFR Jacob (Retd.), former Governor, Punjab & Goa.

- India empowered for me would be at two levels. We are (aam) *Bahu Bhashi* (multilingual) society. When we cease to be parochial about language, and let each regional language coexist with English. As a writer, that would be India empowered to me. On another level, India empowered to me would also be when we resolve the dichotomy between technology and tradition without sacrificing other – Namita Gokhle, Author.
- I have a simple vision of an Empowered India. *Roti, Kapara, makan* and good education is what most people need in this country. Self sufficiency at different levels from agriculture to Industry and entertainment is also crucial – Shashi Kapoor, Actor.
- People usually think of prosperity and empowerment, but for me when every body from the top to Bottom will abide by the Law, that , when India will become empowered – Lord Meghnad Desai, Economist.

HR Forum

- Today's leaders have to do more than merely extract work out of their people. Modern people management has a lot to do with becoming "change artists" and with nurturing the dreams and ambitions of employees with a view to making them realize that their contribution is not just a transaction of work for money. Therefore, the form 'resource' might be misplaced, since it implies top-down activity where in employees have to be handled by the management.
- How cued HR How ROU|I (Return on Investment) and become a more main steam business functions?
- What is the HR managers' role in managing the change within the orgnisation?
- Gauge employees engagement. Empowerment tactics (delegation of authority). Everything that enables leaders to meet the opportunities and the challenges of managing tomorrow's work force.

- Is there is a written down policy for deciding kind of HR practices that need to be adopted by organizations?
  (a) Work but not at the cost of not having fun?
- HR is the eyes and ears of the leaders. It is up to HR to identify leaders and not try to be the power centre.
  (a) The role of HR is to constantly inspire employees towards the corporate purpose.
  (b) It is for HR to understand where the organization is heading.
  (c) What is the best thing it can do for the organization to help it achieve its goals and plan strategies accordingly.
- Talent retention and talent appreciation is the primary function of HR. HR needs to pay close attention to optimizing hearing within the organization, since this will have a very tangible impact on the employees' quality of work.
  Figuring out the resource leakages within the organization is every body's priority, especially HR managers. For this HR managers must play a central role in business operations and have a say in governance and corporate policy.
- The role of HR managers is fundamental, not only for executing a strategy, but also defining it. HR personnel should become business partners and should also play a crucial part of the sales function.
- HR plays a vital role right from getting people on board to identifying the leaders and developing the succession plan.
- HR will make a break through if organisational structure is simplified. Companies are used to fiddling with HR related costs when it is belt tightening time. HR experts agree that people costs are legitimate and must be given as much importance as other investments. Hiring right people is the MANTRA. Recruit people who are comfortable with change. Create culture where people are free to experiment.
- Change in the name of game, HR managers used to be hired for small amount, now it is in lakhs and crores. How ell he

communicates with people, anticipates business needs and employees timely and need based HR initiatives to deal with the change. At the end of the day, change is always difficult to perfect. The fact is every body is clueless about the future. Internal and external factors will ultimately change the environment and if you are not agile enough to meet the change head-on, you are going to face several difficulties.

- The corporate scenario should be such that promotes free thinking and courageous decisions.
- Need of the hour is to improve employee – HR communication. Investment in HR.

Good, Bad Officer

"Who is a good officer?," the oldest member asked in the officers' club. No answer was expected or given. We young ones resignedly kept silent, maintaining a posture of attentive interest. "A good officer is diligent, professionally competent, honest and morally upright. He has an eye for detail but never forgets to keep the big picture before his mind's eye. An inspiration to his subordinates, he is kind to those below him in the administrative hierarchy but firm and unswerving in dealing with those above him in ladder. He will protect his subordinates for their acts of omission and commission if they have been done in good faith, essential nowadays since anyone can fall foul of politicians and senior officers who are politicians-in-disguise. Above all, they must remember the injunction in the *Bhagvad Gita* that one only has the right to action, but not to the fruits of action. A bad officer is of course, none of these things. Both good and bad officers are easily recognisable."

How?" we young ones cried in unison. Looking around, we added, were innumerable cases of bad officers rising effortlessly into the bureaucratic skies, while good officers fell like nine pins by the wayside. The oldest member was unfazed "I was only talking about recognising them", he said. "Not about succeeding in the bureaucracy. That's quite another matter, requiring different qualities and skills. Look around you", he added. "Who are the officers who leave the service prematurely? And those who continue forever after retirement?"

And then came the oldest member's anecdote. His homily continued with a story about how he had taken on the health minister when the latter wanted to appoint a private doctor to head an important commission to study the state's public health problems. He had refused to recommend the doctor's name and the minister was hesitant to do it himself. The minister had expostulated, """But, Doctor so-and-so is a good doctor. He has a large practice". The oldest member had then replied, "Surely, the minister means doctor so-and-so is a successful practitioner". Success in the bureaucracy, it seems, has little to do with being either a good or a bad officer, but being a successful practitioner.

WINNER or LOSER

- The winner is a part of the answer.
- The loser is always part of the problem.
- The winner always has a plan.
- The loser always has an excuse.
- The winner says, "Let me do it for you."
- The loser always says, "That's not my job."
- The winner always sees an answer in every problem.
- The loser always sees a problem in every answer.
- The winner always see a green man every sand trap.
- The loser always sees a sand trap near every green.
- The winner always says, "It may be difficult, but it's possible."
- The loser always says, "It may be possible, but it's difficult."

BOSS and LEADER

- The boss drives his men, the leader inspires them;
- The boss depends on authority, the leader depends on goodwill; The boss evokes fear, the leader radiates love;
- The boss says "I", the leader says "We";

- The boss shows who is wrong, the leader shows what is wrong;
- The boss knows how it is done, the leader knows how to do it;
- The boss demands respect, the leader commands respect;
  So be a LEADER – not a BOSS.

The Vision of Tomorrow

- A world that is at peace,
- And nations that fight no wars,
- Cities that are clean and green,
- And earth carries no scars.
- With humans who believe in harmony,
- And families who know no strife,
- When children with the hope of tomorrow,
- Complete the full circle of Life
- Try not to become a man of success but rather try to become a man of value - Albert Einstein.

Employee Attrition

Employees who play together, stay together, make work more fun always find themselves secured. And when secured, naturally, they are more productive. Even hens give more eggs when they hear light music.

Emotional Connect

- The primary focus of these engagements is to create a forum to connect employees. If employees can be made to feel that they are a family and not individuals only. They tend to stick together.
- It helps to integrate the employees' family with the company, so that they all feel, they belong to that company. They should feel that it is their company. They should feel that they are part of the company.
- The feeling of togetherness motivates the employees and this in turn enhances productivity.
- River Raftering or any other team game. It involves combination

of mental activity and physical vigour. It involves values team work, strategy planning and execution as a team. It teaches leadership and problem sorting skills. Organising activities teach to hone their organising and managerial skills when they manage diverse people.

- Informal atmosphere brings out certain aspects of each other, which they did not know existed. That helps them understand each other better, thus we improve communication, reduce friction and increase productivity.
- If my company is going to spend money to take me and my colleagues out for parties or dinners or to offside in Shimla, we are not going to mind in the least.

President Obama Security

- Multi agency Command Centre
- Mob Command Centers' with very high-tech security devices.
- Bomb containment vans.
- Bomb technicians vans.
- SWAT Team
- Hazardous Materials Response Team
- Under water Search & Response Team
- Crisis Negotiations
- Coastal Guards
- Air Surveillance
- Closure of Roads etc.
- Plain Clothes policemen including 1B etc
- Bomb Sniffing Dogs.
- NBC Teams
- Transportation & Communication units
- Medical Teams with Ambulances

Disaster Management

Ten things to learn from Japan after the recent natural calamity that country faced and how it dealt with it?

- **The Calm** Not a single visual of chest-beating or wild grief. Sorrow itself has been elevated.
- **The Dignity** Disciplined queues for water and groceries. No looting and irrational complaining. Not a rough word or a crude gesture.
- **The Ability** The incredible architectures, for instance: Tall Buildings swayed but didn't fall. Earthquake proof building codes are strictly enforced and followed.
- The Grace People bought only what they needed for the present, so everybody could get something. No reports of hoarding or inflating the prices
- **The Order** No looting in shops. No honking and no overtaking on the roads.
- **The Sacrifice** Fifty workers stayed back to pump sea water in the N-reactors fully aware that they were risking their lives. How will they ever be repaid?
- **The Tenderness** Restaurants cut prices. An unguarded ATM is left alone. The strong cared for the weak.
- **The Training** The old and the children, everyone knew exactly what to do. And they did just that.
- **The Media** They showed magnificent restraint in the bulletins. No silly reporters. No stupid and childish comments. No exploitation of human tragedy for raising TRPs. Only calm reportage.
- **The Conscience** When the power went off in a store, people put things back on the shelves and left quietly.

Productivity Improvement Techniques

- Productivity is the volume of output attained in a given period of time in relation to the sum of direct and indirect efforts expended in its production.
- Productivity is more goods of better quality at lowest cost.
- Productivity is elimination of waste in all forms: energy, cost, time, material, equipment, space, physical and mental effort.

- Productivity is concerned with the efficient utilization of resources (INPUT) in producing goods and services (OUT PUT).
- Productivity is the value added per employee.
- Productivity is a function of providing more and more of every thing for more and more people with less and less consumption of real resources.
- Productivity is the ratio between output and input i.e., Productivity = Output / Input.

Productivity Improvement:

- Productivity may be increased in two ways:
  (a) For a given output reducing the input requirement (cell 4 in the diagram).
  (b) For a given input increasing the out (cell 3 in the diagram).
- Here an attempt is made to indicate causes of low productivity and productivity improvement techniques in the form of snake and ladder diagram.
- For example employee-based improvement (cell 67), task-based improvement (cell 43), material-based improvement (cell 7), technology-based improvement (cell 25) etc are shown as ladders to achieve higher productivity.
- Whereas, low motivation (cell 97), poor working methods (cell 47), obsolete technology (cell 66), lack of training (cell 72) etc are shown as pitfalls of hindrance to productivity.

CIT/Bullion Movement

Rajiv Pandev

Why Is Cash In Transit?

There are two important reasons: A bank gives cash to clients and an ATM machine also disburses cash. This cash has to be brought to banks and machines. Banks and ATMs are also deposite sites and ash has to be taken away to main vaults from branches and ATMs. Cash, therefore, has to move.

Bank Cash In Transit

- A bank's cash is required to be vaulted in safe location (currency chests) approved by RBI guidelines.
- Ever increasing geographical spread of bank's branch network and ATMs.
- Setting up of large number of currency chests not economically viable.
- Cash received over the counter cannot be re-circulated without sorting.

ATM Cash in Transit

- ATMs require regular replenishment of good quality currency.
- Advent of new products such as cash pick-up and
- Cash-drop/door-step banking (for retail chain/fuel filling stations/metro/bullion and diamond merchant and telecom operators etc).
- Need to transport bullion and valuables for the bullion
- dealers / organisers of special events such as exhibition etc.
- Banks need to focus on their core business.

Hazards Associated with CIT

- The CIT industry is inherently dangerous, with catastrophic outcomes. Therefore, careful planning and preparation for the operations is essential.
- Hence it is of utmost importance that adherence to the laid-down SOPs/process & security protocol is ensured.
- Some of the hazards and risks CIT operations are vulnerable to: ***Hazards are not always obvious and can include:***
- The probability of an armed hold-up
- Terrorist/secessionist action
- Manual handling (moving of steel boxes etc)
- Operation of vehicles (road accidents)
- Handling and use of weapons (unintended firing etc)
- Fatigue from shift work (prolonged operations)
- Environmental factors such as extremes of temperature

What are the risks?

Potential Risk

- Armed hold-up leading to death of crew
- Injuries to the crew
- Road accidents resulting in fatality/injury
- Loss of valuables being transported
- Damage to the vehicle
- Reputational risk due to loss of valuable and also in case of

improper/invalid documentation (gun/driving licenses, vehicle fitness, improper verification of crew etc)

Here are some measures to mitigate the risk and the essentials in making CIT operations safer.

Measure to Mitigate Risk

- Safe access and egress for persons involved in cash in transit/ATM replenishment
- Locating surveillance/security devices at vantage points for proactive monitoring
- Adherence to speed limits by the cash vans
- No unscheduled stoppages
- Frequent change in routes
- Protective clothing such as footwear, warm cloths in winter and eye protection gear (sunglasses)

More Measures to Mitigate Risk

- Strict adherence to the manning and other safety norms.
- Allocation of appropriate resources for manning sites
- Training of the personnel involved in CIT operations including correct use of fire arms to minimise the risk in a hold-up/robbery.
- Police/field verification of the credential of the crew
- Period check of documents of the crew/vehicle
- Ensure only authorised and trained personnel are deputed as CIT crew
- Good liaison with local authorities
- Appropriate insurance policies (banker's blanket insurance/fidelity insurance/vehicle insurance)

Securing CIT Operations

- Assessment of risk
- Create risk mitigation plan
- Define monitoring methods

- Placing controls & measuring effectiveness
- Audits to assess process compliance (SOPs & Drills)
- Analysis of non-conformities
- Identify training need and schedule of the personnel
- Training to reduce non-conformities

Assessment of Risk

- Identification of risks
- Defining levels of risk (subjective)
- High/Medium/Low
- Risk profiling/mapping of area of operations
- Terrain
- Law and Order situation
- Support from Police & administration
- General human traits of local people

Creating Risk Mitigation Plans

- Define contingencies
- Create standard operating procedures for contingencies
- Effective two- way communication between CIT & operations staff
- Setup monitoring infrastructure and control mechanism
- Test CIT crew through mock emergencies for contingencies during transit
- Conduct refresher training of CIT crew
- Police/field verification of the CIT crew

Monitoring & Control

- Evaluate present monitoring system (if any)
- Define/demand from CIT operator availability of operational vehicle tracking system
- Setting up a local teams for monitoring and control of CIT.
- Create protocols to monitor availability of crew & operational Vehicles

Audit

- Evolve internal audit procedure for process audits
- Create process for audit of CIT & ATM operations
- Analyze non-conformities
- Assess training need (also weeding out)
- Impart training as required to create a culture compliance (like do we ever enter a temple with our shoes on? We don't. Similarly there are many don't to be followed in cash transfer that should not be violated.)

Following these rules may ensure safer movement of cash, be it to and from a bank or an ATM machine.

Terrorist Threats on Banking Security Preventive Measures

H N Sambharya

Terrorism

Terrorists are like spurious growth in a beautiful garden. If it is cut, it comes up again. It has to be uprooted. Terrorism has existed throughout history and throughout the world. Terrorism refers to extortion, criminal attacks, kidnapping, hijacking and killing by suicide squads to attract wider attention to a particular cause and thus force the targetted authority to concede demands of the perpetrators of terror. Terror tactics are generally adopted by misguided isolated groups who are despaired and demand getting a sympathetic audience for their real or perceived grievances. They generally get arms and ammunition and financial support from groups of community on whose behalf they take up arms to challenge the authorities. The conditions for rise of terrorism exist in many parts of the world. It finds favourable environment to grow in areas located near the international borders. Terrorists get arms, training, strategic and financial support from countries which believe in terrorism for solving their so-called problems. The reasons for emergence of terrorism could be many-any single cause or mix of many of the causes viz. socio-political aspirations, ethnic differences and aspirations, strong religious fanaticism, ideological inspirations, political suppression, fundamentalist urges etc.

Terrorism emerged as a global problem in the late 1960s and despite sustained governmental efforts to combat it, this nightmare remained a serious problem. The problem aggravated in the 1990s and perhaps may continue to confront nations in the current century. With technological development, both at domestic and international levels, and incidents which may involve even the use of weapons of mass destruction, the spectrum of terrorism has assumed an alarming proportion. The magnitude of terrorist acts and the growing concern over them are attributable to many factors. Technological development has enabled the perpetrators of terrorism to act in coordination with such groups located at different centres. Sophisticated means of communication have helped terrorists act swiftly and from remote areas. The net result is that both national as well as international systems are in turmoil. Terrorist attacks cannot be predicted and preventive measures therefore, need to be thought of, planned and structured well in advance. But what has stunned the world recently is terrorism by suicide squads. While state security faces an unprecedented and unimaginable challenge by suicide terror, the success of the attacks comes as a shot in the arm for terrorist and extremist organisations.

The nexus between drug traffickers, arms dealers, money launderers and terrorist outfits create a parallel power structure, holding governments to ransom and challenging the authority of the states. Incidences like attacks on the twin towers (World Trade Centre) in the US, the J&K Assembly, the Indian Parliament, USIS at Kolkata, Bali island, Akshardham at Gandhinagar and subsequent events in Russia and other foreign countries are an eye-opener for the world community.

India has been fighting against a proxy war and insurgency for almost two decades. In recent years, there is a spurt in terrorist activities and armed uprisings in many parts of the country, adversely affecting the law and order situation. Jammu and Kashmir is in the grip of a proxy war for almost two decades. The situation in the North East is far from satisfactory.

Threat to Banking Security

A bank's security management consists of physical security arrangements and also maintenance of other security measures like prevention of frauds, fire security, security in use of computer technology etc. MICR technology and stringent clearing disciplines have been introduced to minimise frauds. Various committees have been constituted from time to time to lay down guidelines on security arrangements in banks. In 1982, the Reserve Bank of India appointed a committee on security arrangements under the chairmanship of M.V. Hate, the then Dy.Governor, especially for security in RBI office premises. In 1983, a committee appointed by the Indian Banks' Association under the chairmanship of Secretary (Economic Affairs), Ministry of Finance, Government of India laid down guidelines on security arrangements in public sector banks. The report was again updated by the Ministry of Finance by constituting a committee under the chairmanship of K. Srinivasan, Jt. Secretary, Banking Division, Ministry of Finance, Government of India which submitted its reports in May 1996. The Ministry of Finance constituted another committee under the chairmanship of Dr. P.D. Ojha, the then Dy.Governor, Reserve Bank of India to review the security arrangements in public sector banks in July 1987. The state-level security committees were formed in all states as envisaged by the 1987 committee. The functions of the state-level security committees are to recommend action on various matters relating to Currency Chest and cash movement. The state-level security committees are convened by respective Regional Directors of Reserve Bank of India and function under the overall guidance and directions of the Central Security Cell set up at the Reserve Bank of India, Central Office, Mumbai. Based on the recommendations contained in various committee reports, security guidelines were prepared by the RBI Central

Security Cell in November 2000 and a copy thereof furnished to all the public sector banks. These guidelines relate to operations and security of Currency Chest branches, opening of new branches and other general guidelines.

The Banking Sector is not well organised, nor sufficiently equipped. It does not have the necessary wherewithal to thwart any form of terrorist attack. Hence banks are considered a soft and lucrative target for any form of terrorist action. At the same time, banking industry will have to live and work in this environment, taking necessary measures to ensure least disruption in its operation and safety of money and valuables of which it is the custodian. They have also to ensure the safety of their personnel and their customers. Terrorist attack on the financial system will result in serious disruption of business, leading to huge financial loss and in the long run, may shatter public confidence and will have an adverse effect on the nation's economy. The security management in public sector banks are mainly manpower oriented, with a mix of minimal security gadgets. Security is not considered as a mainstream management function in these banks. On the other hand, the private and foreign banks rely mostly on modern electronic security gadgets basically for access control. Hence there is a need to address these problems at the highest level.

Present Situation:

In India, there has been increased activities of insurgency by ISI agents along with extremist organizations/anti-nationals/terrorists/naxalites etc. These terrorists get arms and financial help from across the borders. There are intelligence reports that terrorists groups including al Quaida and Taliban have planned attacks on banks and financial institutions. These elements may take advantage of the situation and increase their activities and create panic by organizing bomb blasts and other subversive activities. It is essential to maintain vigil against sabotage by explosives. Bomb threats have become so frequent now-a-days that it has become essential for security managers to be prepared to tackle the problem. They should formulate various drills for evacuation, bomb disposal etc. and also educate the security staff. It is also necessary to bring in awareness amongst the staff of various departments. A healthy liaison with various agencies viz. the nearest police station, bomb squad, sniffer dog squad, fire-services, telephone department, forensic science laboratory, the Army, Navy and Air force, hospitals and ambulance services etc. should be maintained constantly. Apart from the various agencies, which are helpful during the bomb threat, it is the security staff attached to the bank that are going to react first. They should maintain high level of alertness.

There has been considerable reliance so far on the human element in devising and implementation of security plans. The field of security is vast and complex and it is undergoing rapid advancement and sophistication. Reliance on machines and electronic gadgets is increasing and less reliance is being placed on the human element, which is prone to fail in times of need. We cannot afford to remain complacent in a changing environment. We will have to keep abreast of the developments in the field of security technology. Enlightened security chiefs of banks should study the latest technical security devices available, which can be used in security management. The need of the hour is dynamism and capacity for adaptation to a new environment. This is all the more necessary for Security Managers in banks because most of them have changed over from a career in the armed forces/CPOs with its emphasis on regimentation to the one in a civilian environment.

Well, security management is based on threat perception. The banking industry as a whole has been afflicted by a number of dacoities, robberies, hold ups, thefts and other forms of violence/crime. Banks are increasingly being exposed to terrorists insurgent activity and politically- or ideologically-induced violence in the recent past. Banks are attacked not only for the magnitude of the treasure they hold, but also because of the mileage they could derive by way of spectacular and instant publicity. It would be significant to note that threatening letters warning of sabotage by explosives are received frequently by the banks in several parts of the country. We cannot allow ourselves to be overwhelmed into a false sense of foolproof security. There is absolutely no scope for any complacency. We have to be always alert and vigilant. The enemy is not likely to strike at points where we have strong protection. They would watch out for chinks in our armour, where they could strike with impunity. The strength of a chain proverbially lies in its weakest link. We have, therefore, to constantly carry out a systems analysis of our security arrangements, locate the weak links and strengthen the protective cover at those points. Evaluation of the system and risk assessment is not a one-time project. This exercise has to be gone through continuously, because in a dynamic environment, new threats could emerge, posing new challenges to our security administrators.

Under certain emergencies, the police/para-military personnel are withdrawn or reduced in emergent situation, thereby making the bank branches vulnerable when the security cover is most required. A special force dedicated to bank security could be created, subject to cost for such force being comparable to the current police costs levied in various states.

Technological Development

Looking at the present law and order scenario, modern security devices should be used to strengthen the security arrangements. They are

Access Control Measures:

Though all the entry/exit points in various office premises are manned by durwans/security guards and access control is exercised with the help of identity cards, entry permits, material outpasses etc, yet sometimes, outsiders are able to gain entry into the premises without being checked/noticed by the security personnel. There are a number of technologies used for access control and checking illegal intrusion. Computerised Access Control plays a significant role and has proved to be more effective. Use of magnetic proximity cards for opening the doors. Gates at sensitive locations are now computer based. The "Computer Vision" or "Biometrics Control System" enables the machines to scan a fingerprint, identify the ridge characteristics to establish the identity of a person. This technology has also been extended to scanning of faces of persons and voice analysis of human beings. Monitoring and supervision of the performance of security men can also be aided and enhanced with the help of computers. The security guard on duty can be required to press the switches installed at vulnerable places, which will be recorded in the computer along with the time. The computer can produce at the end of the day or night or in given periodicity a list/graph/table of the patrolling done by the security guard in various areas for the benefit of the Security Officer, which will give him the idea of frequencies with which patrolling is done and the sequence in which the locations are visited along with the time of the visit. The shirking of duty by security guards can be detected easily. Further, to have fool-proof check on the visitors entering the premises, it is possible to have entry permit issued with photograph of the person visiting the premises. The system is simple, cost effective, easy to handle and use and the system is able to store data for future retrieval too.

Fire/Smoke Detection System:

It is high time that we have a fire detection system installed in all bank premises. The system will have fire detection control panels with built in communicator, remote, power supply, conventional fire alarm control panels and additional panels and Digital Alarm Communicator Transmitter (DALT). In fact, this is a must in buildings, the height of which is more than 15 metres under the National Building Code.

Alarm System:

It is an important and integral element in physical safeguards against bank dacoities and robberies. Microprocessor-based security alarm systems are more effective. This can also be attached to the auto-dialer system.

X-Ray Machine:

It is an ideal system for detecting contraband, arms and explosives with high efficacy. It is also ideally suited for screening visitor's personal effects to see if any objectionable items are being taken into the office building. This can also point out if costly ornaments or large cash is being carried in or out.

Closed Circuit T V (CCTV):

The system is installed with a view to monitoring the movement and activities of people in security areas like vaults, patrol corridors, parking enclosures, banking halls and to watch the alertness and presence of durwans/security guards and police guards. It is also used for monitoring the operations in processing area like computer room, public counters etc. Any suspicious activity or movement is kept under observation and recorded. The colour CCTV is more suitable and advisable, as it gives more depth and details of the objects under watch.

Carriage Inspection Mirrors:

With this simple equipment, the bottom of the three-/four-wheelers can be observed and anti-sabotage checks carried out i.e., to see whether any explosive material or objectionable articles are kept attached to the bottom of the vehicle. The equipment needs to be used in all premises where vehicle-parking zones are available.

Mobile Phones:

The equipment is handy, cost effective and easily available with one to one speech facility. The Walkie Talkie system can also be used for communications at the gates or by guards who patrol the periphery of the premises or from the T.V.console room etc.

Hot Line:

As per the RBI guidelines, all the Currency Chest branches are required to be linked through telephonic hot lines with the nearest police stations/ police control room and fire stations. It is very useful in the sense that at times one does not get through to the police station/police control room or fire brigade through normal telephone and one may not get enough time to dial the required numbers in an emergent situation. In telephonic hot line, one can straightway get through to the police station/fire brigade and inform them about the emergency. Even if no conversation takes place, the police/fire stations would know from where the hot line/s are and they would react immediately, without loss of time. This can enable the police and/or firemen to immediately get into action and apprehend the culprits or save the premises without any loss of time. In addition to hot lines, banks may also install Auto-Dialers, if found necessary.

Time Lock:

This would be ideal for use in Currency Chests/strong rooms. The doors of the strong room can be locked and opened only at a pre-set time. So far as the Currency Chests are concerned, once they are closed in the evening, these need not be and should not be opened till the next morning. A time lock system at these branches should be ideal. It could also be installed in strong rooms of bigger branches where the cash holdings are relatively high.

Integrated Crisis Management (ICM):

This is the latest security concept on the lines of security measures adopted in the U.S. and other Western countries. A crisis management centre is set up, which is manned round the clock by its staff. All the members of this system are given a code number and all the details of the individual subscribers are fed into the computer installed at the ICM centre. The moment there is an emergency at any of the subscriber premises, the wristband is pressed, the code number flashes on the computer screen and all the details are paged on the basis as to where the emergency exists. The action of informing the police, fire brigade, ambulance, as the case may be, is taken and emergency handled without any loss of time. The procedure is so fast that all the actions take place simultaneously within 2 to 4 minutes.

Magnetic Contacts:

Magnetic contacts/sensors can be installed on all the operable periphery doors and windows as well as the rolling shutters. These are, in turn, connected to the security alarm systems to send loud signals as and when it happens when the alarm system is activated. This in time can also be connected to an auto-dialer. These censors are useful generally during the duration when the unguarded branch is closed for the day and till it is opened the next day morning. These are quite useful and the moment anyone tries to break open the window or roll up the shutter, the alarm is sounded. It will not only activate the alarm system but also the auto-dialer and one can know that someone is trying to intrude into the branch.

Glass Break Sensors:

Glass break sensors are installed on single and multi-paned windows and doors. The moment anyone tries to break open the glass, the alarm is sounded, giving early warning about the intrusion taking place.

Passive Infra-RED(PIR) Movement Sensors:

PIR sensors are installed in the strong room, computer room, etc. An invisible infra-red light travels, covering the entire width in front of the doors of the strong rooms and computer rooms. The moment a person crosses the individual infra-red light, the circuit breaks resulting in a alarm being sounded.

Vibration Detectors:

These devices can be installed covering the strong room walls, computer room walls and at the peripheral walls. This is guarding against the burglary attempts. If anyone tries to hammer and break the wall with the help of a hammer, the vibrations travel and result in the alarm being activated.

12 Bore Pump-Action Gun:

The Gun Carriage Factory, Jabalpur has successfully produced a 12-bore pump-action gun which is being supplied to the public sector banks. These guns have the following characteristics: (a) It is short in length and single barrel, (b) The butt is detachable, further reducing the length of the gun (c) Six bullets can be loaded by pump action, (d) It can fire normal 12-bore cartridges, rubber bullets and tear-gas shells, (e) It is being used by banks and the police in some foreign countries as combat guns. These smaller guns shall prove very successful for security purpose in the banking industry.

Door Frame Metal Detectors and Hand Held Metal Detectors:

DFMDs/HHMDs-Metal detectors are front line devices in anti-terrorist measures. Civil Aviation authorities all over the world depend on this device for safety of millions and millions of their passengers from terrorist threat. This equipment can provide optimum security at minimum cost to the banks also.

Safe Case:

It is a stylish brief case designed specially for the transport of valuables and money. The safe case looks like a normal brief case but has the highest security technology built into it without limiting packaging space. It will not attract undue attention. The system is completely remote controlled with no pressing of buttons, if the case is snatched. It will allow a distance of about 30 meters to be created, thus, allowing the bearer to be clear of reprisal from the snatcher before it activates the following features-

Siren: A loud piercing siren (110 Dbs) will be triggered creating fear for the snatcher

Shock: In addition, whilst the siren is still sounding, a high voltage shock in excess of 40,000 V will be triggered, 7 seconds after the siren has started. The entire case, including the handle, will be alive with this high voltage shock and cannot be held- even with gloves on. In other words "it will kick like a mule" if touched.

Smoke: A coloured smoke/dye will be triggered, 7 seconds after the high voltage shock has been initiated. The smoke will colour the contents of the case and will billow out of the case and colour the snatcher as well, thereby attracting attention of viewers.

The system, once activated, will continue to sound the siren and activate the voltage for approx. 90 minutes, unless automatically deactivated by the bearer.

Computer Crimes and Prevention and the Law

With the increased use of electronic devices like computers in day-to-day operations and for storage of data, crimes in this area have increased. Computer related crimes are far more sophisticated. There are (a) physical crimes (b) data related crimes and (c) software related crimes. We should be very clear in mind that hiding, recognising, investigating, recording and settling computer crimes and getting into legal complexities and attending the courts may result into visible and invisible loss of time and funds to the victims and the organisations. Such courts and legal proceedings take a prolonged time in deciding a case. "Justice delayed is justice denied." Therefore, all this can be avoided, if we take precautions and try our level best to prevent computer crime in the first place.

The worldwide use of Information Technology today is ubiquitous in almost every aspect of life. However, like other technologies, IT too is exposed to risks and criminals to a great extent. Therefore, to safeguard the users of electronics commerce against hackers and criminals, statute is the need of the hour. In the USA, the Counterfeit Access Device and Computer Fraud and Abuse Act, 1984, was enacted to cover computer crimes to prohibit anyone who knowingly accessed a computer without authorisation. The available civil and criminal legal remedies like the Indian Penal Code, Law of Torts, Copy Rights Act, etc. in the present form may not be applicable to computer crime. Understanding the vulnerability of the situation, the Department of Electronics, Government of India, in association with concerned Government departments/ministries and in consultation with industries/users has enacted an "Information Technology Act 2000".

Disaster Management

Disaster management is an action plan related to perceivable disastrous threats. A well-conceived plan practised and executed before, during and after any probable disaster incident could minimise-if not eliminate-the loss, delay and suffering caused by the incident. The success of disaster management largely depends on our ability to mobilise resources that may be required to rescue, salvage and restore valuables and normal activities at that unpredictable moment and within the least possible time. Knowing the variegated nature and varying magnitude of disasters, the required resources (including manpower) cannot be anticipated, nor can it be created and maintained for this purpose alone. A list of the probable tools, equipments and manpower needs may indicate that a large number of the listed tools and equipments will be available within the organisation itself. If the quantity required is high and unaffordable, it may not be difficult to find out other organisations in the vicinity that would be able to provide its use at times of such human distress. The important thing is to know where to find it at that moment of crisis. State agencies would normally work out such schemes and organise the rescue operations when the need arises. This spirit of group security needs to be developed for coping with complex challenges arising before us.

Essentially, a disaster plan will consist of three different stages:

1. Preventive measures
2. Rescue, relief and rehabilitation in the wake of disaster
3. Post disaster rehabilitation, both physical and economical

Since the disaster, particularly the major ones, do not occur frequently or even if they occur in the vicinity, neighbourhood or in far-flung places, a tendency to believe that it would never happen to us is natural. Therefore, there is a greater responsibility on authorities to ensure regular conduct and practice of drills and procedures. Safety days every week/month, safety weeks every month/quarter depending on the seriousness of the threat perception, will be a helpful practice.

Red alert procedures to be followed by the security setup and other in-charges in sensitive areas and hardening the target when threat perception is high should also be practised periodically. Rescue, relief and rehabilitation measure is the most important part of any disaster management plan. The identification and tie-up with different agencies and resources should be so well organised that at the mention of a code word or the press of a switch the whole machinery springs into action with clock like precision. Post disaster attention should gear up to manage what is known as shadow disaster. The after effects of a disaster may appear in the form of an epidemic, low productivity and psychological issues. Experts state that there is a general tendency to avoid attending to these issues consciously and a casual approach is common. This, if neglected, can give rise to more problems in time that may be difficult to handle. Authorities would do well to pre-plan for such an eventuality as well.

Existing Provisions and Guidelines

The current security guidelines are as enumerated in the Report of the Committee to Review the Security Arrangements in Public Sector Banks-1996. State Bank of India has submitted a proposal to the Ministry of Finance, Government of India, suggesting that a fresh committee should be set up to review the security arrangements in public sector banks and come out with recommendations so that comprehensive guidelines can be issued to public sector banks, particularly in the areas which were not covered by the earlier committee which submitted its report in May 1996. The Indian

Banks' Association, at the request of the Reserve Bank of India also convened a meeting of the Chief Security Officers of banks and it was unanimously decided in that meeting to request the Ministry of Finance to constitute a fresh committee to review security measures for banks.

Conclusion

The fact that the Banking industry has no wherewithal to prevent terrorist attacks have come into sharp focus. However, all preventive measures need to be taken within the resources available. Disaster management will play a significant role to reduce the effect of terrorist attack, should such an attack materialize and facilitate resumption of operations at the earliest. A well thought-out security plan as well as disaster management scheme will go a long way to face the likely terrorist attack against banks and financial institutions.

Cash Management Services: The New Paradigm

Vipin Jain

Banking is the worlds oldest industry. Until the early '90s, traditionally banking and its cash management services were conducted in a manner where the customer had to come to the bank's doorstep for everything and anything.

However, as the economy progressed, and with the arrival of foreign and private banks with their superior and innovative delivery service to the end customer, there has evolved a new phase to efficiently utilize cash through coordinated management of payments, collections and cash balances. The objectives is to reduce and economize on costs, enhance control and optimize returns.

Faced with dual pressure of increased competition and coping with increasing compliance and transaction costs, banks and other allied sectors were forced to outsource their delivery channels to third-party agencies who acted as the extended arm of the business.

Gradually this sharing became pivotal, leading to the emergence of a new service paradigm called the Cash management Services which until very recently only existed in other countries where lead players had to closely work with bankers and non-bankers as their partners.

Today Cash Management Services has become "A Must To Hire Service" Due to fthe ollowing reasons:

At the macro level

- Robust growth in banking, insurance, retail and other allied sectors
- Competitive survival pressures from other players in the market
- Crossing of boundaries, whereby the world has become a global market for opportunities and returns
- Maintaining upward graph trend on yielding profitability
- Client pressure for convenient and friendly delivery models
- Technology driven solutions become affordable

At the micro level

- Labor costs and trouble
- Lean manpower and staffing policies
- Lack of adequate space and infrastructure; Inability to penetrate in rural and remote areas
- Quality and security issues
- Seasonal variations in requirements
- Rapid ramp up requirements; Transfer of risk and liability burden to TP

Due to the underlying factors, the banking industry and the CMS will go grow strong by leaps and boundL

- ATM user population increased from 100 to 150, 00 in just 2 year
- lAll major banks now offer door step services for cash
- All Banks offer off -site services
- Rural banking is growing in numbers as well as quality
- Penetration of credit cards/ debit cards is still low and cash still remains important

- Regulatory ease up of third party cash handling with increase in NDI (Net Domestic Income), lifestyle has improved
- Two & Three Tier cities are emerging at a fast pace
- Organized retailing and chains are increasing
- Communications and utilities sector is growing
- Private petroleum distribution and high-way services are spreading.
- Aviation sector is booming and is reaching out to large sections of society
- Insurance penetration is increasing
- Crime scene affecting banking and cash is deteriorating fast

A Few Fact on the Cash Industry

- Cash logistics business grew by 250% in last 2 years
- Public sector units including Banks now outsource 10 times more services than 5 years ago
- All these put together is just 10% of total potential business in space of outsourced service
- CIT companies can generate many business models taking advantage of their spread and service

ATM Protection for Today's Threat

S J S Duggal

Refreshing ATM Protection for Today's Threat

Total Estimated Losses in INR (Crores)

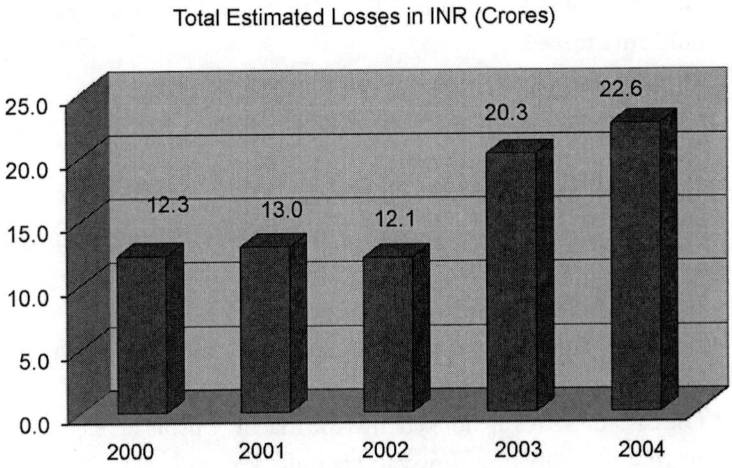

Source: American Special Risk, LLC

Top 10 Loss Locations by %

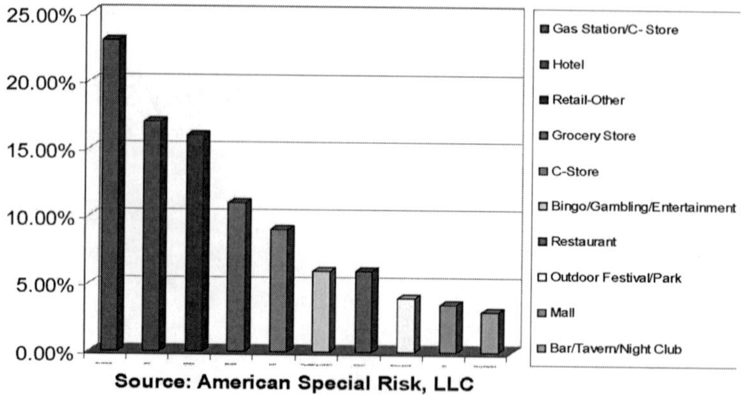

ATM Security Research Brief

- Procedural vulnerabilities - Attack # 1
- Software vulnerabilities - Attack # 2
- Physical vulnerabilities - Attack # 3

Attack #1 Procedural Vulnerability

Gaining access to the cash in an ATM: Can it be achieved using brains and not brute force ?

The first obstacle – a simple lock on the "vanity" plate

- A simple low–security in–tumbler lock protects access to the safe door and the combination lock

Access can now be gained to the safe door

- But surely now comes the hard part?... Safe cracking requires a locksmith. doesn't it?

Bingo! The "shelved mode" combination works!

- An ATM safe in shelved mode does not audit who opens the safe
- The cash cassettes are locked into the machine using an electronic locking mechanism. How can we unlock them?

The cash cassettes can be recovered

...surely there's physical cash cassette protection?

- Apparently the dye spraying mechanisms are not widely used, either because of cost or in case they cause injury to the individual retrieving the cash – we live in litigious times.

Attack # 2 Software vulnerability

Implanting a software Trojan horse into an ATM

Trojan House – Background info

- Prince Paris of troy kidnaps queen Helen of Greece
- The Greeks are not too happy about this
- A huge battle ensues outside Troy – lasts for 10years
- Greeks build a wooden horse and hide in it.
- The Trojans think it's a present from the gods
- They take it into Troy – big party – every one falls asleep
- Greeks jump out – kill Trojans – rescue Queen Helen
- The term "Trojan Horse" is generally applied to a piece of software that hides in an operating system and silently performs some malicious functionality

Attack Assumptions

- Physical access can be gained to the ATM PC
- Software can be introduced to the PC via some mechanism – Floppy / CDROM / USB

The attacker has a maximum of 60 seconds physical access to the ATM internals to install the Trojan

Attack # 3 Physical vulnerability

A physical attack against an ATM

… No it was not brute force, but using intelligence and exploiting a weakness

Site Selection

The following risk assessment should be made before placement of ATMs:

- Safety of all staff, ATM users, and the public;

- Crime history of area and site itself;
- Site conditions i.e. lighting, visibility, traffic etc;
- Existing security measures i.e. alarms, gates etc.

ATM Position

- Away from store fronts/windows;
- Against well-built walls;
- Limit vehicle access;
- Highly visible and well-lit area that allows maximum surveillance by passing traffic, counter staff and other customers.

What should be done?

- An overall risk assessment to determine where the risks are and what to do about them
- An information security health check to identify the areas where procedural failures are manifesting
- A remediation process to put right the policies processes and standards that are flawed
- Regular penetration testing to check that the policies, processes and standards are working properly
- Regular system health checks to ensure that the procedural failures have been rectified
- Ongoing assistance with risk assessment and management of change to the ATM design, deployment and management regime.

Fraud Prevention in Banking Industry

Shreedhar Behera

Legal Definition of Financial Fraud

The criminal offence of knowingly executing, or attempting to execute a scheme or artifice to defraud a financial institution, or to obtain property owned by or under the control of a financial institution by means of false or fraudulent pretences.

In other words, it is a deliberate act of omission or commission

- by any person, carried out in the course of banking transaction;
- or in the books of accounts maintained manually; or
- under computer system in banks, resulting into wrongful gain to any person for a temporary period or otherwise, with or without any monetary loss to the bank.

There is scope for convergence of these various methods of perpetrating frauds.

Modus Operandi

- Financial institutions are susceptible to frauds from outside the institution and from within.

- Internal frauds are mostly committed by the employees who are well aware of the operational procedures and are, therefore, in a position to exploit the lacunae in the system.
- External frauds are committed either totally by outsiders or in connivance with insider(s). These are most prone to happen when the outsiders are able to detect the systemic flaws or when the employees fail to perform their duties properly.

Nature of Frauds

- Misappropriation / Criminal breach of trust
- Fraudulent encashment through forged instrument/Manipulation of books of accounts or through fictitious account/conversion of property
- Unauthorised credit facilities extended for reward/ for illegal gratification
- Negligence and cash shortage
- Cheating / Forgery
- Irregularities on foreign exchange transactions
  - ⇒ Opening of fictitious account
  - ⇒ Acquisition of Cheque Books wrongly
  - ⇒ Forged HV Operation and Closure of Account
  - ⇒ Bills of Exchange supported by false documents
  - ⇒ Fake Title Deeds
  - ⇒ Unauthorised handling of dormant accounts
  - ⇒ Tampering with specimen signature
  - ⇒ Kite-flying transactions
  - ⇒ Multiple financing to the same party against same security
- Cases of Theft, Burglary, Dacoity and Robbery
  - ⇒ These are the most serious crimes and may involve the loss of life also. The use of force is implied and often the law enforcement agencies would have to be involved from the outset
  - ⇒ Computer frauds
  - ⇒ ATM related
  - ⇒ Net-banking

⇒ Credit Cards
⇒ Cyber frauds.......

Prevention of fraud

- Frauds strike at the very root of the financial system and shake the confidence of the general public.
- In most cases (except where, these may be "white collar" crimes where the perpetrators, even if caught, would be liable only to a limited jail term.
- As a central banker, the RBI is entrusted with the statutory task of securing monetary stability.
- To prevent and preempt frauds the RBI has put in place a tough administrative and legal framework.
- Guidelines Issued by RBI:
  ⇒ Risk Management Area
  ⇒ POML / KYC
  ⇒ Fraud Monitoring
  ⇒ Compliance
  ⇒ Supervisory Set-Up at RBI:
  ⇒ Onsite Inspection
  ⇒ Offsite Inspection
  ⇒ Various Returns
  ⇒ MIS & Exception Reporting
  ⇒ Penalty / Fine Imposed

Prevention of fraud

- Risk management framework
- Fraud monitoring cell
- Dedicated efforts for KYC / POML - FIU
- Returns to RBI and compliance issues
- Internal control mechanism
- Prevention and detection mechanism
- Thrust on effective auditing including IS audit
- MIS and exception reporting

- Internet working / Core-banking

Internal Control Systems

- The RBI periodically reviews the steps taken by the public sector banks in the internal control area, through analytical reports covering the following areas:
- Reconciliation of inter-branch accounts
- Reconciliation of inter-bank accounts
- Reconciliation of nostro accounts, and
- Status of balancing of books of accounts
- Reconciliation of clearing differences

Prevention by Banks

- Banks are required to ensure that the practice of forced matching of inter-branch entries should be subject to appropriate checks and balances
- Strengthening of internal audit /control system
- Audit system in banks
- Complaints
- Change in incumbency
- House keeping/Balancing of Books
- Audit & Inspection
- Visits of RO/ZO functionaries
- Scrutiny of returns
- Presence of mind and efficiency of staff

Control at the Bank level

Fraud monitoring

The system of internal control and follow-up in respect of cases of large frauds of Rs.1 crore and above reported to the RBI is reviewed periodically.

Banks are cautioned about the details of individuals/companies/firms/ proprietary concerns involved in perpetration of frauds, furnishing details of their directors/partners /guarantors/associates.

With a view to expediting the investigation of fraud cases, RBI reports cases involving Rs. 1 crore and above as also those revealing inter-state ramifications irrespective of the amounts to CBI.

The banks have been advised to scrupulously follow the time limit laid down by Chief Vigilance Commissioner (CVC) and the position of adherence to CVC guidelines reviewed by their board on a quarterly basis. If these guidelines are not strictly followed, the concerned banks should furnish a report to the CVC.

Scope for Convergence

- Consultative process
- Risk-Based supervision
- Prompt corrective action
- Consolidated supervision
- Upgrading reporting systems
- Skills upgradation

On the Fake Currency Trail

Shilpan Patel

Part - I

The economy of India is the eleventh largest economy in the world by nominal GDP and the fourth largest by purchasing power parity (PPP). It is one of the most attractive destinations for business and investment opportunities due to huge manpower base, diversified natural resources and strong macro-economic fundamentals. Following strong economic reforms from the socialist inspired economy of a post-independence Indian nation, the country began to develop a fast-paced economic growth, as free market principles were initiated in 1990 for international competition and foreign investment.

India is an emerging economic power with a very large pool of human and natural resources, and a growing large pool of skilled professionals. According to the book *Contours of the World Economy 1-2030 AD'* by Angus Maddison, India was the largest economy from the year 1 AD until the colonial period whereupon it was taken over by other countries such as China and the UK Economists predict that by 2020, India will be among the leading economies of the world.

According to the BRIC report, published by Goldman Sachs, India will be the second largest economy after China by 2043.

India was under social democratic-based policies from 1947 to 1991. The economy was characterised by extensive regulation, protectionism, public ownership, pervasive corruption and slow growth. Since 1991, continuing economic liberalization has moved the country toward a market-based economy.

A revival of economic reforms and better economic policy in the first decade of the 21st century accelerated India's economic growth rate. In recent years, Indian cities have continued to liberalize business regulations. By 2008, India had established itself as the world's second-fastest growing major economy. However, the year 2009 saw a significant slowdown in India's GDP growth rate to 6.8% as well as the return of a large projected fiscal deficit of 6.8% of GDP which would be among the highest in the world.

Currency

The Indian Rupee is the only legal tender in India. It is accepted as legal tender in the neighboring Nepal and Bhutan, both of which peg their currency to that of the Indian rupee. The rupee is divided into 100 naya paise. The highest-denomination banknote is the 1,000 rupee note; the lowest-denomination coin in circulation is the 50 paise coin (it earlier had 1, 2, 5, 10 and 20 and 25 paise coins which have been discontinued by the Reserve Bank of India).

The Reserve Bank of India (RBI), the country's central bank, was established on 1 April 1935. It serves as the nation's monetary authority, regulator and supervisor of the financial system, manager of exchange control and as an issuer of currency. The RBI is governed by a central board, headed by a governor who is appointed by the Central government of India.

Currency notes in circulation have increased significantly since the time RBI was established 75 years ago. The value of notes in circulation in the country has increased from about Rs.172 crore in 1935 to more than Rs.700,000 crore in 2009. In terms of volume, the notes in circulation have increased from 124 million pieces in 1935 to more than 51 billion pieces in 2009. In fact, after China, India is the largest producer and consumer of currency notes.

As the economy grows, people need more currency and other payment instruments to settle their transactions. Notwithstanding several innovations in the field of payment and settlement, common people in our country, as indeed in many other developing countries, still use paper currency for their routine financial transactions. The ratio of currency with the public to GDP which was 12 per cent in 1951 is currently around 13 per cent, demonstrating that currency still remains an important mode of payment in the country. It is the Reserve Bank's responsibility, as the sole issuer of notes, to make available good and clean notes in adequate quantity to the public.

History and Evolution of Production of Notes in India

Currency/bank notes are among the most mass-produced commodities in the world. The genesis of paper money is generally attributed to the token money that evolved around the 10th century in China.

Use of paper money started in the West in the 17th century. However, paper currency did not catch on in India because of the political turmoil following the collapse of the Mughal Empire in the 17th century. Early currency in the form of 'I owe you / promissory notes' issued by banks or royal courts made appearance in India only in late 18th century. Use of official Government of India paper currency commenced in 1861, with the enactment of the Paper Currency Act. In 1935, Reserve Bank of India was created to preside over the function of issuing bank notes in India.

Indian Currency notes were printed in England till late 1920s. Recognizing that production of currency notes is a strategically important activity, the then Government of India set up a currency printing press at Nashik in Maharashtra in 1928. This was followed by the setting up of another press at Dewas in Madhya Pradesh nearly fifty years later, in 1975. Meanwhile, in 1967, a security paper mill with a capacity of 1,500 metric tonnes per year was established at

Hoshangabad in MP. By the late 1980s, the demand for currency notes exceeded the capacity of the two Government note presses. To meet the demand-supply gap, at the instance of Government of India, the Reserve Bank established, in 1996, two currency presses-one in Mysore and the other at Salboni in West Bengal. These were set up through a wholly-owned subsidiary of RBI viz. the Bharatiya Reserve Bank Note Mudran Pvt. Ltd. (BRBNMPL). By 1999, the BRBNMPL's two new presses started working to their full capacity making the country self-reliant once again in currency note printing.

Counterfeit Currency

Counterfeit money is currency that is produced without the legal sanction of the state or government, to resemble some official form of currency closely enough that it may be confused for genuine currency. Producing or using counterfeit money is a form of fraud.

Counterfeiting of money is almost as old as printing of currency. At some period in history, it was considered treasonous enough to warrant punishment by death. Before the introduction of paper money, the most prevalent method of counterfeiting involved mixing base metals with pure gold or silver. A common practice was to "shave" the edges of a coin. This was known as "clipping". While not itself counterfeiting, the exponents were able to use these precious metal shavings to create counterfeits. A fourree is an ancient type of counterfeit coin, in which a base metal core has been plated with a precious metal to resemble its solid metal counterpart.

It was in 1650 AD that paper money was developed and counterfeiting flourished, especially within America where counterfeit money was more common than genuine money. Counterfeiters had become so skilled that when the first federal coins were issued by the US Government in the 1780s, they had the dies cut by an ex-counterfeiter. However, it was the advent of colour copiers and other electronic devices in late twentieth century that made counterfeiting easier. Around the world, governments are locked in a fierce race with counterfeiters to keep that one crucial step ahead in terms of technology and security features. Governments are also tightening measures to check counterfeiting, apprehend counterfeiters and impose deterrent and harsher punishments.

Data available in the public domain suggests that the incidence of counterfeiting varies across different countries. As for the Euro, there was roughly about one counterfeit per 14,600 bank notes in circulation (2008). At home here in India, fake notes reported as detected by banks and fake notes found in remittances received by RBI during 2008-09 amounted to eight per one million notes in circulation. The data, however, does not include the counterfeits that are seized by police. The above data shows that, by an international metric, the incidence of counterfeit notes in India is not alarming. Nevertheless, counterfeiting per se is a matter of serious concern for the Government and the Reserve Bank.

Last year, some newspapers had erroneously quoted a figure from the Nayak Committee Report for estimates of forged currency notes in circulation. The Nayak Committee, which was set up in 1988 to go into the dynamics of currency management, did not make any estimate of fake currency. What it estimated was the projected value of fake notes in circulation in the year 2000 which was Rs. 1,69,000 crore. The media incorrectly reported this as the number of fake notes in circulation.

Modern counterfeiting began with paper money. Nations have used counterfeiting as a means of warfare. The idea is to overflow the enemy's economy with fake bank notes, so that the real value of the money plummets.

Instances

In 1926, a high-profile counterfeit scandal came to light in Hungary, when several people were arrested in the Netherlands while attempting to procure 10 million francs worth of fake French 1000-franc bills which had been produced in Hungary. After 3 years, the state-sponsored industrial scale counterfeit operation had finally collapsed. The League of Nations' investigation found Hungary's motives were to avenge its post-WWI territorial losses and to use profits from the counterfeiting business to boost a militarist, border-revisionist ideology. Germany and Austria had an active role in the conspiracy, which required special machinery. The quality of fake bills was still substandard, however, due to France's use of exotic raw paper material imported from its colonies.

During World War II, the Nazis attempted to implement a similar plan (Operation Bernhard) against the Allies to destabilise their economy by flooding the countries with forged banknotes. The Nazis took Jewish artists in the Sachsenhausen concentration camps and forced them to forge British pounds and American dollars. The quality of the counterfeiting was very good, and it was almost impossible to distinguish between the real and fake bills. The Germans could not put their plan into action, and were forced to dump the counterfeit bills into a lake. Most of the bills were not recovered until the 1950s. It was the largest counterfeiting operation in history and has been fictionalised in books, the BBC comedy-drama miniseries Private Schulz and a 2007 Oscar-winning Austrian film, The Counterfeiters (Die Fälscher).

During WWII, the U.S. counterfeited notes throughout the war in part to destabilize the local economy, thereby demoralizing the Japanese, and to supply guerillas fighting the Japanese. General MacArthur asked the Office of Strategic Services (OSS) to replicate the Japanese currency in the Philippines for his eventual return. "Toy Horse" was a classified operation where counterfeit Japanese banknotes would be printed in San Francisco and then shipped to Sacramento for numbering, cutting and wrapping by the State Printing Office hidden in the Governors Hall of the State Fairgrounds.

Today, some of the finest U.S. counterfeit banknotes are called Super dollars because of their high quality and likeness to the real US dollar. There has been a rapid growth in the counterfeiting of Euro banknotes and coins since the launch of the currency in 2002.

In 2006, a Pakistani government printing press in the city of Quetta was accused of churning out large quantities of counterfeit

Indian currency, The Times of India reported the story based on Central Bureau of Intelligence investigation. The rupee notes were then smuggled into India as 'part of Pakistan's agenda of destabilising (the) Indian economy through fake currency,' the daily said. The notes were 'supplied by the Pakistan government press (at Quetta) free of cost to Dubai-based counterfeiters who, in turn, smuggle it into India using various means,' the report said. This money was allegedly used to fund terrorist activities inside India. The investigations into the recent terrorist blasts and attacks in major Indian cities of Bengaluru, Hyderabad and Mumbai were allegedly funded using fake currency printed in Pakistan.

How fake currency destroys our economy?

i. Reduction in the value of real money

ii. The fake currencies will be used to fund the terrorist operations

iii. It will create a fear among the people that fake notes are in circulation. Indian currency will lose confidence among the public. It will force the RBI to withdraw certain currencies

iv. The fake currencies will increase the money supply and thereby result in inflation disturbing the economic growth. This will also add more to the already existing parallel economy (black money or unaccounted money in circulation) in the country

v. Decrease in the acceptability (satisfactoriness) of money-payees may demand electronic transfers of real money or payment in another currency (or even payment in a precious metal such as gold)

vi. Productivity losses, due to stoppage of work

vii. Fear complex among the people and reduction in tourism

viii. FDI outflow

In these days, counterfeiting has also been used to promote and sponsor terrorism. In India, counterfeit currency has long been a source of funding for terrorism. Investigations into at least four cases — Hyderabad bombings of August 2007; the attack on the Indian Institute of Science, Bangalore, in December 2005; the Ahmadabad bombings of July 2008; and the 26/11 terror attack on Mumbai — revealed a link.

What Are Other Countries Doing?

Innovation has intensified the race between increasingly sophisticated counterfeiters and banknote designers. The improving performance and decreasing cost of information technology have reduced "barriers to entry" in counterfeiting. Thus, to control this menace, bank note designers worldwide have introduced a number of features to deter counterfeiting. Most banknotes incorporate several security features, including holograms, micro printing, serial numbers, and watermarks. Most notes also include one or more visual accessibility feature, including different sizes and principal colors for different denominations, oversize high-contrast numerals, and tactile features such as embossed numerals or recessed/raised dots.

The goal of secure or 'intelligent' printing is to find features which are prohibitively expensive to counterfeit. The 'foundation' of banknote security is paper. High quality paper is required for reasons of durability. Also, at least 20 countries in the world use plastic notes, which are supposed to be more durable, being made of non-porous polymer with a special protective coating that prevents absorption of moisture. Such notes are said to be more counterfeit-proof. Australia has started issuing plastic banknotes which contain clear plastic 'windows' (performing a function similar to watermarks in paper). But this single layer of polymer (basically polypropylene film) failed in many specifications. Eg; in countries where punching a hole or stapling is more prevalent, it failed miserably. Also, the security features available in paper, like security fibers, security water mark, security thread, etc, were never possible in polymer. Since 2010, the latest innovation is to make hybrid bank note substrate of paper on both sides and hot molten polymer in the core. Other features that are added during manufacture are, e.g. watermarks and ultraviolet (UV) fluorescent fibres – the security thread. The next layer of security is in the printed design. Inks which are difficult to obtain are commonly used, which can only be printed using high quality printers. The texture of the printed surface is also controlled: the raised writing on notes ('Intaglio'), which also requires special printing presses. Another graphical security feature is 'registration', where images printed on the front and back of notes coincide exactly when held up to the light. Basically, the proposal is to keep the low level forgers to be out of the race by making the Capex more expensive for them, and to keep the state sponsored forgers to be forewarned.

More 'exotic' (and expensive) security features are also available and introduced by various countries. 'Optically Variable Ink (OVI)', is used, which changes colour depending on the angle of view. Foil patterns of various complexities can be stamped onto a note. More advanced and difficult to counterfeit non-printed features include, advanced optical devices, such as holograms, and the Kine gram. These holograms are essentially a three-dimensional drawing or photograph. Security holograms are mass produced, but the replication process requires specialized, expensive equipment to pull off. This is an advanced security feature utilized by many currencies such as the British Pound, the Euro, Canadian Dollars, Japanese Yen, the South Korean Won etc. Also, there is much research into new kinds of machine-readable features- that may prove very difficult to counterfeit. For example, 'biological tagging' using minute quantities of genetic material (DNA or RNA), and 'phase masks' which are high security laser-readable devices. In this analysis, we focus on currency design features that enhance counterfeit deterrence. All currencies issued worldwide contain some of these design features but, interestingly, different countries have made different choices.

Security Industries Role

Secure printing is in a state of constant evolution, as counterfeiters learn how to defeat increasingly sophisticated techniques. There is much research into new kinds of security feature–mostly machine-readable-that may prove very difficult to counterfeit. For example,

Currency Features - Features to assist authentication and denomination (Anti-counterfeiting measures)	Australia	Canada	Euro	Hong Kong SAR	Japan	India	Singapore	Sweden	Switzerland	UK	USA
Background printing offset	Y										
Braille codes							Y				
Clear window	Y										
Color changing number / Color shifting inks			Y								Y
Concealed image / denominations				Y							
Engraved Portrait							Y				
Fine line patterns		Y									Y
Fluorescent ink properties	Y										
Fluorescent machine-readable barcode				Y							
Fluorescent / UV light tests		Y		Y		Y					
Holographic Stripe / Hologram patch / Holographic Window thread / Hologram / Kinegram / Foil-strip Hologram / Hologram & Foil		Y	Y	Y	Y		Y	Y		Y	
Iridescent images				Y							
Intaglio Priniting / Raised Printing	Y	Y	Y	Y	Y	Y		Y	Y		
Intaglio feature : non-reflective under UV light							Y				
Latent Image					Y	Y					

Contd...

Currency Features - Features to assist authentication and denomination (Anti-counterfeiting measures)	Australia	Canada	Euro	Hong Kong SAR	Japan	India	Singapore	Sweden	Switzerland	UK	USA
Lithographic Print							Y				
Low vision feature											Y
Machine readable feature											Y
Microlettering						Y		Y		Y	
Micropriniting	Y	Y	Y		Y	Y	Y				
Motion feature								Y			
Optically variable ink				Y		Y			Y		
Peal Ink / Shimmering mother of pearl ink					Y			Y			
Perforations			Y					Y			
Security thread			Y	Y		Y	Y	Y		Y	Y
See through windown							Y				
See through registration device / See through number / See through feature / Asymmetrical serial number	Y	Y	Y	Y			Y				
Serial Number		Y									
Shadow image	Y										

Contd...

Currency Features - Features to assist authentication and denomination (Anti-counterfeiting measures)	Australia	Canada	Euro	Hong Kong SAR	Japan	India	Sinagpore	Sweden	Switzerland	UK	USA
Tactile marks			Y								
Transparent register									Y		
Ultra fine line priniting					Y						
UV and Metallic digits									Y		
UV light tests			Y							Y	
Watermark / Watermarks portrait		Y	Y	Y	Y	Y	Y	Y	Y	Y	Y
Window color shifting thread		Y									

'e-watermark', 'Nano particle tagging' using nano particles as taggants, 'biological tagging' using minute quantities of genetic material (DNA or RNA), 'Windowed Banknote Substrate' can be used with transparent window and 'Security fibers' which are high security fluorescent fibers with special optical properties.

E-Watermark It is a process in which the currency notes are watermarked for having a common overt and covert security feature, i.e., for example the Mahatma Gandhi Watermark, by traditional dandy roll and a ghost image which is embeded at the short former level and can be read using an electronic device. This ghost image can also have DNA Taggants, for forensic investigations.

Windowed Banknote substrate Windowed banknote substrate offers a new feature to the market: a transparent window and high durability. An example of this kind of product is Durasafe®.

It is made using combination of paper and polymer, where a central polymer core is added between Two thin security paper layers (cotton base) which has transparent die-cut window where the polymer is easily visible in the form of a transparent clear window. Some benefits of using Windowed banknote Substrate are:

- Special security substrate available only to security printers
- Photocopies & digital prints cannot have access to windows–easy to identify fakes
- High Capex for small-time fraudsters
- Overt and covert features
- Special hot molten polymer used to manufacture; Can incorporate DNA or other taggants within windows
- Windows can be overprinted, by security printers
- No over lacquers needed to protect prints as paper on both sides
- Long life and easily stapled– if needed and if allowed

Properties of a windowed substrate paper:

- Touch and feel of paper
- Real cylinder mould-made watermark and electrotype watermark

- Substrate-integrated transparent windows
- Paper-based and window-based security features

Function of paper surface

- Ensures print ability
- Carries watermark and paper-based security
- Gives typical banknote touch and feel

Function of polymer core

- Forms transparent windows, inherent to substrate
- Provides strength and durability

Security Fibers Special quality security fiber which are fluorescent security fibers with advanced optical properties (like polarized absorption/emission) can be used in the banknotes. These special optical properties can be visualized by aid of a special optical devices (like rotating optical polarizer). Depending on the orientation of the polarizer with respect to the orientation of the security fiber, the security fibers show fluorescence or remain dark (bright/dark-effect). An example of this kind of product is Polarisafe®

Highly secure and hidden features for security fibres and security threads:

- At first sight looks like a UV fibre
- Linear atomic structures visible under polarized light

Some benefits of using special polarised security fibers and threads (e.g. Polarisafe, from Landqart):

- These special security fibers features two levels of security: In addition to showing fluorescence under ultraviolet light, it is sensitive to polarized UV light. This property is a hidden feature and becomes only apparent by using the appropriate test equipment
- Under ordinary UV lamps and document testers, these features appear like ordinary fluorescent security features. With special test equipment, these features show a dynamic, blinking and twinkling effect
- These effects are directly linked to the structure of the feature and has an inherent superstructure of its own-a property that

cannot be imitated by common printing techniques

Special Iridescent security features Iridescent security features have proven to be effective for a long time. This kind of stripe varies in colour when the note is tilted. An example of this kind of product is Irisafe®

Some of the benefits of the Iridescent security feature are:

- IRISAFE® is an optically variable security feature detectable by naked eye without further devices
- IRISAFE® has high brilliance & distinct colour change effect
- The colour flip cannot be reproduced, neither by scanners nor by colour copiers
- High visibility of iridescent lines upon tilting
- Exclusive colour combinations are possible
- We can for e.g. choose our national colours as a colour combination
- Is easily integrated into the print design. And can be overprinted by any printing process.
- Very durable security feature. Even on heavily circulated and soiled banknotes, the distinctive IRISAFE® effect is still very visible
- A cost-effective first-level security feature

Nano Particle Taggants (custom made to portray India Flag) Sometimes what can't be seen can make all the difference in protecting something. Nano Particle taggant particles are microscopic. Each particle can be uniquely encoded like a fingerprint and can be detected in multiple ways, starting with an inexpensive, handheld readers to complex computerised algorithms.

Some Commonly Used Formats of Nano Particle Taggants are:

- Compounded plastic resins
- Security inks
- Security threads
- Paper

Some commonly used readers to detect Nano particle taggants are:

- Laser Pen

- UV Lights
- Audible Detector
- Microscopes
- Computerised Readers

Secure DNA Mark It is a biotechnical tagging system that applies unique codes to a wide variety of liquid and solid materials. Marked items can be identified unequivocally to provide proof of ownership or source, which facilitates the detection of fraud, theft or illegal manufacture.

For the purpose of tagging, DNA is synthetically produced and the base sequence provides the unique code. A base sequence of 100 nucleotides gives over 1×1060 unique codes.

Some security tag characteristics of the DNA Mark are:

- Infinite number of tags.
- Harmless to environment.
- Totally secure.
- Used in minute concentration.
- Stable and permanent.
- Cost Effective.
- Acceptable as evidence by the judiciary.

How is DNA Mark verified?

- DNA mark is composed of two chemical components. One of a variety of overt or covert markers to act as a beacon to indicate the presence of the unique taggant
- DNA-mark beads are one method of indicating the presence of the unique taggant. They are in the range of 1-10 microns with a variety of physical, chemical and surface properties dependent on application. Each bead can be fluoresced allowing easy detection..DNA Mark can also be identified by a specially supplied scanner. This forms a separate semi-covert field test.

How and where we can use DNA Mark? Paper Pulp Slurry

- Minute quantities of DNA Mark can be added in the pulp slurry
- DNA Mark is used in inks and coatings

- Conventional pigmented inks: solvent based, water based UV inks
- Invisible inks
- Over-lacquers

DNA Mark can be used with a wide variety of printing techniques

- Direct film casting process
- Silk screen printing
- Rotogravure and flexo printing
- Offset printing
- Ink jet printing
- Tampon printing

Conclusion

A currency is a medium of exchange of paper for services or goods. Not accepting this "paper" is like loss of confidence in the particular country.

The main intention is to control the currency from duplication by "interested parties" (read parties who want to wage a war on our country). Controlling is one thing, identifying the source, and bringing them books (through FATF or other world bodies), is another.

The security feature should be overt (for common man), covert (for law officers and approved machines/readers with banks etc) and forensically provable in the court of law.

While the cover security features and forensic security features should be known to only the relevant people, nationally and internationally, the overt features, necessarily have to be communicated to the general public. Even these overt features need to be special and the technology needs to be controlled by Indian entities, who are accountable. Some of the relevant and high-technology features should be home grown and should have an unique "Indian flavour" and if imported, the same should be manufactured within geographical boundaries of India.

Currency is widely used in the payment systems of all countries. In each system, there are a large number of participants–households, retail merchants, financial institutions, high-volume currency processors, and the central bank or currency-issuing authority. We may believe that the above precautions will make India a country of zero counterfeit currency and accelerate the growth of our economy, however, the way, we in India, can tackle this problem is to exercise vigilance on the part of every citizen. "If men were angels, no government would be necessary." This battle against counterfeiting is not only for the strong alone; but for the vigilant and the active.

Part - II

Indian Currency

- The word Rupee is derived from the Sanskrit word रौप्य (raupya) meaning "silver" or "made of silver".
- The issuer of this is the Reserve Bank of India.
- The unofficial user of this currency are two neighboring states of India, Bhutan(along with Bhutanese Ngultrum) and Nepal(along with Nepalese Rupee).
- Recently on July 15, 2010 the Indian Government adopted it's official Currency Symbol.

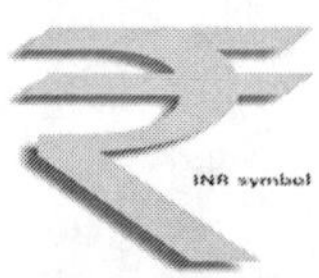

With the adoption of it's unique symbol **Indian Rupee has now achieved parity with major international currencies** such as the dollar, euro, pound sterling and yen in one respect and has a distinct identity.

- Money is considered an intrinsic component of the cultural heritage of a country mirroring its socio-economic history.
- **India was one of the earliest issuers of coinage in the world (*circa* 6th Century BC)** and has been home to many-a-monetary experiment recorded in history.
- Historians believe that the **first 'rupee' was issued by Emperor Sher Shah Suri in the 15th century**. Where one rupee was equivalent to 40 copper paisas.

Indian Currency - History

Financial Instruments and 'Hundies' in India have a venerable history.

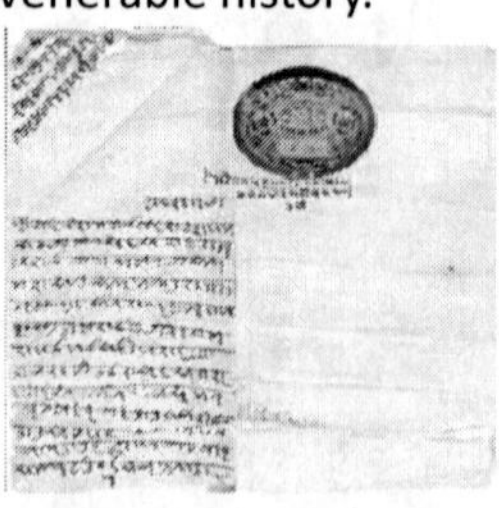

A British India Hundi

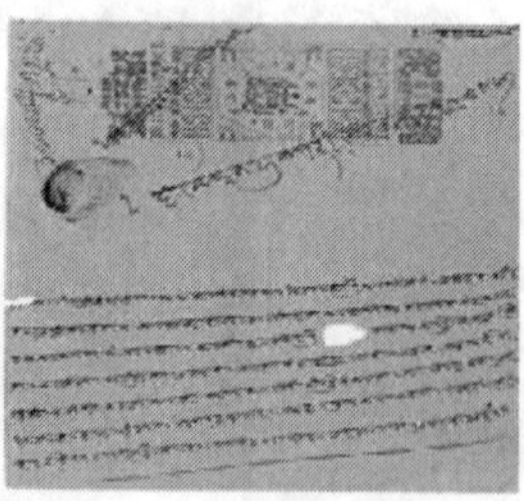

A Princely State Hundi

- **Paper Money**, as we know it today, was introduced in India in the **late Eighteenth Century**.
- Among the earliest issues of paper rupees were those by the ***Bank of Hindustan*** (1770–1832), the ***General Bank of Bengal and Bihar*** (1773–75) and the ***Bengal Bank*** (1784–91), amongst others. Until 1815, the **Madras Presidency** also issued a currency based on the fanam, with 12 fanams equal to the rupee.
- Following independence in 1947, the **Indian rupee replaced all the currencies of the previously autonomous states**. Some of these states had issued rupees equal to those issued by the British (such as the Travancore Rupee). Other currencies included the Hyderabad Rupee and the Kutch Kori.

Indian Currency - History

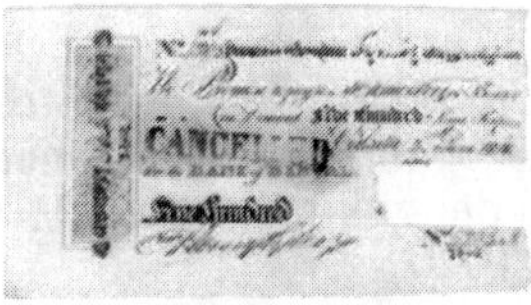
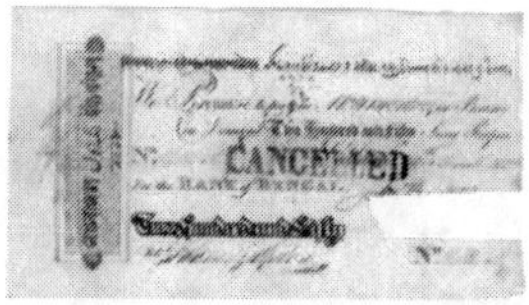

The **Unifaced** (printed on one side only) Notes of the Bank of Bengal

The **Unifaced** (printed on one side only) note issued by the Bank of Bombay

9

Indian Currency - History

The Indian rupee replaced the **Danish Indian Rupee**(issued by the Danish East India Company, used in the Danish India) in 1845, the **French Indian Rupee**(issued by France's Banque de L'Indochine, used in French India) in 1954 and the **Portuguese Indian Escudo**(issued by Banco Nacional Ultramarino, used in Portuguese India) in 1961.

A French One Rupee Banknote

A Portuguese 30 Escudos Note

The Paper Currency Act of 1861 gave the British Indian Government the monopoly to issue notes in India.

- The first set of British India notes were the 'Victoria Portrait' Series issued in denominations of 10, 20, 50, 100, 1000
- These were **unifaced** (**printed on one side only**), carried **two language panels** and were **printed on hand-moulded paper manufactured at the Laverstock Paper Mills** (Portals).
- The security features incorporated the **watermark** (GOVERNMENT OF INDIA, RUPEES, two signatures and wavy lines), the **printed signature** and the **registration of the notes**.

The Victoria Portrait series was withdrawn in the wake of a spate of forgeries and replaced by the **unifaced (printed on one side only) 'Underprint Series'** which were introduced in 1867.

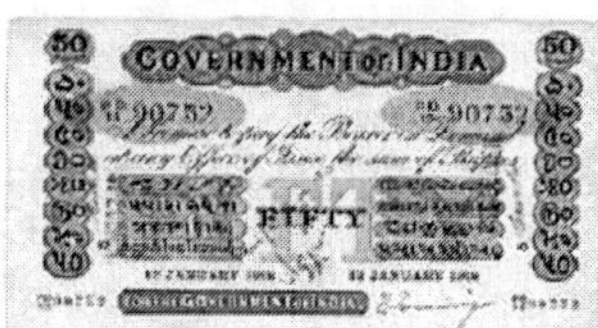

- The Underprint Series notes were **printed on moulded paper** and carried **4 language panels (Green Series)**.
- The languages differed as per the currency circle of Issue. Language panels were increased to **8 in the Red Series**.
- The improved security features included a **wavy line watermark**, the **manufacturer's code in the watermark , guilloche patterns** and a **coloured underprint**.

The **Reserve Bank of India was formally inaugurated on Monday, April 1, 1935** with its Central Office at Calcutta.

<u>This was also the first time that the notes were printed on both the sides.</u>

- The first Governor, Sir Osborne Smith did not sign any bank notes; the **first Reserve Bank issues were signed by the second Governor, Sir James Taylor**.
- During the **WWII war, Japanese Operations to destabilise Indian currency involved high quality forgeries**, largely of Re 10 notes signed by **Governor C.D. Deshmukh**.
- This necessitated a **change in the watermark and obverse design** from the profile portrait of George VI to his full frontal portrait. As an added security feature, the **security thread was introduced for the first time in India**.

When on the **Midnight, August 15, 1947 India was heralded into independence from colonial rule. The Reserve Bank continued to issue the extant notes**.

Rupees Ten - Ashoka Pillar

Rupees Hundred- Mahatma Gandhi Series

- **Symbol for independent India** consensually chosen was the **Lion Capital, Ashoka Pillar at Sarnath**.
- In **1953, Hindi was displayed prominently on the new notes**. The debate regarding the Hindi plural of Rupaya was settled in favour of Rupiye.
- The lean period of the early sixties led to considerations of economy and the **sizes of notes were reduced in 1967**.
- Cost benefit considerations prompted the Bank to **introduce Rs. 20 denomination notes in 1972 and Rs. 50 in 1975**.
- With the advancement of reprographic techniques, traditional security features were deemed inadequate. It was necessary to introduce new features and a new '**Mahatma Gandhi Series**' was introduced in 1996. A **changed watermark**, **windowed security thread**, **latent image** and **intaglio features** for the visually handicapped are amongst the new features.

- The **Rupee and its subsidiary coinage was current at various times in East Africa, Arabia and Mesopotamia**. The usage of the Rupee in East Africa extended from Somalia in the north, to as far south as Natal. In Mozambique the British India rupees were overstamped, and in Kenya the British East Africa Company minted the rupee and its fractions as well as pice. In Somalia the Italian colonial authority minted 'rupia' to the exact same standard, and called the pice 'besa'.
- With **Partition of India**, the **Pakistani Rupee came into existence**, initially **using Indian coins and Indian currency notes** simply **overstamped** with "**Pakistan**".
- In previous times, the **Indian rupee was an official currency** of other countries, including Aden, Oman, Kuwait, Bahrain, Qatar, the Trucial States(which later became United Arabs Emirates in 1971), Kenya, Tanganyika, Uganda, the Seychelles, and Mauritius.

- The **Indian government introduced the Gulf Rupee**, also known as the **Persian Gulf rupee** (XPGR), as a replacement for the Indian rupee for **circulation exclusively outside the country** with the Reserve Bank of India [Amendment] Act, 1 May 1959.
- A separate series of notes exclusively for circulation in the Gulf (Kuwait, Bahrain, Qatar, and the Trucial States (now the UAE) were issued by the Indian Government and the Reserve Bank of India. The notes **retained the contemporary design** but were **different in colour** and **carried the prefix 'Z'**.

The Gulf Rupee issued by RBI

Fake Currency

- If Intelligence Bureau is to be believed the amount of fake currency in India is shocking at ₹170,000 crore (₹17 trillion).
- Reserve Bank of India official figure for the total currency available with the Indian public was ₹603,000 crore (₹63 trillion) (as on July 2008)
- If what the IB is saying is true, then it would mean that 28 per cent of the currency in the country is fake(**though Reserve Bank of India officials dispute this figure**).

Ref-http://www.rediff.com/money/2008/dec/19mumterror-how-fake-currency-funds-terror.htm and "The Week", 24,October,2010

Fake Notes Detected by RBI Across India

Denomination	Number of Notes			Face Value (In Rupees)		
	2006-07	2007-08	2008-09	2006-07	2007-08	2008-09
₹ 10	110(-)	107(-)	68(-)	1,100	1,070	680
₹ 20	305(0.1)	343(-)	341(0.2)	6,100	6,860	6,820
₹ 50	6,800(1.2)	8,119(1.5)	12,792(2.6)	3.4L	4.05L	6.39L
₹ 100	68,741(5.1)	1.1L(8.2)	1.33L(9.7)	68.74L	1.1Cr	1.33Cr
₹ 500	25,636(5.7)	66,838(12.7)	2.19L(35.6)	1.28Cr	3.34Cr	10.98Cr
₹ 1000	3,151(3.4)	10,131(7.2)	31,857(16.6)	31.51L	1.01Cr	3.18Cr
Total	**1.04L(2.6)**	**1.95L(4.4)**	**3.98L(8.1)**	**2.31Cr**	**5.49Cr**	**15.57Cr**

Note: Figures in parentheses show pieces per million banknotes in circulation; Data is exclusive of the counterfeit notes seized by the police.

Fake Currency

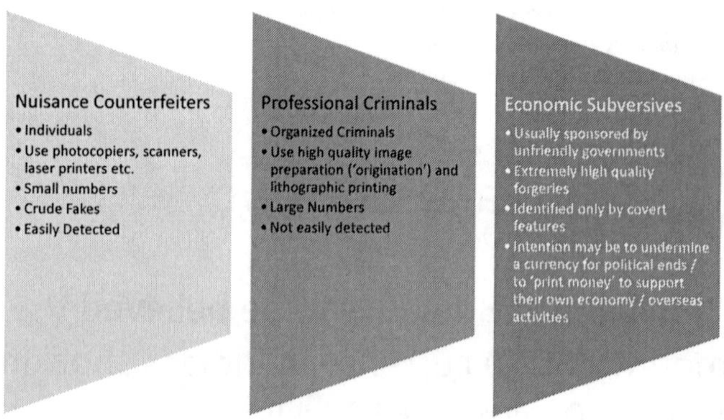

Some of the ill-effects that fake currency has on society are:

- Reduction in the value of ***real*** money.
- Reduced **confidence** in currency.
- Increase in prices (**inflation**) due to more money getting circulated in the economy - an unauthorized artificial increase in the money supply.
- Decrease in the **acceptability** of money - Globally - payees may demand electronic transfers of real money or payment in another currency (or even payment in a precious metal such as gold)

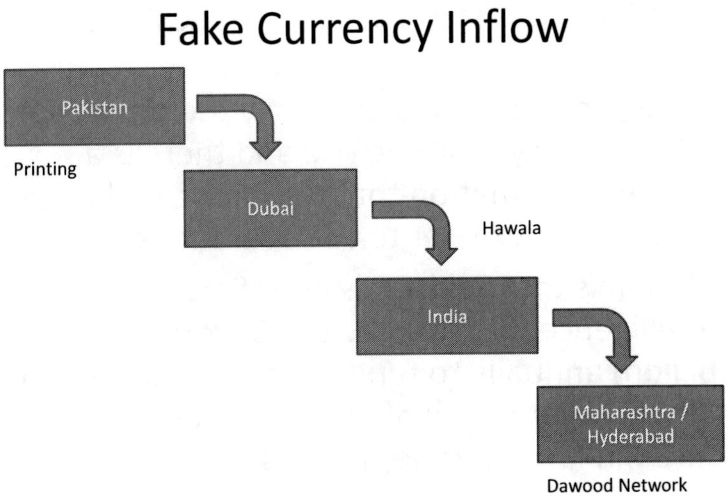

- **Labourers**, who go to Dubai in search of employment, are the usual targets. When they return to India to visit relatives, they are lured with incentives to carry the fake currency. The notes are **covered in carbon paper and stashed in suitcases and covered with perfume, clothes, packed in photographic albums**, etc.

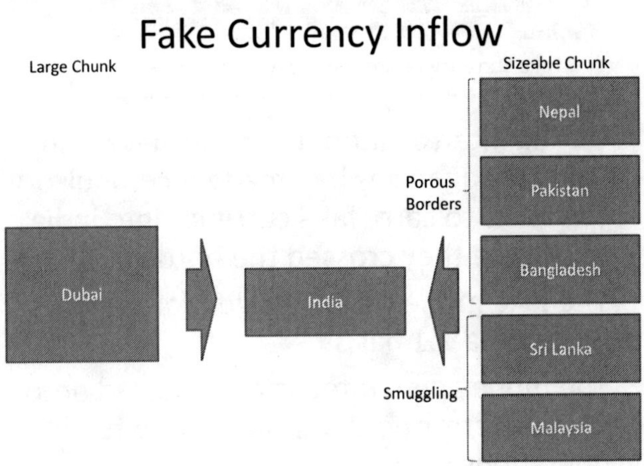

Fake Currency For Terrorism

- Intelligence Bureau sleuths say the menace of fake currency is on the rise and there is a specific information that this money is being used extensively for terror operations.
- IB claim's that Pakistan's Inter Services Intelligence (ISI) raises ₹ 1,800 crore (₹ 18 billion) annually to fund terror operations and that a major chunk of this amount comes in through fake currency rackets.

Indian Institute of Science, Bengaluru

- ₹ 30 lakh of the ₹ 50 lakh
- Fake currency racket

Hyderabad blasts

- ₹ 5 crore
- Distribution of fake currency

Mumbai Attacks

- Fake currency rackets and *hawala* channels

- During interrogation, terrorists have said that Pakistani agencies had made it compulsory for terrorists to carry fake currency into India each time they crossed the border.
- The fake money is exchanged for original notes on a 2:1 basis.
- The money generated is then passed onto various terror networks in India to fund operations.

Present Security Features of Indian Currency

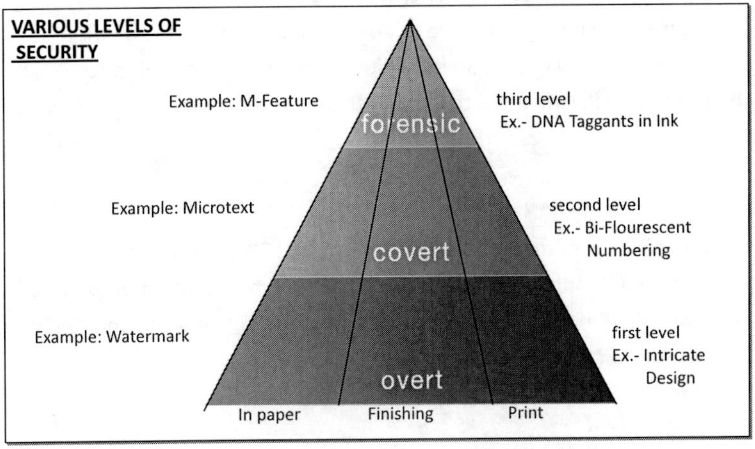

The main Overt security features of the current banknotes are listed below:

- **Security thread** - All notes except for ₹1000 have a security band with inscriptions visible when held against light which reads Bharat in Devanagari script and RBI in English. The security thread of the ₹1000 banknote contains the inscription 'Bharat' in the Devanagari script, '1000' and 'RBI'.

- **Latent image** - On notes with denominations of ₹20 and upwards, a vertical band on the right side of the Mahatma Gandhi's portrait contains a latent image showing the respective denominational value in numeral which is visible only when the note is held horizontally at eye level.

- **Microlettering** - Numeral denominational value is visible under magnifying glass between security thread and latent image.
- **Identification Mark** - On the left of the watermark window different shapes are printed in Intaglio for various denominations . This also helps the visually impaired to identify the denomination.

Rs.20 Rs.50 Rs.100 Rs.500 Rs.1000

- **Intaglio** - On notes with denominations of ₹20 and upwards, the portrait of Mahatma Gandhi, the Reserve Bank seal, guarantee and promise clause, Ashoka Pillar Emblem on the left, RBI Governor's signature are printed in intaglio i.e. in raised prints.

- **Fluorescence** - The number panels of the banknotes are printed in fluorescent ink. The banknotes also have optical fibers. Both can be seen when the banknotes are exposed to ultra-violet lamp.

- **Optically variable ink** - Notes of ₹ 500 and ₹ 1000 have their numerals printed in optically variable ink. Number appears green when note is held flat but changes to blue when viewed at angle.

- **Watermark** - White side panel of the banknotes contain the Mahatma Gandhi watermark with a light and shade effect and multi-directional lines and an electrotype mark showing the denominational numeral 10, 20, 50, 100, 500 and 1000 appear in this section respectively in each denomination banknote and these can be viewed better when the banknote is held against light.in the watermark window.

- **See through register** - Half the numeral of each denomination (10, 20, 50, 100, 500 and 1000) is printed on the obverse (front) and half on the reverse. The accurate back to back registration makes the numeral appear as one when viewed against light.

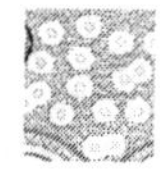

- **EURion Constellation** - A pattern of symbols found on the banknote helps software detect the presence of a banknote in a digital image so that it can prevent its reproduction with devices such as color photocopiers.
- **Optically Variable Ink (OVI)** - The font size of the numeral 500 and 1000 in ₹500 and ₹1000 denomination banknotes is reduced, as compared to older Mahatma Gandhi series banknotes issued in these denominations earlier in the year 2000. The colour of the numeral appears green when the banknote is held flat but would change to blue when the banknote is held at an angle.
- **Year of Printing** - Year of printing appears on the reverse of the banknote.

- In addition to these largely **overt security features,** there are **covert features,** known only to a few key personnel. Covert features provide an **'ultimate' test of authenticity**, and examples are inks with special spectroscopic characteristics, magnetic inks, radioactive inks, isotopic composition of the paper and ink, microscopic structure of the paper, M-Features, India Specific DNA Taggants, etc.

Security Concerns for Indian Currency

FINDINGS OF RBI OFFICIALS, WHO EXAMINED THE PAK-ISI SPONSORED COUNTERFEIT CURRENCY

Sl. No.	Findings	Remarks	Recommendations
1	The Series Prefix and Distinctive Numbers are smaller in size	Post Printing Issue	Distinctive DNA taggants can be mixed in Ink for covert proof
2	Alignment of Series prefix and distinctive numbers is not in line when carefully examined	Post Printing Issue, could have been resulted since absence of Attention to Detail	More of a "mind set" issue of Security Printer, Will possibly get corrected in future "super fakes"
3	Thick lettering has been used for printing the issuing authority's name i.e., 'Reserve Bank of India' and guarantee and promise clauses	Post Printing Issue, could have been resulted since absence of Attention to Detail	More of a "mind set" issue of Security Printer, Will possibly get corrected in future "super fakes"

4	Continuity of Security Thread is not maintained	Security thread has to move – This is technical requirement of Papermakers	Insert security thread in between long former and short former using a Hydro Phyllic film
5	Alignment of the register on the left hand side of the watermark is not proper	More of a "Attention to detail" issue. Common man does not know	E – Watermarking
6	Watermark at the left hand side bears a thicker effigy of Mahatma Gandhi and the eyes and spectacles in the effigy are thicker in size	More of a "Attention to detail" issue. Common man does not know	E – Watermark embedded within the 2 layers of web. Overt and Covert features, with DNA taggants
7	Intaglio printing is absent	Digitally Printed Notes on newgen Printers and scanners	EURion Constellation (Omron) will control this on new age printers and scanners.
8	The optical fiber marks are present when exposed to UV lamp but these are very few when compared to genuine notes	Does general public know the number of fiber per note?	Low tech "Print technology" fibers should be replaced by high Tech Polarised UV & Machine readable Polarisafe Fibers. Take guarantee from producers / collaborators that they will not supply or divulge technology to "enemy" countries. Inform Citizens about number of fibers per note.
9	Security thread does not glow under UV lamp	If it does not glow then the values and 'RBI' can't be read under UV.	Change colour to glow to unique "Pink" or "Black" or "Red" or have dual colour glow
10	The paper used for the purpose seems to have been made of wood pulp while compared to the security paper, cotton and special ink used in the manufacture of the notes by the RBI	How can a common man find out this paper difference?	Use Banknote made with Windowed Banknote Substrate (a combination of paper and polymer) which has a Clear Transparent Window. Ex. – Durasafe (Best of Overt and Covert Security features)

Suggestions for Safeguarding the Indian Currency

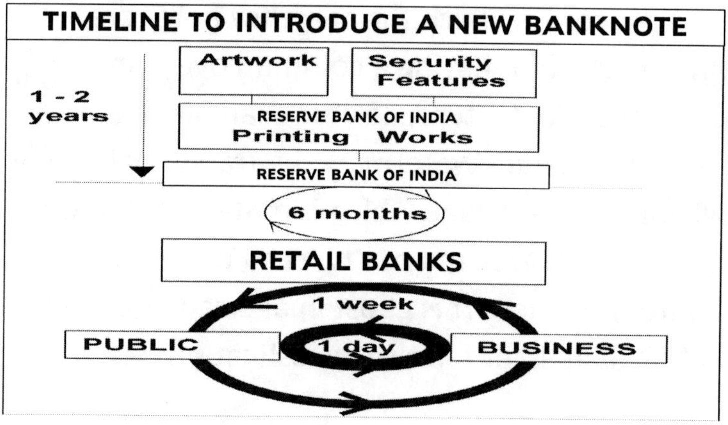

Secure printing is in a state of constant evolution, as counterfeiters learn how to defeat increasingly sophisticated techniques. There is much research into new kinds of security feature – mostly machine-readable - that may prove very difficult to counterfeit. For example, **'e-watermark'** ,**'nano particle tagging**' using nano particles as taggants, **'biological tagging'** using minute quantities of genetic material (DNA or RNA), **'Windowed Banknote Substrate**' can be used with transparent window and **'Security fibers'** which are high security fluorescent fibers with special optical properties.

Suggestions for Safeguarding the Indian Currency – E-Watermark

E-Watermark

It is a process in which the currency notes are watermarked for having a common overt and covert security feature, i.e., for example the Mahatma Gandhi Watermark, by traditional dandy roll and a ghost image which is embeded at the short former level and can be read using an electronic device. This ghost image can also have DNA Taggants, for forensic investigations.

Suggestions for Safeguarding the Indian Currency - Durasafe

Windowed Banknote substrate

Windowed banknote substrate offers a new feature to the market: a transparent window and high durability.

An example of this kind of product is **Durasafe**®

How is it made?

It is made using Combination of paper and polymer:

- Two thin security paper layers (cotton base)
- Central polymer core
- Transparent die-cut window

Suggestions for Safeguarding the Indian Currency - Durasafe

Why Windowed Banknote Substrate?

- Special Security substrate available only to Security Printers.
- Photocopies & Digital prints cannot have access to windows—easy to identify fakes.
- High Capex for small time fraudsters.
- Overt and Covert Feature.
- Special Hot Molten Polymer used to manufacture. Can incorporate DNA or other taggants within windows.
- Windows can be overprinted, by Security printers.
- No overlacquers needed to protect prints as Paper on both sides.
- Long life and easily stapled– if needed and if allowed.

Windowed Banknote Substrate, Example - Durasafe®

Production Method

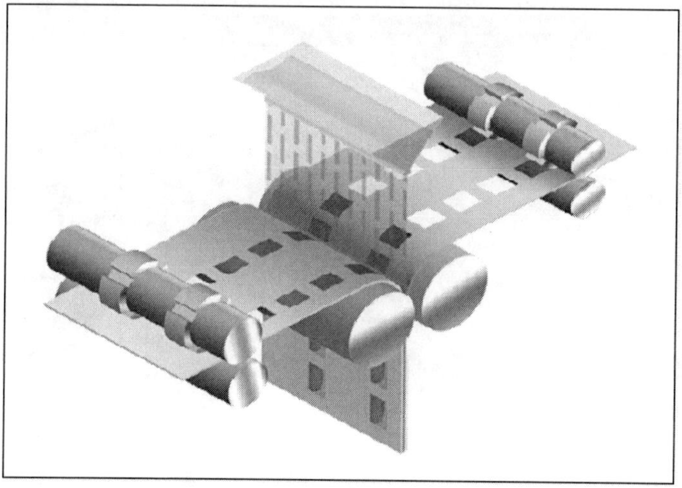

Windowed Banknote substrate, Example - Durasafe®

Production Process

- Die-cutting in registration with watermarks
- Registration of front- and reverse paper layer
- Hot molten polymer between paper layers
- Polymer is introduced as liquid polymer melt
- Super chilling and high pressure is applied
- Polymer infiltrates the paper fibers to form an even substrate
- Polymer forms inseparable bond
- No plastic film, no adhesive, no lamination is used

Windowed Banknote Substrate, Example - Durasafe®

Electron Microscopy – Lateral Cut of Cross-Section

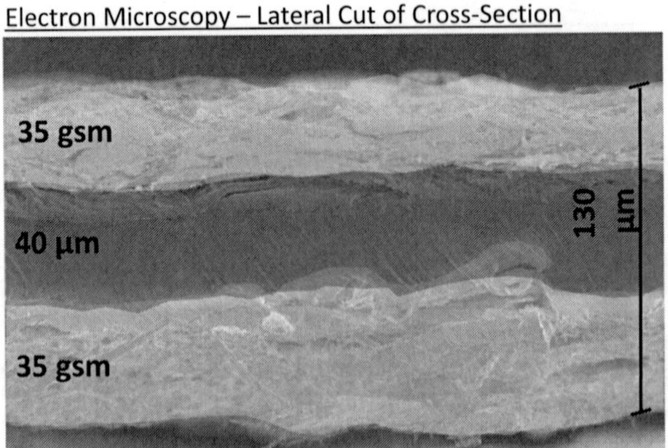

Windowed Banknote substrate, Example - Durasafe®

Properties of a Windowed substrate paper:

- Touch and feel of paper
- Real cylinder mould-made watermark and electrotype watermark
- Substrate-integrated transparent windows
- Paper-based and window-based security features

Function of paper surface:

- Ensures printability
- Carries watermark and paper-based security
- Gives typical banknote touch and feel

Function of polymer core:

- Forms transparent windows, inherent to substrate
- Provides strength and durability

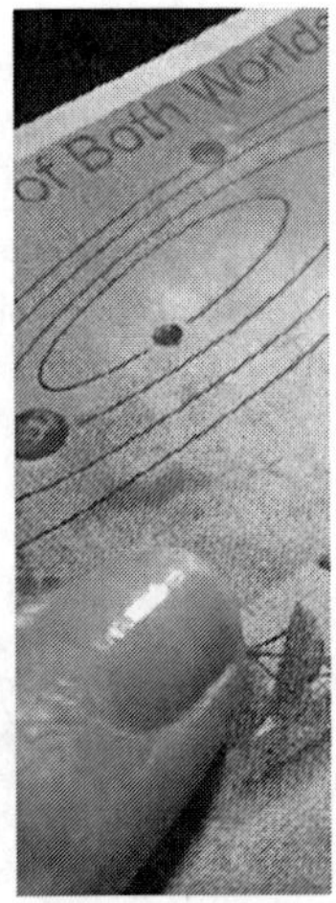

Windowed Banknote Substrate, Example - Durasafe®

Window Design

- Well-defined shapes possible
- Multiple windows possible
- Almost any window position possible
- Combination of windows with security features

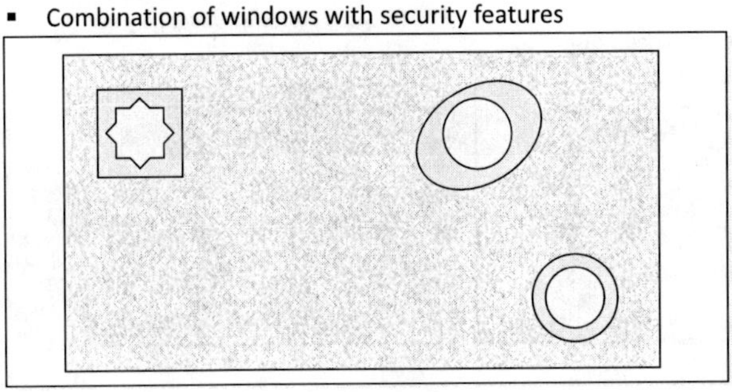

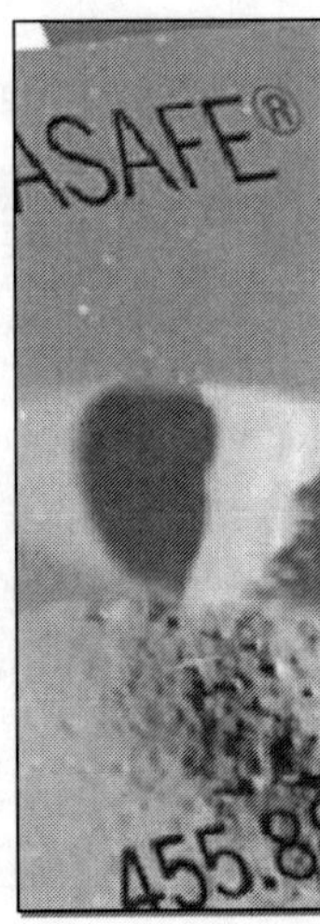

Windowed Banknote substrate, Example - Durasafe®

<u>Window Design – Type 1</u>

- Similar window geometries on front- and reverse side
- Overlap generates large transparent window area

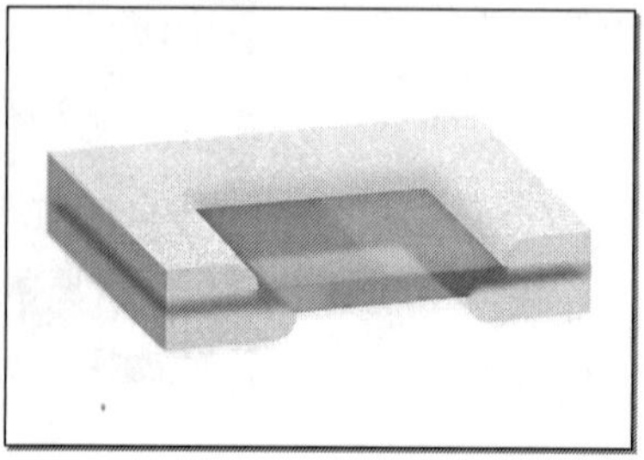

<u>Window Design – Type 2</u>

- Different window geometries on front- and reverse side
- Formation of transparent, semi-transparent and fully opaque areas

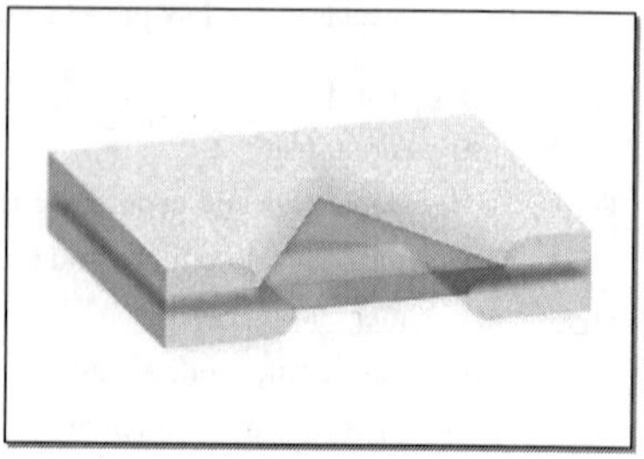

Windowed Banknote Substrate, Example - Durasafe®

<u>Window Design with Security–Type 1</u>

<u>Watermark in Semi-Transparent Window</u>

- Easy to check, watermark visible against dark background
- No need to hold against the light
- Semi-transparent in the main watermark area
- Keep the confidence during a cash transaction

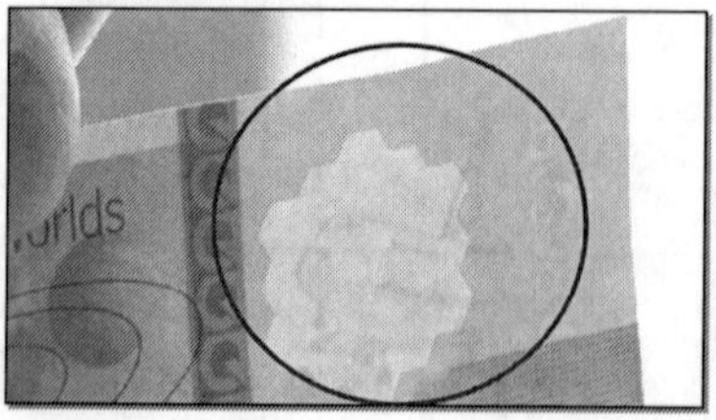

<u>Window Design with Security–Type 2</u>

<u>Security Thread Through Window</u>

- De-metallized 6 mm colour switch thread
- Without wobble zone, flatness of sheet still good
- Thread is protected under polymer

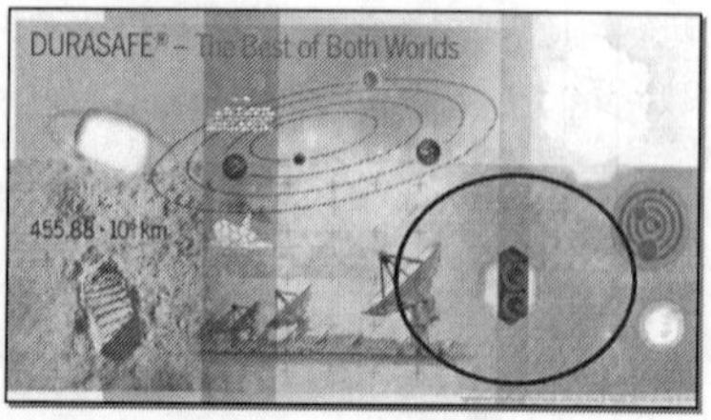

Windowed Banknote Substrate, Example - Durasafe®

Two Sided Intaglio Printing

- Durasafe® retains more tactility.
- Durasafe® shows much less distortion

- Paper loses tactility when printed on the reverse side.
- Paper forms a trapezoid during intaglio printing

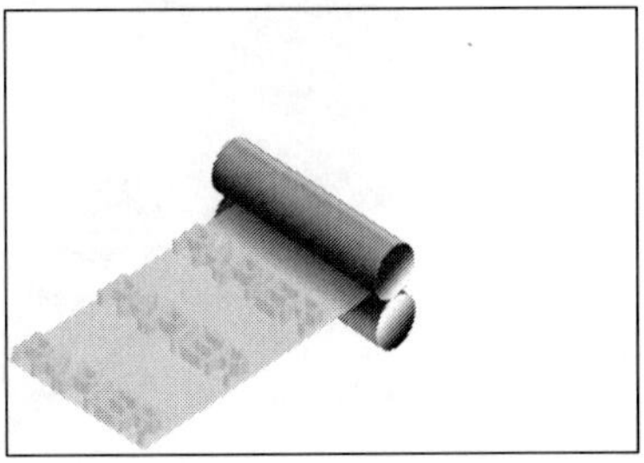

Windowed Banknote Substrate, Example - Durasafe®

Reverse side intaglio relief

Paper   Durasafe®

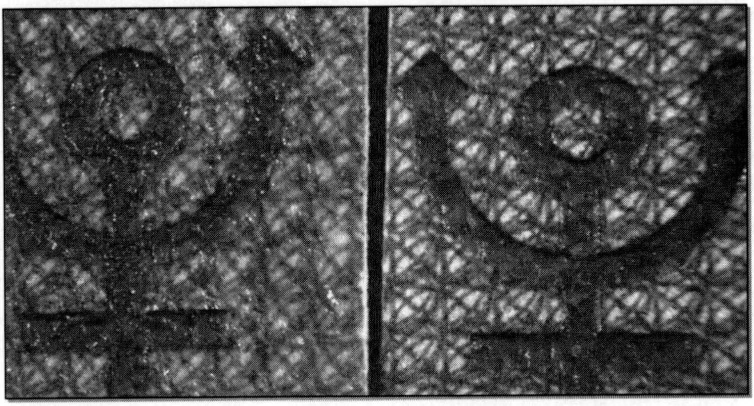

Windowed Banknote Substrate, Example - Durasafe®

Your increase in precision

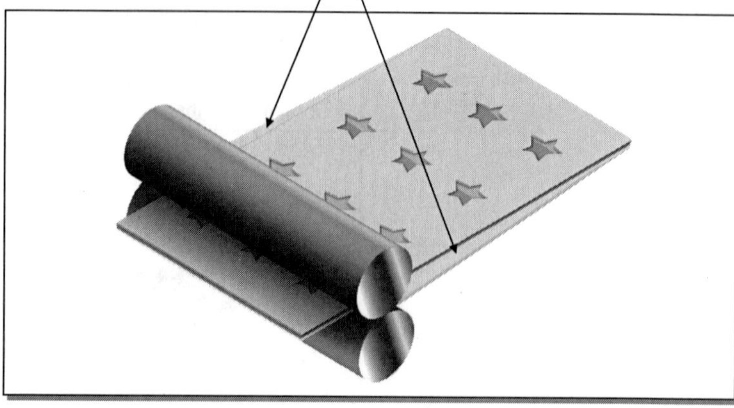

Suggestions for Safeguarding the Indian Currency - Polarisafe

Security Fiber

Special quality security fiber which are fluorescent security fibers with advanced optical properties (like polarized absorption/emission) can be used in the banknotes. These special optical properties can be visualized by aid of a special optical devices (like rotating optical polarizer). Depending on the orientation of the polarizer with respect to the orientation of the security fiber, the security fibers show fluorescence or remain dark (bright/dark-effect).

An example of this kind of product is **Polarisafe®**

Highly secure and hidden feature for security fibres and security threads.

- At first sight looks like a UV fibre
- Linear atomic structures visible under polarized light

Polari***safe®*** ***is more secure than common security features:***

- ***Common fluorescence is easily imitated***
- ***The*** Polari***safe®-effect comes from the structure:***
  This structure can not be printed

Polari***safe®*** ***can not be imitated by common printing techniques!***

Polari***safe®*** ***interacts selectively with polarized UV light***

- ***special dye molecules***
- ***special carrier materials***
- ***special processing conditions***

... lead to unique superstructure
... gives rise to Polari***safe®-effect***

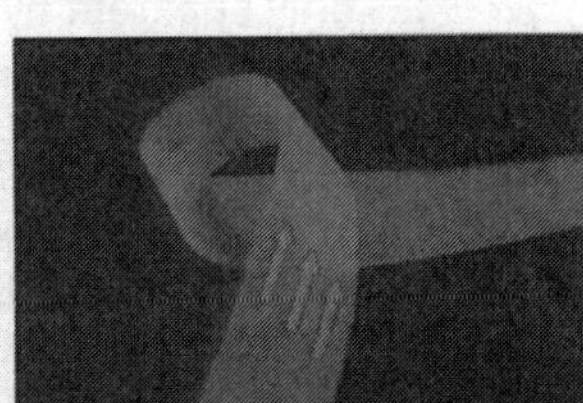

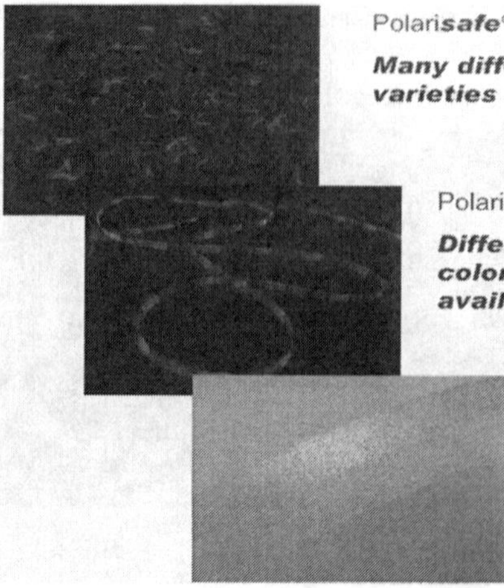

Polari**safe® *Security Fibers***

Many different colors and varieties available

Polari**safe® *Security Thread***

Different colors and even multi-color varieties and logos available

Polari**safe® *Coating***

Different colors and combinations with iridescent pigments available

Security Fibers

- Security fibers are available in many different colors, lengths and thicknesses.
- The fibers can be homogeneously distributed in the paper, or can be applied in well-defined stripes. Even combinations of several stripes with different varieties of security fibers are possible.

Security Threads

- Security threads are introduced in the paper making process as windowed threads.
- The varieties range from threads that show a single fluorescence color to threads with multi-color fluorescence and even threads with fluorescent multi-color text and symbols.

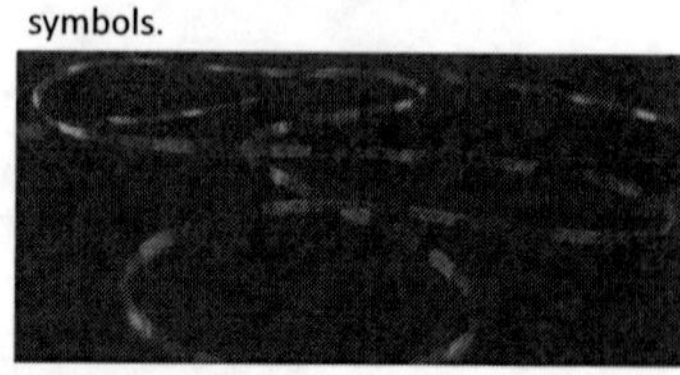

- These special security fibers features two levels of security: In addition to showing fluorescence under ultraviolet light, it is sensitive to *polarized UV light. This property is a hidden feature and becomes* only apparent by using the appropriate test equipment.
- Under ordinary UV lamps and document testers, these features appear like ordinary fluorescent security features. With special test equipment, these features show a dynamic, blinking and twinkling effect.
- These effects are directly linked to the structure of the feature and has an inherent superstructure of its own - a property that can not be imitated by common printing techniques.

Suggestions for Safeguarding the Indian Currency - Irisafe

Special Iridescent security features

Iridescent security features have proven to be effective for a long time.

This kind of stripe varies in colour when the note is tilted.

An example of this kind of product is

Irisafe®

Special Iridescent security features, Example - Irisafe®

- IRISAFE® is an optically variable security feature detectable by naked eye without further devices
- IRISAFE® has high brilliance & distinct colour change effect
- **The colour flip cannot be reproduced, neither by scanners nor by colour copiers**
- High visibility of iridescent lines upon tilting
- Exclusive colour combinations are possible
- We can for e.g. **choose our national colours as a colour combination**
- Is easily integrated into the print design. And can be overprinted by any printing process.
- Very durable security feature. Even on heavily circulated and soiled banknotes, the distinctive IRISAFE® effect is still very visible
- A cost-effective first-level security feature

Suggestions for Safeguarding the Indian Currency – Q-Check

Infra Red Security Feature, Example - Q-Check® . No Subjectivity.

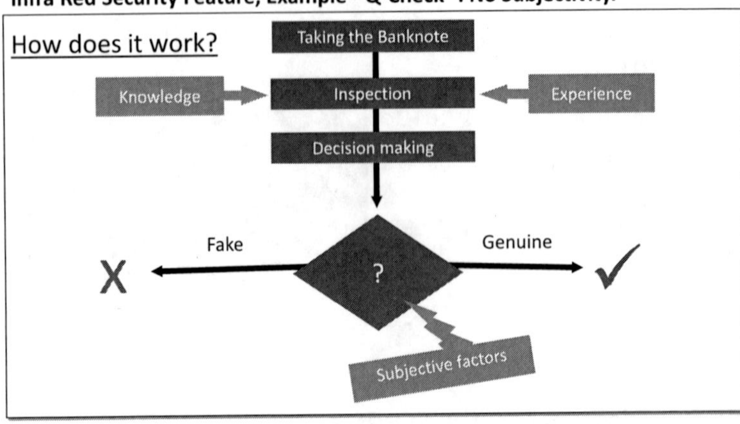

Infra Red Security Feature, Example - Q-Check®. No Subjectivity. High Speed.

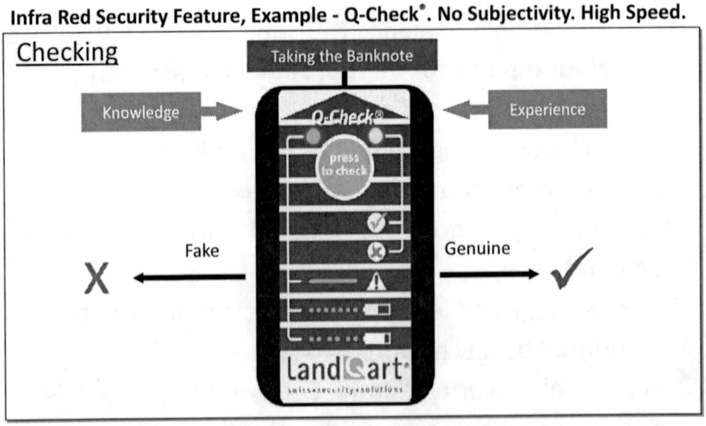

Infra Red Security Feature, Example - Q-Check®

OEM

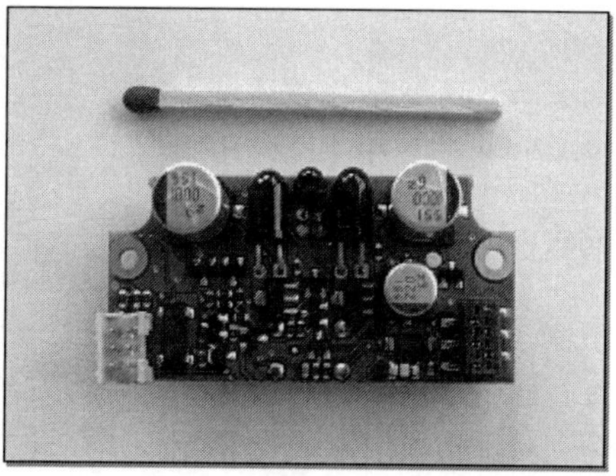

Technology

- Similar to UV dull paper
- Q-Check® Paper has unique special IR properties

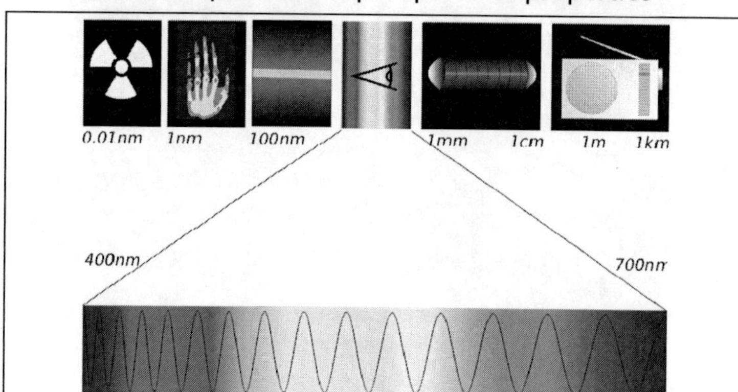

Features

- Quick, checking time
- Easy, in training and use
- Clear, automatic decision-making
- Secure technology, for banknotes
- Trouble free
- Non toxic material, entirely safe
- Affordable

Suggestions for Safeguarding the Indian Currency

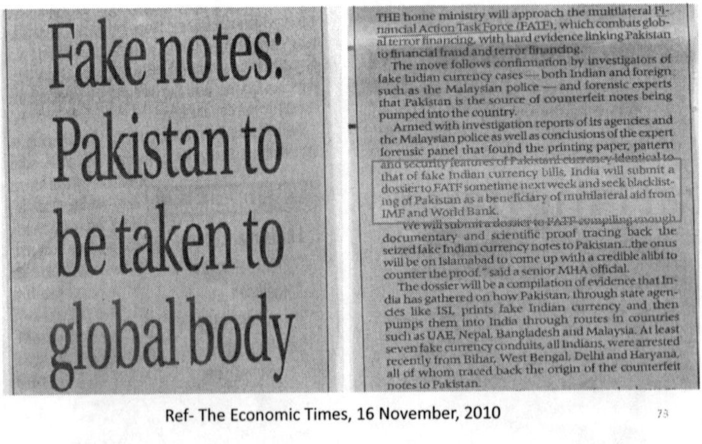

Fake notes: Pakistan to be taken to global body

THE home ministry will approach the multilateral Financial Action Task Force (FATF), which combats global terror financing, with hard evidence linking Pakistan to financial fraud and terror financing.

The move follows confirmation by investigators of fake Indian currency cases — both Indian and foreign such as the Malaysian police — and forensic experts that Pakistan is the source of counterfeit notes being pumped into the country.

Armed with investigation reports of its agencies and the Malaysian police as well as conclusions of the expert forensic panel that found the printing paper, pattern and security features of Pakistani currency identical to that of fake Indian currency bills, India will submit a dossier to FATF sometime next week and seek blacklisting of Pakistan as a beneficiary of multilateral aid from IMF and World Bank.

"We will submit a dossier to FATF compiling enough documentary and scientific proof tracing back the seized fake Indian currency notes to Pakistan...the onus will be on Islamabad to come up with a credible alibi to counter the proof," said a senior MHA official.

The dossier will be a compilation of evidence that India has gathered on how Pakistan, through state agencies like ISI, prints fake Indian currency and then pumps them into India through routes in countries such as UAE, Nepal, Bangladesh and Malaysia. At least seven fake currency conduits, all Indians, were arrested recently from Bihar, West Bengal, Delhi and Haryana, all of whom traced back the origin of the counterfeit notes to Pakistan.

Ref- The Economic Times, 16 November, 2010

73

Suggestions for Safeguarding the Indian Currency—FATF?

- Like It has been made mandatory by Governments to use taggants in the explosives, FATF should form a database to identify source of banknotes.
- The most common are microscopic polymer particles and PCR readable secure Synthetic DNA marks, which identifies the source of bank notes and are legally enforceable.

Suggestions for Safeguarding the Indian Currency

<u>What are Taggants and How they can help?</u>

- Taggants are microscopic or nano materials that are uniquely encoded and virtually impossible to duplicate—like a fingerprint. They can be incorporated into or applied to a wide variety of materials.
- A single taggant can be used for an application, or multiple taggant technologies can work together to create a higher level of security.
- Taggants can be used for simple yes/no identification and authentication or more complex identification purposes.

Suggestions for Safeguarding the Indian Currency – Nano Taggants

Nano Particle Taggants

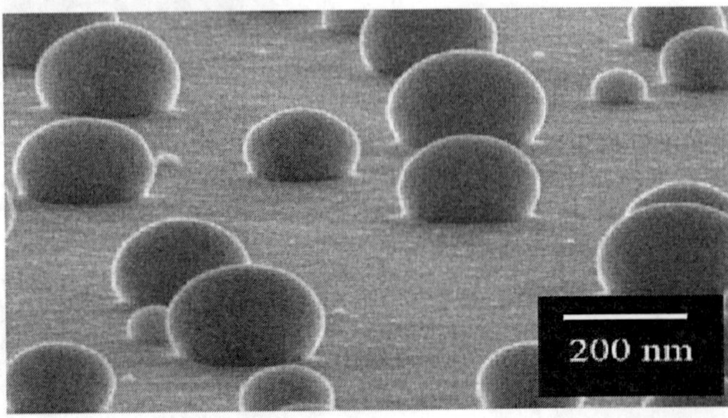

Nano Particle

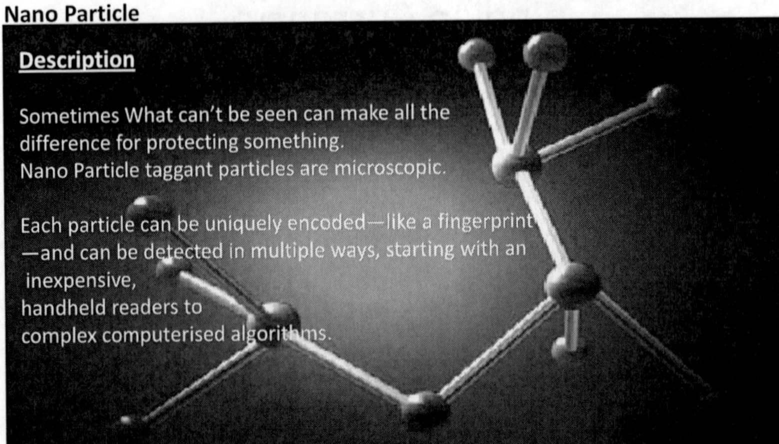

Nano Particle

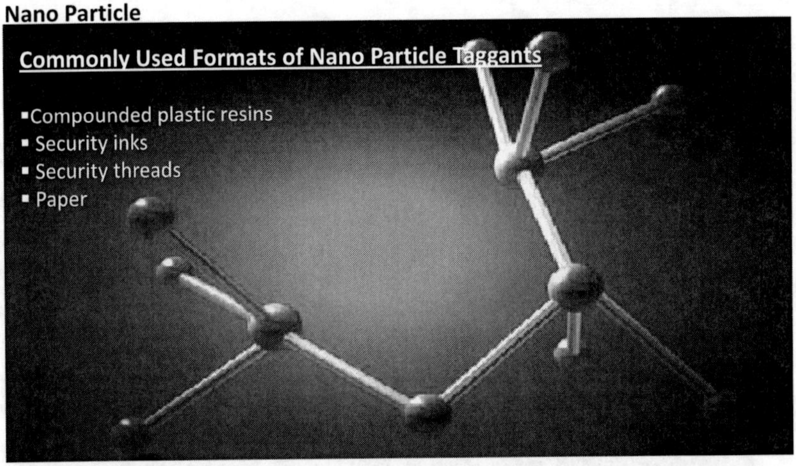

Nano Particle

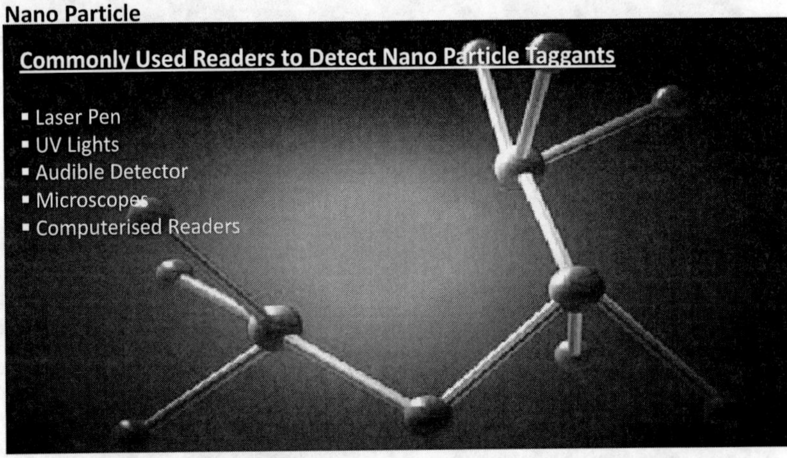

Secure DNA Mark

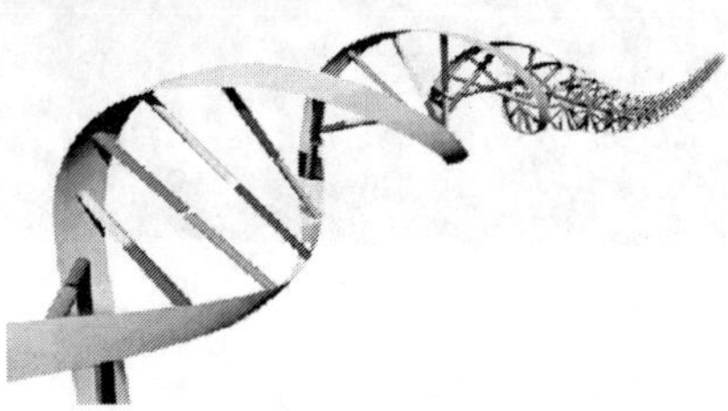

Suggestions for Safeguarding the Indian Currency – DNA Mark

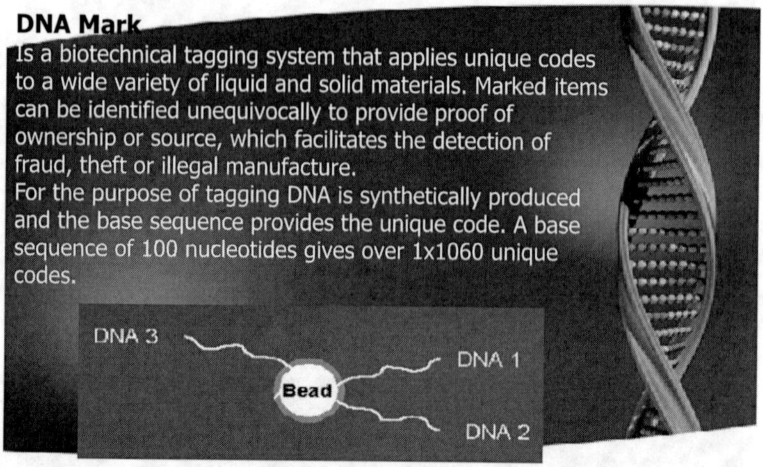

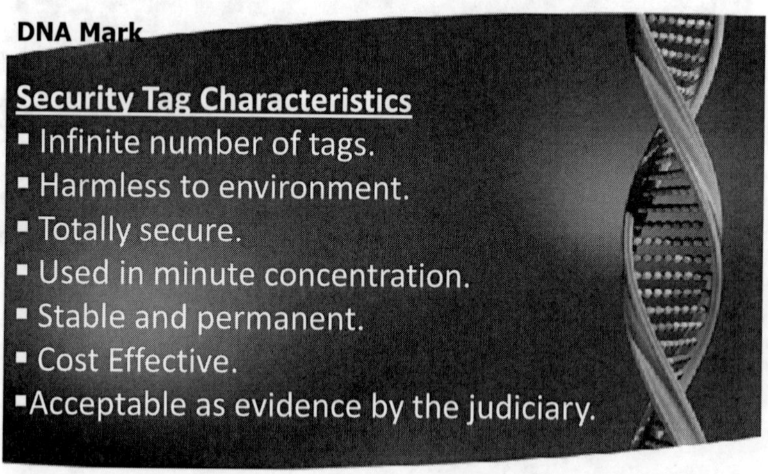

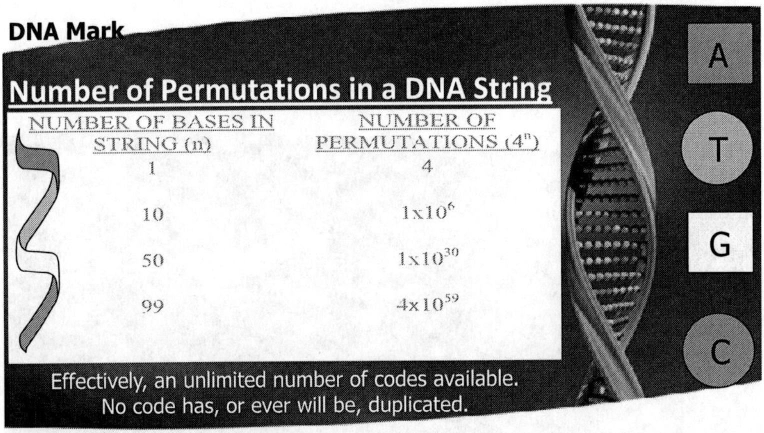
DNA Mark
Number of Permutations in a DNA String
NUMBER OF BASES IN STRING (n)
NUMBER OF PERMUTATIONS (4^n)
1 — 4
10 — $1x10^6$
50 — $1x10^{30}$
99 — $4x10^{59}$
A
T
G
C
Effectively, an unlimited number of codes available.
No code has, or ever will be, duplicated.

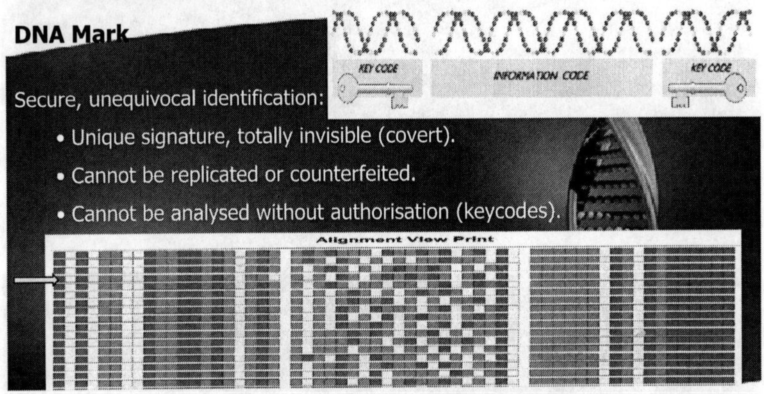
DNA Mark
KEY CODE
INFORMATION CODE
KEY CODE
Secure, unequivocal identification:
• Unique signature, totally invisible (covert).
• Cannot be replicated or counterfeited.
• Cannot be analysed without authorisation (keycodes).
Alignment View Print

DNA Mark
DNA Amplification Equipment
Taqman 7700 qPCR for amplification / analysis

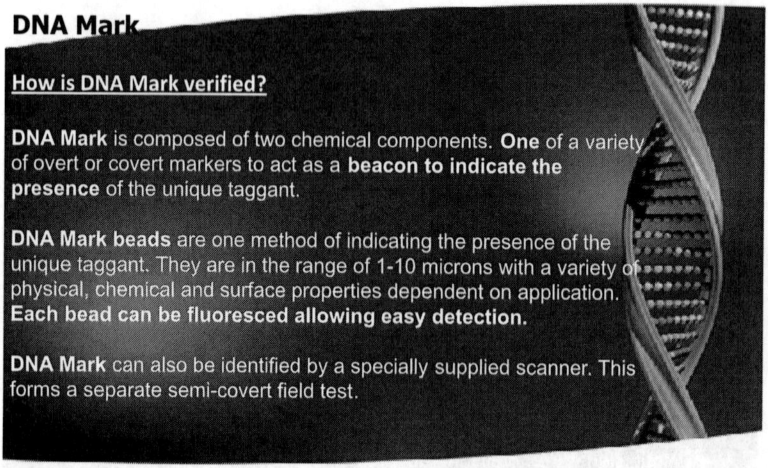
DNA Mark
How is DNA Mark verified?
DNA Mark is composed of two chemical components. One of a variety of overt or covert markers to act as a beacon to indicate the presence of the unique taggant.
DNA Mark beads are one method of indicating the presence of the unique taggant. They are in the range of 1-10 microns with a variety of physical, chemical and surface properties dependent on application. Each bead can be fluoresced allowing easy detection.
DNA Mark can also be identified by a specially supplied scanner. This forms a separate semi-covert field test.

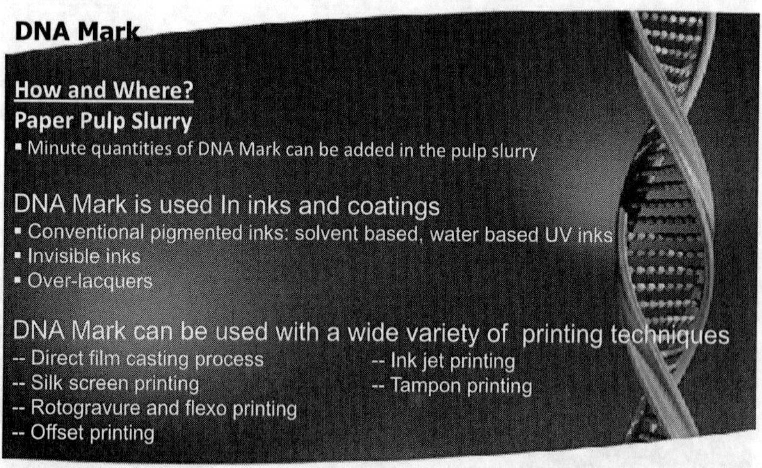
DNA Mark
How and Where?
Paper Pulp Slurry
▪ Minute quantities of DNA Mark can be added in the pulp slurry
DNA Mark is used In inks and coatings
▪ Conventional pigmented inks: solvent based, water based UV inks
▪ Invisible inks
▪ Over-lacquers
DNA Mark can be used with a wide variety of printing techniques
-- Direct film casting process
-- Silk screen printing
-- Rotogravure and flexo printing
-- Offset printing
-- Ink jet printing
-- Tampon printing

Suggestions for Safeguarding the Indian Currency

Some more Suggestions

- Chalk out a way to control the base paper used to make currency notes.
- Embed all security features which are unique for India, within geographical boundaries of India.
- Stress should be on having an Overt as well as Covert Security feature which is people friendly.

Some more Suggestions

- Look for a way to use "Rare Earth" found in India to be used in the paper/ink and design algorithms in a way that they read these parameters in milliseconds.
  - Readers can be made very cost effective.
  - Specifically designed in India and mass produced within India.
  - Algorithm and Security application Module should be in Indian control.
- If paper needs to be made outside India-then supply the paper manufacturer with the features specific for India, from India to the paper makes in a controlled way(controlled supply chain), and make them guarantee that these features are not being used for any other client of theirs.

Case Study: Wage Fraud

A D Van Eden

It is of the utmost importance to note that in any investigation, the investigator must obtain a full understanding of the various operational procedures, in order to arrive at a credible conclusion.

In this case study, the nature of the client's operation is the cultivation of mushrooms. It is estimated that they grew in excess of (65) sixty five tons per week. The harvesting operation is labour intensive, as all the picking and packing is done by hand.

The growing of mushrooms is cyclical and as a result of this, it is necessary for the company to engage casual workers to assist in the harvesting. There are around 130 permanent employees and between 60 and 80 casual workers that are employed as the harvesting need dictates.

Some of the casual workers are employed on permanent /casual terms. They would be required to submit their banking details so that payment can be made directly into their accounts. This information is communicated directly to the wage clerks.

Employees had free access to the farm and would proceed to a clock station where employee's clock cards were used to register their attendance. The normal hours worked and overtime were calculated manually. In some instances employee's clock cards; times of arrival and departure, were completed manually. On a weekly basis the completed clock card would be signed by the supervisors as proof that the employee was at work. The clock cards were then forward to the wage office.

Wage office staffing and procedures

Two females were employed, one as senior wage clerk and the other as assistant wage clerk. Two procedures for the payment of employees were in operation:-

- Permanent employees and permanent/ casual workers were paid directly into their bank accounts. (Referred to as a TT.)
- Those casual employees, who did not provide banking details or were on short term engagement, were paid in cash from the casual wage box.

In some instances, permanent staff members were also paid from the casual wage allocation. This would occur if, for any reason, the permanent employee was short paid in the amount transferred to his/her bank account. The difference would then be paid from the casual wage allocation.

A lockable cashbox was used and an amount of R10, 000.00c was allocated to the casual wage account. The box with the cash was entrusted to the wage clerks and secured in a safe, the key to which was held by the wage clerks.

The wage clerks were responsible for the preparation of the wage transfer TT to the employees' accounts. In addition to this, they were responsible for preparing pay packets for the casual workers and also carried out the function of paymasters.

Wage packets preparations

The wage clerk would receive, from the various supervisors, the daily clock cards of all the employees including the casual employees that were on duty during that specific week. (As mentioned above, some clock card's time and attendance entries were hand written.)

The wage clerks would then apply the wage formula to calculate the payments to be made and prepare the TT or the individual cash pay packets for those workers without banking details.

A pay voucher was prepared for each individual payment with details of the employee name and amount paid. This was then signed by the employee when they received their pay packet. These documents were used to audit amounts paid out from the cash box.

The wage clerk prepared a spread sheet of all the casual employees paid that week and calculated the total amount to be reimbursed to the casual wage box, in order to bring it back to R10, 000.00c. She would present the spreadsheet to the Administration Officer who would draw a cheque in that amount.

Casual wages audit

The auditing of the casual wages was either carried out by me on random days when I visited the farm, or by the Administrator. The cash was counted in the cash box and compared with the vouchers paid out for the casual wages.

Shortfalls in the wages of any permanent staff member were also reimbursed from the cash box. These errors would be picked up by the employee when he received his wage advice slip.

The name of the employee and details of the error, i.e. short payment on overtime, would then be added to the spread sheet and in addition to this, a pay voucher and a pay packet prepared for the permanent employee.

Investigation

I carried out an unannounced audit on the cash wages and found that the box contained R4, 288.87c. for the week ending 05/12/03. I asked the wage clerk for the vouchers representing the balance of R5, 711.13c. She replied that she could not do it immediately as she had a deadline to meet.

On the following week, the wage clerk presented wage packets in the amount equal to the difference of the previous week. When she was asked why the workers were not paid for the week under investigation she broke down and confessed that she had taken the cash. A few hours later the assistant wage clerk asked to see me. I requested the Operations Manager to be present as I had a feeling what was coming.

She then confessed that she had received R1, 000.00c per week from the Senior Wage clerk. I then carried out a full investigation and compared every casual wage pay out from 4th October 2002 until and including the 19th December 2003 against the TT payments made.

I discovered that casual employees who had submitted their bank details were paid by TT from details on the spreadsheets but that their names were also used to create false payments from the cash box by the two wage clerks. I further noted that some of the clock card times were written in by hand, the excuse being that the clock machine was out of order. This became an issue in the investigation as fictitious clock card were used as part of the scam.

I found that the clerks had misappropriated cash from the cash box in the amount of R214, 349.16c, during the period under investigation.

Disciplinary hearing

Legal and criminal action considerations

Note: I have added this section as I believe it will assist companies and investigators regarding what action and steps they can take to recover losses which occur.

The disciplinary hearing was held with the result that both accused pleaded guilty and were found guilty, resulting in immediate dismissal. The company could not lay claim to either of the accused' Provident Fund Contributions in order to recoup some of the money misappropriated, without obtaining a court order. This is a very costly exercise when civil court action is taken. As criminal action was instituted against the accused the court would be requested to make a ruling on compensation in term of the Criminal Procedure Act.

The court case and plea bargaining

To assist the state public prosecutor and the police to prepare for the court case, I completed schedules of each individual illegal transaction. In addition to this, I took the relevant statements and admissions made by the accused and handed this in as well. This speeded up the prosecution procedure. Both the accused had been in the company's employment for 18 years.

Both were single mothers with minor children.

It was agreed with the senior public prosecutor and the accused' legal advisors that the company would not disagree to a plea bargaining action, providing a court order in terms of the Criminal Procedure Act in favour of the company is made.

The court found the two accused guilty of the theft and sentenced them to, inter alia; to forfeiture of their Provident Fund contributions, to the company, in order to recoup some of the money stolen.

Accused no 1 was further sentenced to a period in goal, suspended on condition, that she repay the company R500.00c per month until the amount of R18, 000.00c was repaid.

Insurance claims and details of recovery

This section illustrates that even with insurance cover, the company incurred financial losses.

Most companies are covered by fidelity insurance, but there is usually an excess clause in the policy.

In this instance the excess was R175.000.00c.

The Loss Adjuster's fee was added to the claim figure. I strongly disagree with this action as he was appointed by the Insurer to investigate the claim and as such should be paid by them.

Of the R214, 489.16 less R3, 763.12c found in the safe, the total claim then amounted to:

Claim:	R 210, 726.00c
Add Loss Adjuster's fee for claims preparation cost:	
	R 16,099.00c
Sub Total :	R 226,825.00c
14% Vat :	R 31,755.00c
Total Claim :	R 258,580.00c
Received from the Insurer (excess R175.000.	
	R 83,580.00c
Add received from accused Prov. Fund:	R 30,000.00c.
Accused No 1 repayments court ruling:	R 18,000.00c
Total recovered:	R 131 580.00c.

The company showed a direct loss in the amount of R 127 000.00c.

Note: The Provident Fund Administrators had first deducted outstanding housing loans before the balance was paid to the company.

The findings and comments

The most obvious detail arising from the investigation was the non-segregation of the duties in the wage office. The wage clerks preparing the pay roll were also acting as paymasters. An unhealthy state of affairs and, in this case, led to corruption. It also allowed the two accused to carry on their theft over a period of time without being detected.

The pay-out vouchers did not indicate the details of the employee's work numbers but only their names. The lack of using employee numbers in the wage spreadsheet created opportunity for the accused to carry out the crime. The fact that hand written clock cards were accepted into the system also gave opportunity for the pay roll to be manipulated by the accused, introducing fictitious clock card on the casual wage pay roll, using the names of casuals already on the TT pay-roll.

No cross reference checks were carried out between those employees paid by TT and those paid in cash from the casual wage cash allocation.

I recommended that in all incidents, employees will be allocated with a work number which must be reflected on all the payroll details. Further, to distinguish between permanent and casual employees, they were to be allocated differently coded employee numbers. All casual employees must have bank accounts in to which their wages can be paid. I further recommended that the existing time and attendance method be changed from the antiquated clock-card system to a more advance system whereby each employee is issued with a numbered disc for clocking in at both the turnstile and then at their work station. The one will not operate without the other. This will ensure that the employee is present on site and at his work place. This is then automatically captured onto the payroll system.

Payments from the cash wage box would only be made in exceptional cases. For instance when a new casual is employed and had not yet obtained a bank account.

These payments must be approved and authorised by the Administration Officer.

The amount the cash box was reduced from R10, 00.00c to R5, 000.00c.

Author's note

Ever since this case was investigated during December 2003, a considerable technological system change has taken place to improve security in the wage pay-out procedures. The main improvement is the segregation of staff responsibilities in the wage office.

A further update during 2010 will be that the existing time and attendance system will again be upgraded. The system will be replaced with biometric fingerprint readers, located at the turnstile access point and at the various work stations. I wonder how many companies still operate with the old clocking system.

Motivating For Result

Katherin Xin

In tough times, money is scarce and motivation becomes ever more critical. We will show you how to improve motivation two ways at no cost beyond that you already incurred. Can you improve your situation without extra spending? Yes.

Every manger can benefit from an increased understanding of motivation. Managers responsible for safety have an even greater advantage from understanding motivation, which we will explain in some detail. Basically, you want to increase your ability to set up an environment of motivation in your organization for two quite different reasons.

First, safety mangers, as with every practicing manager, want to have as productive an organization as possible. Public officials and managers alike want the nation, your nation, to be as reductive as possible. The better we can deal with this subject, the better off will be our workers, our organizations, our society. With this in mind, we will review some classic ideas about motivation, and we will see how they can apply to you today.

Second, as managers in the safety arena, we have special needs. One of those needs is to ensure that those at the top of the ladder know about the dangerous situations or practices at the bottom. You need to know about things that may be happening, which may lead to hazard, or even to disaster. But, in some organizations, the climate is such that no one wants to tell the boss that the company safety policies are not being followed. People fear that the person who reports a problem or potential problem may come under attack. Perhaps this is not a new or isolated problem: we remember the ancient Roman leader who gave the order to "slay the bearer of bad tidings". Are there dangers hidden in your organization that you do not even know about? In some cases, does "everyone else" know about these but does social pressure, or the unwritten policies of intermediate supervisors, prevent this information from getting to you? We will discover how to assess your organizational climate in this dimension, and we will actually help you conduct a preliminary test of that climate.

Motivation for Productivity

In the past, the major forms of "motivation" took the shape of fear of punishment – physical, financial and social. But today, many theories of motivation exist that managers can use to improve their understanding of why people behave as they do. None provides a universally-accepted explanation of human behavior. People are far too complex. There are many theories of motivation. I will discuss some of what we know about motivation from two perspectives : Content theories and process theories.

Content theories of motivation are concerned with identifying what it is within an individual or the work environment that energize and sustain behavior. Simply, what specific things motivate people? On the other hand, process theories try to explain and describe the process of how behavior is energize, directed, and finally stopped.

Process theories try to answer three questions: (1). Should I work hard? (2) How hard do I need to work? (3) How long do I have to keep this pace?

In the following paragraphs, I will first discuss two content theories: Maslow's need hierarchy and Herzberg's two-factor theory. Second, two process theories, Vroom's expectancy theory and Skinner's reinforcement theory, will be reviewed.

Maslow's Hierarchy of Needs Theory:

There are many theories of motivation. One of my favorites has little or no statistical validity, little or no scientific basis, yet seems to help practicing managers understand their employees better. This is the theory of Abraham Maslow, who wrote his ideas over fifty years ago. Maslow's need hierarchy theory has enjoyed widespread acceptance since it was introduced. He identified 20 needs, which are hypothesized into five levels of needs.

Basically, Maslow held that individuals are driven by different kinds of needs at different times and in different circumstances, depending on the situation. He divided needs into a hierarchy of needs. (1) First, physiological needs drive behavior. (2) Second, safety and security needs. He was probably not aware of the India Institute of Safety and Security Management when he wrote, but he did group these two together, and said they were the MOST important needs, after the survival needs such as food and water in the physiological needs category. (3) Third, social needs also motivate. (4) Fourth, Maslow held that people are motivated by a need for self esteem, or ego satisfaction. (5) Fifth and the last, we are motivated by the desire for self actualization.

There are some important aspects to Maslow's theory. For one thing, he suggested that typically, humans would be driven to satisfy these groups of needs in order. When an individual has nothing, the physiological needs will dominate. The first priority of a person without food is to get food. Physiological needs are the driving force at that time. However, once a person has food, new and higher needs come to drive behavior. That is when the human being starts to focus on safety and security needs, according to Maslow. A key aspect of this description is that once a group of needs are somewhat satisfied, the next class of needs seems to dominate. For example, if a person has physiological needs met, and also has met safety and security needs, then social needs will tend to drive behavior. If this group of needs are basically satisfied, with the person content with his or her group of friends, then ego or self satisfaction needs tend to take center stage. Although, neither social or ego needs can ever be fully satiated, when these needs are basically taken care of, the need for self actualization comes into play. Maslow had a tough time defining self actualization, and I cannot really do better than the author of the idea. But, to me, self actualization is doing the thing you always wanted to accomplish, for no reason other than to prove to yourself that you can. The person who climbs a Himalayan mountain peak must be driven by the need of self actualization.

There is an important aspect of Maslow's theory that has to be mentioned here. A satisfied need is not a motivator. Once a person has enough food, food will not motivate. Further, safety and security are critical, but once satisfied, these areas will not MOTIVATE. However, the areas of social, ego or self esteem, and even more so, self actualization, can never be fully satisfied. The implications for management are significant. Social, ego and self actualization can always motivate. And, if you think about it, you can help your employees reach social goals, and ego goals, without cost to your organization. To the extent you allow people to choose their own work groups, they may be able to meet social goals. Of course, you do not want to sponsor a permanent party or celebration, but when we discuss the next theory, you will see that the team will feel more motivated if they are accomplishing.

Herzberg's Two-Factor Theory

Another theory that practicing managers find worth studying is that of Frederick Herzberg, developed from studies conducted in 1959. He based his theory on a study of need satisfaction and on the reported motivational effects of these satisfaction on 200 engineers and accountants. The theory is referred to as the two-factor theory of motivation. Based on the study, he reached two conclusions: (1) Some conditions of a job operate primarily to dissatisfy employees when they are not present. However, the presence of these conditions does not build strong motivation. Herzberg called these maintenance factors. (2) Some job conditions build high levels of motivation and job satisfaction. However, if these conditions are not present they do not prove highly dissatisfying. He described six of these motivational factors.

A key point here is that the factors in one group are not the same as the factors in the other group. Hence, the "two- factor theory". The distinction between motivational and maintenance factors is similar to what psychologists have describe as intrinsic and extrinsic motivators. External factors, called hygiene of maintenance factors, can be manipulated only to eliminate dissatisfaction. To motivate people, organizations need to address motivational factors. And, the lucky thing is, the motivating factors typically cost you, the manager, nothing.

The basic ideas of this Herzberg theory and the Maslow theory, which preceded it, are sound. They can help you motivate, without spending extra money, which is always an important factor in tough times. These content theories, even though quite old, are still referred to by thousands of practicing managers. They were not really developed scientifically, but they have a 'common sense' appeal. They can help you as well.

Process Theories

In contrast to the two content theorists-- Maslow's 'need hierarchy' and Herzberg's 'two factors', expectancy theory and reinforcement theory are process theories. They concentrate on how motivation occurs, is directed, sustained and stopped.

The expectancy theory of motivation was initially presented in 1964 by psychologist Victor Vroom who views motivation as a process governing choices. He suggests that individuals are motivated at work to make different choices, such as the decision to participate, and decision to participate at a certain level. The logic of expectancy motivation is that individuals will exert work effort to achieve performance that will result in preferred rewards. The key concepts of Vroom's expectancy theory are balance, instrumentality and expectancy. Sometimes people call it the VIE model.

Reinforcement theory is another widely discussed process theory of motivation, based largely on the work of psychologist B.F. Skinner. Reinforcement theory considers the use of positive and negative reinforces to motivate or create an environment to motivate. This theory of motivation is not concerned with needs or why people make choices. Instead it focuses on the environment and its consequences for the person. Reviewing all the motivational theories discussed above, they all contain the theme that motivation is goal directed. Although the theories use different terms and appear to be quite different they are not completely in conflict with each other. Basically they look at some segment of overall motivation or look at the same aspect of motivation from a slightly different perspective. Professor Lyman Porter and Edward Lawler offer an integrating mode of motivation, based on all the theories discussed above.

The Porter-Lawler model points out the relationship or performance, satisfaction, and rewards and introduces the importance of having individuals performing jobs for which they have the proper skills, abilities and traits. There is also an issue of performance measurement. Performance must be measured accurately and systematically so that rewards can be distributed equitably. If no meaningful difference in rewards is made between high and low performance, high performers will lose motivational intensity and probably cut back on their performance. In sum, motivation theories discuss what motivates people at an individual and organizational level. Of course, we are living in a global era. People from different cultures may have different needs and expectations. Organizations from different culture might employ different motivational strategies. But in every culture, certain basic ideas prevail. You can use these ideas to help your organization improve productivity.

At the same time, it is important not to overstate the importance of motivation. It takes more than motivation to accomplish organizational, or personal, goals. Edgar Schein put it simply. Schein reminded us that the ability of the person, the nature of the work setting, the tools and materials available to do the job, the nature of the job itself, and the ability of management to coordinate employee, group, and departmental efforts – all enter into organizational effectiveness. So, when you apply the ideas discussed here, remember that there are other things in the equation also, such as the state of your equipment.

Motivation for an Open Environment

In addition to studying motivation for enhanced productivity, safety and security, managers need to be concerned about motivation of a very different kind. If you do not know policies are being violated, your organization many run into serious problems. A survey of some maritime accidents in the USA reveals some interesting points.

In each of these four accidents, accident summaries reviewed one common denominator, crew or human error. In each accident, failures in upward communication flow had a bearing on the results.

Accident #1: The ramming of the U.S. fishing vessel Chickadee by the guided-missile frigate USS Richard L. Page in the Atlantic Ocean Virginia beach, Virginia on April 21, 1987. The page officer on deck (OOD) failed to treat reported radar contact with a vessel in part because of fatigue and stress. The ODD did not have confidence in the ability of the radar operator and thus did not acknowledge the operator's reports. THE OOD failed to communicate his concerns to the Commanding officer (CO) about the authenticity of the radar reports. The lack of information flow upwards was one casual factor in this accident.

Accident #2: The ramming of the Sidney Lanier Bridge by the Polish bulk carrier Ziemia Bialostocka at Burnswick, Georgia, on May 3, 1987. The pilot of the Zieam Bialostocka misjudged the turning capability of the vessel because he did no make himself aware of and use all available information. The pilot did no have knowledge of the technical parameters that affected the maneuvering characteristics of a vessel, information which was known to others on the ship. The lack of information flow upwards was one causal factor in this accident.

Accident #3: The ramming of the Spanish bulk carrier Urduliz by the aircraft carrier USS Dwight D. Eisenhower at Hampton Roads, Virginia on August 29, 1988. The probable cause of the accident was the delayed and insufficient action to correct the Eisenhower's deviation from the intended track by the navigator and the OOD, because of inexperience in piloting the vessel through the resurrected channel in Hampton Roads. The OOD was overly concerned with arriving precisely on time at the harbor and slowed down the vessel in order to "look professional". In addition, a pilot was not utilized in this case. Most naval vessels do not utilize the services of pilots, at least in part, because they believe that the use of the pilot implies that the crew does not measure up to the navigation task. Expert guidance was available, but not used. And finally, the CO's attention had been diverted from the vessel's navigation to other duties during a critical period (an Admiral came on board). All the above cultural norms functioned in such a way that they overshadowed the proper navigation of the vessel. In addition, lack of information flow from those who knew the channel to those making navigational decisions, was one casual factor in this accident.

Accident #4: The ramming of the French tank ship Camargue by the Swedish auto carrier Figaro in the Gulf of Mexico Galveston, Texas on November 10, 1988. The probable cause of the collision was the Figaro pilot's determination to overtake the tank ship in the entrance channels to Galveston Bay and the master's and pilot's lack of action to abort the overtaking. The Pilot of the Figaro and the pilot of the Camargue did not exchange information regarding the speed of their vessels. Once again, there was a general lack of communication and overconfidence on the part of the pilot. If all concerned reported what they knew, this accident could have been prevented.

These little case stories are from one small area, naval ramming. However, information from a wide variety of settings leads to painfully similar conclusions: too often, those who need critical information do not receive it. And, more times than we would like, incidents occur, incidents which can be in part attributed to the lack of upward communication of ideas and facts. Frequently, the information is withheld in spite of policies that "bad news should be transmitted upwards", but this does not take place. Why?

Recent findings show that one key factor is the organizational climate. To achieve a safe organization, you need an open organization. There are several ways to improve openness. First, however, we recommend each organization assess the climate to determine openness. The use of a sample survey form will help such assessment.

Conclusion

Each of us is interested in motivation, especially in tough times. As managers responsible for safety and security, we have an even greater need to motivate employees. In our case, it may be a matter of life or death at times. Fortunately, social scientists have given us some tools to work with, and hopefully these will help us do our jobs better.

Anti Terrorsim By System Design

Richard P Grassic

Designing a security system which effectively responds to terrorist and other threats presents a formidable challenge to the security system design engineer. System success will be based on the effectiveness of individual components to counter threat elements and reduce vulnerabilities.

System design engineers must visualize security threats and risks, anticipate the worst situation and ultimately weigh the cost of any countermeasure recommendation against the perceived benefit gained. Determination of cost effective protective measures and their integration is the result of a structured decision process which considers the individual and collective contribution of each assessor protection strategy according to the complete system's requirements.

Role of the Security Designer

The designer strives to achieve a synergistic relationship among the various components and subsystems selected. Selection of appropriate equipment, procedures, manpower levels, facilities and information is accomplished on the basis of the most reliable and capable combinations to meet the known and expected capabilities of the threat.

However, the designer is constrained by limited and possibly decreasing budgets, soaring personnel and equipment costs and ever-increasing external and internal threats. This demands a comprehensive systemic approach to countermeasures selection and integration which minimizes asset vulnerability, minimizes initial system cost and keeps subsequent costs under control.

In the final analysis, the designer selects and integrates protective measures from the following range of subsystem options:

- Facilities and architectural barriers designed to deter and delay an adversary
- Physical security equipment designed to assist detection and assess intrusion attempts and unauthorized activities
- Communications systems that collect, integrate, transmit, and display alarm and other data for operator response and control response forces
- Security personnel to conduct day-to-day security programme operations, management and provide system support and respond to non-routine events.
- Security procedures that guide security operations and provide direction and control

Countermeasures Selection

Experience has shown that the countermeasures selection and overall system integration process must be structured and front – loaded in order for the designer to arrive at a valid security concept. The process is based on a thorough analysis of threats and the relative exposure of individual assets to these threats. Thus, the initial accomplishment of thorough requirements analysis is critical to developing an optimum system configuration and allow for the relative cost-effectiveness of various protective design strategies and countermeasure options.

Initially, assets that need protection are identified. And their criticality to the facility and its function are determined. Next, the attractiveness of these assets to potential threats and the likely modes of attack are evaluated. Finally, areas in which existing countermeasures do not adequately address the threat are identified as facility vulnerabilities.

In order to be applied effectively, countermeasures must be selected for each asset in terms of an applicable design based threat. Likely modes of attack in terms of the potential use of tools,, weapons and possibly explosives to be used at specific severity levels is also considered. A critical assumption of the process is that an asset of highest criticality to the user, coupled with its high attractiveness to an aggressor, will prompt a likely and probable aggressor to employ more force in an attack on that asset.

Likelihood of attack is expressed for each asset and potential aggressor(s) either as high, medium, low or very low. This forces the designer to determine what is to be protected, its value to the user and aggressor alike, and its attractiveness to various aggressor types. This is usually expressed in terms of design-based threat parameters for each asset.

For security upgrade projects, countermeasures identification and selection can only occur after the designer has determined existing measures in place that can effectively be integrated into the system solution to deter, delay deny detect assess and respond to attacks. Finally an assessment is made of the financial regulatory and operational constraints to candidate countermeasures. Based on the results of the on-site requirements analysis, asset-specific physical security countermeasures are applied to various points in and around the facility or asset to be protected. Selection of individual countermeasures is made based on an initial statement of system objectives and functional requirements such as detecting unauthorized entry and controlling access.

Individual countermeasures are selected by the designer and integrated into a cohesive protection solution. Preliminary cost estimates for the initial and expected total life cycle of the complete system are also established. Costs for those physical security countermeasures necessary to meet operational and vulnerability reduction objective are always a prime consideration for the designer.

Determining required protective measure: once the appropriate design basis threat parameters are selected for each asset, the designer is ready to determine required protective measures. The structured approach allows the designer to consider appropriate protective measures for each mode of attack and severity level and then consolidate them for each asset. Protective measures are normally divided by the designer into mutually supportive subsystem such as:

- Access entry control measures
- Detection measures
- Structural architectural measures
- Assessment surveillance measures
- Command, control and display requirements
- Operations and manpower considerations

These mutually supportive subsystems are further defined by the designer in terms of countermeasure application at the asset facility or site level. Asset specific measures are applied within the room housing the asset or within close proximity to an asset. Facility specific measures are those applied where assets are housed. Site specific measures are those applied between the facility and site perimeter.

Asset specific protective measures can include a wide range of countermeasure options. Architectural measures may include interior barriers combined with enhanced structural features that provide the desired level of protection. Detection and assessment measures may include a combination of point and area sensors along with duress alarms, CCTV surveillance assessment and area lighting. Interior control measures may include personnel access control within the facility and access restriction at or near the asset. Security personnel should be positioned to be available for response to intrusion attempts while asset specific procedures may require the periodic check of asset locations by security patrols.

Multiple assets are usually housed in various locations within a facility. Common requirements among groups of assets make the designer's job of protective design development much easier. When considering countermeasures for a group of assets within a facility, the designer should also consider other selection variables before arriving at specific measures. These variables might include the possible movement of the asset, local mission constraints, environmental design criteria for establishing defensible space and acceptability of physical security options within the organization.

The process of compartmentalization allows the designer to define inner perimeters of a larger controlled space and build security measures inward from the points of access and egress unique to the protection requirements of the asset. The perimeter typically will be defined by physical barriers through which access is monitored electronically. Within the facility, several compartment may be established within the common space to limit costly manpower allocation or to maximize electronic access control and detection through the creation of a single zone. Groups of facilities that share a common boundary or perimeter require that the designer focus not only on the asset and the individual facility, but also on the site. Generally sites with multiple facilities will have common or shared security requirements and some sites will even have a perimeter fence line and manned guard booth at an entry point to separate the area from the general public.

Countermeasures cost-effectiveness

The designer's consideration of countermeasures options will depend to a large extent on the cost-effectiveness of individual countermeasures. Cost-effectiveness criteria that might be used by the designer include operational restrictions nuisance alarm susceptibility, installation cost, maintenance cost, probability of detection, mean time between failure, contribution to manpower reduction, contribution to asset vulnerability and reduced risk, normally expressed in monetary consequence of loss or destruction.

While any one of these criteria may result in selection or rejection of a countermeasures alternative, the range of acceptable countermeasures must be linked together to form a system level impression of overall cost and effectiveness. Whether the designer considers either individual or collective countermeasures' cost-effectiveness, the following design issues must be analyzed:

Operational impact

- Lost through put time for identification alternatives (hrs/s)
- Estimated cost of physical reconfiguration
- Impact on safety and operational efficiency

Vulnerability reduction potential

- Estimated saving due to reduction in known loss experience
- Increased reliability and coverage of physical security versus manpower
- Reduced risk of loss

Cost of operation

- Estimated installation and operations cost
- Estimated life cycle maintenance cost
- Contribution to overall organizational efficiency
- Savings in security manpower cost over life cycle of system
- Ancillary advantages (e. g use of fiber optic data link for voice data and other operational functions unrelated to security)

User confidence

- Nuisance alarm versus probability of detection
- Deterrence value versus perceived intrusiveness and inconvenience of countermeasures
- Acceptability of system approach for increased safety of users

Conclusion

The security designer must determine the appropriate protection to be afforded critical assets in the face of terrorist and other threats.

Selection and ultimate integration of the various components sub-systems in the design process is totally dependent upon a variety of resource and policy issues. Cost-effective protective measures and their integration can only result from a structured decision process which considers the criticality of assets, the capabilities of potential threats, the likely outcome of attack attempts, and the collective contribution of individual asset, facility and site protection strategies.

Motivating Different Levels of Personnel

Renu Mattoo

The workplace of the future will fundamentally and permanently alter the relationship between mangers and workers. These traditional adversaries will become partners. Managerial control will give way to employee self-control. Authoritative, directive and controlling management will die out. No longer will mangers seek quality performance from workers through forced obedience. Instead, managers of the future will seek to empower employees to rights and responsibilities of partnership. These workers will themselves be responsible for the products and the services they produce. They will perform their own inspections, identify defects and causes of poor quality, and make adjustments that they deem necessary. They will monitor their relations with customers' needs, most of which they will anticipate in advance, and be able to rapidly create products and services to meet these needs. Most importantly, worker-partners will be flexible, willing to take on any assignment or perform any tasks necessary to help their company succeed. They will do what needs to be done when and where it needs to be done. They will adapt to and learn to love change.

Worker–partners will willingly do all of these things because of the way they will be motivated. The workplace of the future will require that employees take imitative, respond rapidly to changing circumstances and saturations, and be mentally alert and focused on the current organizational imperative. Rigid hierarchies will be dismantled, as will the ceremonial trappings of power. The goal will be to attach people mentally and emotionally to the workplace.

The difference between the traditional, control – oriented, scientifically managed workplace and the commitment-oriented workplace of tomorrow are many and varied. The traditional workplace emphasizes individual responsibility for individual performance; has fixed jobs and job contents; causes coordination and control to flow form top to down and thus, legitimizes status and position, making adversaries of workers and managers.

In tomorrow's workplace emphasis will be on shared responsibility for group performance; jobs will be fluid and flexibility of paramount importance. Control will be shared and coordination will flow from shared goals and values; workers and managers will be partners.

Motivation will be of prime importance because the human resource will become something much more than an asset to be merely counted. It will be tabulated, used, moved and expended. Moved importantly, the human contribution will become more critical for success because the production and delivery system of the future will be chaotic, unpredictable and even perhaps, irrational. Overt domination and control by a managerial elite will become ineffective.

The importance of people rather than technology as the key, important for success in the workplace of the future, is well illustrated by the themes of some of America's most prominent future-oriented companies:

Apple computer's Mike Campi says: "… the best way to keep great people is to allow them to feel like they make a difference.

What makes Apple a good place to work is the company's commitment to empowering people at all levels. Campi explains, "it's not the traditional supervisor telling the line operations people what to do. It's really the line operations people working with the supervisor to make sure that all obstacles that might block their objectives are removed–that means giving them the right tools, working with them. That is what we mean by really giving people responsibility and empowering them with the authority to meet their objectives."

Form the CEO on down, the company is very frank about it's business directions and new product strategies. While that candour may sometimes result in the competitions learning a bit too much, it also shows Apple's employees that the company is willing to share important information with them, showing them another sign of their power and value.

Digital's Bill Hanson says "At Digital, we fell very strongly that people will do the right thing… when they're given a sense of vision or a sense of direction, have access to information, are given responsibility. We trust the individual. "In Digital's future, employees will look less like employees and more like employers, more like partners in the business as the employee-employer relationship becomes similar to that of customer-supplier. With well defined and obvious benefits and independence for each party."

Thus, a company that trusts its employees, an open corporate culture, and an energetic, future-oriented work environment makes Digital a great place to work in.

Hewlett Packard's Harold M Edmondson says "The heart of the thing is treating people as individuals and trying as hard as you can to satisfy their needs."

The result is an atmosphere where employees are challenged. Are urged and expected to be creative, to think individually, to take risks. "We try to make our engineers feel the sky is the limit," Edmondson says. "We give them a substantial amount of technical and intellectual freedom to do the right things.

"We try to create an atmosphere in which employees can enjoy themselves and prosper and make significant contributions. We also try to be up front about what their future is likely to be, not only in terms of financial rewards. We all share a genuine desire for the individual to lead a full an rewarding life."

What instructions then can we give to mangers on the "new styles of motivating people?"

1. Make people feel like champions, the way Apple Computer does. Create an environment where he or she can make a difference. Make every person feel personally significant.
2. Give people a mission. Make it not just any mission, but something truly special. Such as "changing the world". Make working at the company something much more than just an economic exchange.
3. Empower people through involvement. Make the role of managers and supervisors a "helping" and "facilitating" role. Act on the premise that people want to achieve – that they want to help the company succeed. Instead of having of managers and supervisors try to control employee behavior, have them focus on removing obstacles to employee performance. Assume that people can and will do extraordinary things, if institutional barriers to performance are removed.
4. Be frank and open about the company's business strategies and direction. Make sure everyone understands what "we" as a company are trying to accomplish. Don't be concerned if a competitor finds out about a particular strategy. Above all else, don't keep secrets. Make sure everyone knows everything.
5. Trust people to do the right thing. Assume that, given enough of the right information and enough self-control, people will act in the best interest of the company and presumably in their own best interest.
6. Create a unique culture and indoctrinate people from the start to practice in that culture. Don't let an informal social system just develop over time. Visualize what the company should be like, and share that vision. Make sure everyone knows how to behave, consistent with that vision, and reward people who do. If someone doesn't act in concert with the vision, express your

disappointment and encourage him or her to change or leave. Such might be the prescription for motivation in the workplace of the future. But what do they mean for the individual worker? On the positive side, they mean that the workplace will be purposely orchestrated to have greater meaning and significance for each worker personally than ever before. Working will be more than an economic exchange. It will be a search for daily meaning as well as daily bread, for recognition as well as cash, for astonishment rather than torpor; in short, for a sort of, rather than a Monday through Friday sort of dying. To that extent, the workplace will be much better. But being given "daily meaning" in the work one does, also carriers a price.

The workplace of the future will demand more from every worker, more than ever before, it will also give more meaning, responsibility, purpose, autonomy, self-control. Each employee will have to decide on the value of that exchange.

The Migration of Fraud to Customer provided Equipment Fraud

John E Venn

Fraud characterstics are the same whether we are discussing a con artist who has bilked a person out of their life's savings or a person unlawfully using another's calling card, a person obtaining illegal welfare payments or a person fraudulently selling another's phone service.

Ever type of fraud shares some basic characteristics. They all look similar. These characteristics are:

1. There is minimal risk of the suspect being apprehended
2. The fraud preys on a weakness
3. There is usually little sympathy for the victim.
4. It is usually not viewed as a serious crime
5. It is lucrative

If any of the five charactestics are absent, the fraud becomes less likely to occur. If the likelihood of arrest is high, the suspect is discouraged from committing the crime. If the suspect cannot find a weakness to exploit (a human weakness or a system weakness) the fraud will not occur.

If there is sympathy for the victims there will be pressure exerted by the public on the police to apprehend the suspect/s. Further, the media will inform the public of the fraud (and how to avoid becoming victim), making it more difficult for the criminal to repeat the crime. If the public or the police view the fraud as serious crime, steps will be taken to effectively control it. Most importantly, if the suspect is not going make money through the fraud, he she will not commit it.

Telecommunications fraud has migrated over the years in response to changes or advances in telecommunications technology. For every action by the telecommunications industry to control fraud, there is a reaction from telecommunications criminals. Some times, these reactions are predictable.

Telecommunications fraud varies from opportunity to opportunity. The industry moves to eliminate a weakness in the network and the fraud community immediately moves to discover a new weakness to place or sell their fraudulent calls.

Fraud Migration

Clip-On Fraud

One of the first discovered types of fraud is called the clip-on fraud. Clip-on fraud required little expertise on the part of the fraud suspect. The suspect only had to know how to attach a telephone to a working telephone service, belonging to another person. The suspect then used the service to place calls. The suspect left the attachment in place (which increased the likelihood of detection) or equipped it with alligator clips and made a connection only when they wished to place a fraudulent call.

Losses due to clip-on fraud were / are minimal because the fraud suspect only makes one call at a time.

Coin Telephone fraud

The coin telephone became a target of fraud shortly after the introduction of the first coin systems. Older coin phones were ground start, which means the systems had to put a ground on the telephone line to draw a dial tone. The ground was caused when coins were deposited into the set. Some industries person found that if a small hole was drilled into the face of the phone, and a small wire inserted they could cause a ground on the lines (piercing the handset cord, breaking the armored handset cable etc.). After this, coin phones were changed to loop start the completion of an electrical loop draws dial tone which eliminated the fraud.

An enterprising electronics buff designed an electronic device called a red box (because the first one seized by the police was red), which took advantage of another weakness in the security of the coins telephone. Coin telephones used three different audio signals to indicate to the network when a nickel, dime or quarter was deposited. The red box duplicated these coin telephones tones. Coin telephones, at the time, did not isolate the voice path from the handset and a person using a red box could use the handset to send the coin signals through the coins phone.

The mechanical fix which defended against the red box was to isolate the hand set voice path when the coins were deposited.

Another type of coin telephone fraud was known as coin chute stuffing. It was a low tech crime in which the fraud suspect would open the coin return slot, stuff tissue up into the coin and wait for the dial tone. When they did not receive dial tone, they would release their coin but the coin would stop at the tissue. The fraud suspect would return at a later date and release the chute, collecting the coins. Coins phones were changed so the chute could not be stuffed when the coin return was open.

One of the simplest types of coins telephone fraud was coin refund fraud. Fraud suspects in some areas were paying their rents and making their car payments through coin refund fraud. A fraud suspect would call the operator from a coin phone and tell the operator that they (the fraud suspect) had just tried to place a call to a distant location, had paid for the call and had been disconnected. The fraud suspect would ask for a refund to the suspect. Some fraud suspects were receiving over a hundred checks a month from various telephone companies. Then telephone companies began auditing refund reports and refused to refund abusers.

Theft of calling cards

A large part of past and present telecommunications crime is very organized. It is because it is lucrative and there is little risk of apprehension. One of the most organized types of fraud schemes is the sale of fraudulent calls at coin telephones. A distributor of stolen calling card numbers sells the numbers to fraud suspects. They take the coin on phone location so they can sell calls to willing buyers for about 10% of what the call would cost if made legitimately.

This type of operation is referred to as call/ sell and it depends on a steady supply of a stolen calling card numbers to maintain the operation.

The distributor uses several methods to obtain the calling card numbers. One method is referred to as hawking or shoulder surfing and involves looking over the shoulder of a person. Using a calling card number at a coin telephone. The hawk writes down the number and immediately phones it into the distributor is it can be used to place fraudulent calls. Hawks have even used video cameras to video record persons placing a call, in an attempt to capture the calling card number.

Another means used by call / sell operators to obtain calling card numbers is known as the Tony White scam. The distributor calls unsuspecting subscribers and tells them, "My name is Tony White and I am an investigators with the telephone company. Have you made several calls to Brazil recently? We have several calls to Brazil on your bill."

The customers reply that no calls were made to Brazil. The fraud suspect then states, "I will investigate for you, but to begin the investigation, I need your PIN (Personal Identification Number) and the last four digits of your calling card numbers."

Some subscribers give the fraud suspect their PIN, and since the suspect already knows the telephone number, usually the first ten digits of the calling card number is the telephone number, the suspect now possesses the calling card number. The distribution immediately calls his sellers and provides them the calling card numbers so they can be begin fraudulent calls to it.

Distributors have also paid people to steal calling cards from mail boxes or form homes.

Electronic Boxes

Towards the end of the 1960's, an enterprising electrical engineering student found a weakness in the telecommunications network. The weakness involved the internal signaling between long distance switches used to initate and terminate and for routine calls. The student designed an electronic box, commonly referred to as a blue box, which emulated the tones internal to the network and allowed the user to place toll-free long distance calls.

The users of a blue box would usually call toll free number (either long distance information and/ or 800 –xxx-xxxx) and before the called number could answer, the person placing the call would use the blue box to drop the called party off, still controlling the trunking (series of lines / channels that are connected when a call placed to provide an end-to-end voice path). The fraud suspect would then use the blue box to dial a telephone number, anywhere in the world. The call would not be billed by the network.

The black box was another electronic box, designed to allow a person to accept a free call. The black box took advantage of the fact that a called number or to in a machine or to an operator, information regarding the status of a loop or trunk. The four service conditions that supervisory signals convey are idle circuit, busy circuit, seizure, supervision.

A black box was built into the fraud suspect's telephone company central office. The black box lowered the current drawn by the telephone to a point that it would not draw supervision, and the ringing would continue even after the phone was answered. Built into the black box was a switch which when activated, produced a quick short on the line and caused the ringing to stop.

Changes in the network have all but eliminated the use of blue boxes and black boxes.

Computer Hacking

Around at the time American telephone and telegraph was divesting, a number of long distance companies were entering the market to compete with AT&T. Many of these companies rushed to deliver their long distance product to the market place. They could not connect directly to the wire companies like AT&T. They had to create access points for their customers to call. The service companies offered was referred to as Feature Group A(FGA) and a later, similar service Feature Group B (FGB). Their customers would dial the company access telephone number, (usually a local or toll free telephone number) or dial a reassigned personal identification number (PIN) (initially these numbers were 4 digit long) and follow it with the called telephone number. If the PIN was validating by the computer, the call would go through, if it did not validate, the call would not go through. Security of their networks was weak. They could not identify a telephone number calling into their networks. About this time, the personal computer industry was also booming. Computers enthusiast were using their computers to communicate over a telephone lines throughout the world. The vast majority of these computers enthusiasts were honest but a few were not.

These few--often referred to as computers hackers--designed computerized blue box programmes to pay for their telecommunications expenses, but as the network was improved, blue boxes became less and less dependable. Computers hackers then designed programmes which took advantage of the security weakness of the FGA and FGB companies. Hackers initially designed two types of hacking programmes. One, often called a JOSHUA or war games dialer, was used to dial every telephone number in a prefix, identifying all numbers answered by a computer. The hacker could probe the identified computer later or use the numbers as the terminating number for a calling code hacking program. Calling code hacking programmess were designed to call the access number of a FGA or FGB company, try a PIN and dial a number known to be answered by a computer. If the calling computer recognized the modern tone from the called computer, the calling computer recognized the call had gone through and the PIN worked. The calling computer would then send the PIN to memory. If the call did not go through, the computers would try another PIN.

Hacking programmes were widely distributed on computer bulletin board systems discussed below. urther they were easily duplicated and knowledge of programming was not necessary to operate them. FGA and FGB companies soon began to work on their networks security. They lengthened their PIN, installed hacker software to survey their systems, restricted system use geographically, provisioned their to receive information on the calling number and they began providing law enforcement with sufficient evidence to arrest some of the hackers. Hackers then began to realize that there was risk of arrest associated with hacking some of the FGBand FGA companies.

Many businesses purchased Private Branch Exchange (PBX) later as it is customer-provided equipment and they equipped with a feature known as Direct Inward System Access (DISA). DISA is a PBX feature which allows a user to call into switch from a remote location, input a PIN assigned by the business and if validated, place an outbound call which is charged to the business. DISA works just like a FGA or FGB system.

Most Business that activated DISA on their PBXs never anticipated the risk they were assuming. Some didn't even use PINs. They felt a non-published number was protection enough. Hackers quickly migrated from FGA and FGB hacking to IDSA hacking. The companies who fell victim to the hackers often did not realize they were a victim until they received their phone bills. Some were victimized for over a million dollars. Further, they were responsible for the bills, the telephone companies would not write the fraud off.

DISA fraud continues to be a major telecommunications problem plaguing business.

Computers Bulletin Boards

Computers bulletin board systems (CBBS) were developed shortly after the beginning of the personal computer boom. They are computer programmes loaded on a computer, designed to allow callers to call the bulletin board and leave/read/ browse information. Most CBBS are legitimate and exchange information (and ideas) on subject matter on bulletin boards are computers information, games, investing, pets etc. Some CBBs are used to exchange illegal information (often referred to as hostile bulletin boards), including stolen calling codes, hacking programmers, business and information on perpetrating illegal scams.

Hostile CBBS were used extensively to exchange stolen calling codes numbers. Telecommunication company and law enforcement investigators would monitor the bulletin boards' activity to gather evidence necessary to prosecute the CBBS operator. When sufficient evidence was obtained it would be presented to either the local District Attorney or the US Attorney and search warrant would be issued for the location housing the offending CBBS would be seized.

Today hostile CBBs use high levels of security to ensure that only other hackers or phreakers (individual who refers to themselves as phreakers and who attempt to find and compromise weakness in the telephone network) have access to the illegal information resident in their systems. Further, may hackers and phreakers now use voice mail systems (I will discuss this later in this paper) to distribute their stolen calling codes.

Social Engineering

Telecommunication companies and business, due to attacks on their systems by persons intent on committing fraud, have hardened their system, making them more difficult to compromise. Criminals found the mechanical systems were difficult, if not impossible to penetrate.

They had to find a new weakness to compromise, so they began attacking the human element. Social engineers call telephone companies and businesses, pretending to be someone the are not, in an attempt to gain valuable information. They may want information on how the company's computers system works. How many digits are there in the company directs Inward System Access (DISA), how the company voice mail system works, how a portion of the telephone network functions, information on an employee, etc. Any information possessed by a telephone company or business may be of value to such a social engineer.

The social engineer is really saying, 'Hi! Please give me your valuable proprietary information. So I can take advantage of your company.' They use subterfuge to gain information that would not be given to them if their true identity were known. Social engineering continues to be a very popular way for criminals to obtain information necessary to commit fraud.

Mobile Cellular Fraud

One of the first mobile telephone systems,s know as the Improved Mobile Telephone System (IMTS) IMTS, used a negative validation system to identify those numbers not authorize to place a call through the system. The negative validation system does not validate these users who should be on the system. If a person used a number, any number that was not on the bandit list, the call would go through and would continue to go through until someone at the mobile company noticed the number was being used. It would then be placed on the bandit list. Some people equipped their mobile phone with thumb wheels which could go through and would continue to go through until someone at the mobile company noticed the number was being used. It would then be placed on the bandits list.

Some people equipped their mobile phone with thumb wheels which could be turned to change the originating number of the mobile telephone. They could make a fraudulent call, change their number and make another call without any risk of detection.

IMTS was replaced by the cellular telephone system. There are still some IMTS systems in use which provide the users with greater systems capacity and improved signaling characteristics. Two numbers are required by the cellular system to recognize the originating cellular set. One is the Electronic Serial Number (ESN), which permanently identifies the cellular company and is programmed into the phone when it is installed or activated in the case of portables. The early models of cellular telephones were constructed in a manner that made removal or changing of the ESN impossible. In later model telephones, cellular telephones were constructed to allow the ESN to be removed and changed.

Unscrupulous installers began fraudulently installing an ESN and MIN assigned to a legitimate cellular customer into the cellular telephone of a person willing to pay for the fraudulent service. The service usually would work for a billing period (30 to 45 days) when the legitimate customer reported it, after seeing it on their bill to the cellular company.

Cellular companies have improved network and are becoming better at detecting imposter fraud, but it continues to be a problem for cellular companies.

Subscription Fraud

Telephone companies have prided themselves as being easy to do business with. Subscribers can usually call, from any location, to have new service installed, features added to have a line repair etc. from any location to have a new service installed, features added, to have a line repaired etc. Even people who have not had a prior account with the telephone company usually have little difficulty in obtaining new service. In some areas, the respective public Utilities Commission (PUC) dictate what identification must be presented by a person requesting telephone service and normally those requirements are easily met. The PUC also usually directs the phone company to contact a subscribers either verbally or in writing, and wait a certain amount of time before disconnecting the service. The ability to obtain telephone service with little or no proof of identity, and requiring the telephone company to wait a certain amount of time before disconnecting a fraudulent service are system weaknesses.

Some countries do not allow calls to be made to other designated restricted countries for political reasons. If a person wishes to place a call to a restricted country, they must call through a country that allows telecommunications with both countries. Some criminal organizations realized if they somehow could sell fraudulent telephone calls from their both country to the restricted country, they could become rich. They found they could exploit the 'three-way conference calling' feature and the way telephone companies conduct business.

Here is the way subscription fraud works. Organized rings of telecommunication criminals in a restricted country send their agents to the United States. The agents rent apartments and business locations (fraud shops), paying cash whenever possible. They install telephone service in the residences and business they have rented, providing the telephone company with fictions identifications information.

They also set up business in their home country and advertise that they will place calls to the restricted country for a fee.

Their counterparts in the United States furnish the fraud shops with two or three desks with re more telephones, a business ledger and a clock which delays the time in the home country. They then hire people to staff the telephones. People come into the business in the home country and request to place a call to the restricted country. A call is placed to the fraud shops (usually collect or using stolen calling code). The person answering the phone at the fraud shop in the USA writes down the time of the call, number of the calling agent and destination of the call (for billing purposes). The person at the fraud shop then uses three-way conference calling card to connect the calling party with the numbers in the restricted country. The criminal in the home country collects money from the person wishing to make the call.

When the telephone company becomes aware of the calling

activity, originating from the fraud shop, a telephone company representatives calls. The manager of the fraud shop will try and stall the phone company from disconnecting service. Since the manager of the fraud shop knows approximately how long it will take the telephone company to disconnect service he /she begins setting up the next fraud shop location. Just prior to the telephone disconnection, the new fraud shop begins operate.

The loss to the long distance providers can be as much as $100,000,00 per line, and since the fraud operation has no intention of paying the bill, the overhead is low.

Telephone companies have taken steps to tighten their identifications requirements, improve their network surveillance systems and have worked with the PUCs to allow immediate disconnection of service when fraud is identified.

Customer Provided Equipment Fraud

The term Customer Provided Equipment (CPE) refers to any type of telephone equipment owned by a telephone company customer and connected to the telephone line. It could be a computer company customer and connected to the telephone line. It could be a computer, an answering machine or a large telecommunication computer called a Private Branch Exchange (PBX). For the purpose of my discussion, I will focus on CPE fraud associated with PBXs.

A PBXs is a computer that functions in much the same way as a telephone company switching computer. In fact, PBXs used by many business are identical to the switching computers used by telephone companies. A PBX is usually purchased and used by a business for one reason, to save them money. Utilization of a PBX allows a business to purchase fewer incoming and outgoing lines from the telephones company but still provides the same level of calling service to the business employees and customers; further a PBX provides the user with a number of useful telecommunications features. Some of which are: Call Director,. Voice Mail and Direct Inward System Access or DISA.

Call Director

A call Director allows a business to screen calls and route them to the correct telephone number. Most of us have listened to a call director at one time or another time Usually the first thing heard when a call director answers is if you are calling from a touch tone phone, 'please press 1 now…'. The call director recording then advises the caller of the available options and the extension to call to contact them. A call director recording will usually have a maximum of five or six options. Any more than that and the caller will hang up.

Someone discovered that some Call Directors, when 8 is dialed and not being programmed, would hand the call to the PBX. An 8 to most PBX is the telephonic command for an outside line. Once caller had an outside line, they could call anywhere the PBX allowed them to and the call would be billed to the PBX. A call director should be tested to ensure that it will any route calls as desired and will not respond to any commands but those programmed in.

Voice Mail Hacking

Voice mail has become as common in business today as reaching a receptionists was ten years ago. It is used so often by business that most business persons, when asked cannot recall when voice mail was installed. The designers of voice systems tried to make them as user friendly as possible. They developed features like call transfer capability, auto page capability and the capability to access voice mail messages from a remote location. Some voice mail features and/ or procedures have created security weakness in the system that have been comprised by criminals.

Most businesses issue a new Voice Mail box to a user and utilize the last four digits of the user's voice mail box telephone number as the initial password. The user is instructed to change the password, some do but others do not. Hackers are aware of this practice. They obtain a telephone directory belonging to a large business. Usually listed in the directory will be the Voice Mail telephone number that can be used by employees and access their mail box when they are away from the office. The hacker will call the voice mail access number, the system will ask for the telephone number and password of the user, some times in reverse order. The hacker will use a telephone number out of the directory as the requested telephone number and will use the last four digits of the telephone number as the password and he has found a good password and he will change the password and use the box.. If the system doesn't allows him access, he will try another telephone number from the directory, continuing until he is successful.

Hackers will also attempt to take administrative control of the system. If they are able to gain control of a system they can create as many Voice Mail boxes as they like. Hackers use pirated boxes to exchange stolen calling code numbers, exchange messages exchange computer password, exchange stolen credit card numbers.

Voice mail hacking is easy to prevent. Never allow an administrator or employees to assign the voice mail box telephone number as the password. Always assign the box's password (do not allow the employment to select it because the employee will use a number they can easily remember, like their extension number. Require at least an eight digit password. Do not allow the computer ability for remote administrative control of the system to exist.

Another features that is often compromised by hacker is the voice mail call transfer feature. This feature allows voice mail caller to command the systems to provide dial tone and make business calls from the office to obtain dial tone and make business cells from the systems saving the business money. Hackers and call/sell have used the feature to place long distance calls which are billed to the business. A voice mail system should not allow any caller to obtain dialer tone.

Direct Inward Systems Access

Direct Inward System Access System (DISA) was explained earlier in the Computer Hacking section. DISA allows a business to provide its employee with the capability to place long distance calls through the companies PBXs while away from the office. Bussiness usually do not protect their DISA activity as well as they should, nor do business survey their DISA system adequately. Both of which make DISA numbers very popular with call/ sell operations (much more popular than telephone cards numbers).

DISA codes are used by telecommunications criminals for a number of purposes. They sell them. They use them to call through, when committing a telecommunications crime (hacking annoying calls) to hide their telephone number (a call trace of the suspects call will show the DISA port telephone number, and not the suspect's telephone number). They are used by organized crime to conduct various types of fraud. US telephone Customer Protection Plan require the following of their customers systems:

Use a minimum of eight digits for each DISA code

Eliminate all voice mail external transfer capabilities, including the ability to transfer or route traffic to the trunk level

Install a security, for example, call back on all CPE remote maintenance ports. Delete all manufacturer and vendor installed default passwords. I further recommend the following:

- Use a non- published number for DISA ports

Allow the DISA number to ring 4 or 5 times before answering it, this makes it more difficult for hackers.

- Assign the authorization codes randomly, on a need to have basis. One code per person
- Use the longest possible authorization code.
- Deactivate unassigned codes
- Change codes on a schedule basis.
- Instruct users to keep the DISA telephone number and authorization code secure
- Block out of hours and weakened DISA activity if it is not required
- Restrict the DISA geographic dialing area to only those areas to do business
- Monitor the PBXs call detail reports closely

And know your equipment and vendor. The vendor should be advised to call your telecommunication manager if a similar PBX has fraud problems. This allows you time to fix the problem before you become a victim.

Investigation Process

A CPE fraud investigation cannot be planned when a business becomes a victim a fraud. If a business has not planned how to respond to a telecommunications fraud, the fraud loss will be a far greater than with a business that has developed an action plan.

An investigate action plan must accomplish a number of tasks First the key contacts must be identified. These key contacts would probably include the security manager, the telecommunication manager, a representatives of senior management, a manger who can render an immediate business-affecting decision and an expert PBX resource. Other contacts to be familiar with are the vendor, a representatives of local law enforcement, a representative of the local telephone company's security department, a company attorney, a media relations expert.

The key contacts should meet as a team and develop a strategy on how to recognize fraud at an early stage, or that they may be the victim of a fraud. This usually involves utilizing or developing surveillance software and the PBX. It also usually involves educating the employees (since they are usually the first to recognize that something unusual is occurring). The employees must be encouraged to report unusual occurrences and must be told who to report them to. They should be rewarded when they take the time to report an occurrence is reported the team must decide if it is an equipment problem or a crime. If it is a crime, senior management must be decide whether they want to immediately protect the systems or attempt to apprehend the criminal. Not protecting the system at an early stage of the fraud may be vary costly. I recommend immediately securing the system, even if it means the criminal will not be apprehended this time. A criminal's luck will eventually run out, they will make a mistake and be caught breaking into another system. If the decision is to apprehend the criminal, the legal department contact and telephone contact have to be notified. A police report has to be filled and the company will have to begin attempting to identify the originating telephone number and the company attorney should be kept advised about what documents are being released to law enforcement. If the suspect is arrested, the police will need to be quickly notified of the loss, include in the loss amount of labour required to investigate the fraud and protect the system.

Lastly, when the case goes to trial the business may have to provide the prosecutors with witness who can explain to a jury how he victim system works and how the fraud was perpetrated.

Fraud occurs in the same manner as many others crimes do, Fraud seeks out an easy victim. They do not care where the victim is located, who the victim is, who the victim knows. They only are interested in whether or not they can make a significant amount of money with little or no risks of apprehension. Like other crimes, fraud does not stay within geographic boundaries or jurisdictions and we cannot either. We must be prepared to share information about fraud with other business. We must be willing to help our competitors when it comes to fraud. If businesses properly safeguard their telecommunications equipment, stay informed and share information on current fraud schemes, telecommunications fraud will feel the impact of our actions.

Managing Performance

Sharu S Rangnekar

Managing performance means managing relationships and relationships have to be managed continuously, on a day-to-day basis. Whether in the work place or outside, fear is no longer an effective way of managing people, neither is the incentive system. There are three things with which we can replace them-- the first is a sense of identity, the second a sense of importance and the third a sense of development. Motivating people to perform is the best way of managing performance.

In any organizations, performance depends on two factors: One is technology, the other is relationship.

Technology and Relationship

Technology is by and large a matter of investment and to that extent the company is able to get funds and invest them and choose the right technology, there will be performance in that organization. However, high technology doesn't always mean high performance. In fact, take the case of the Binny company, which invested a lot of money in getting the latest technology but ultimately went bankrupt. There have been only two organizations in the world which have gone bankrupt in spite of a very high reputation for quality: Rolls Royce and Binny. And their cases are worth looking at. Here was a company investing very heavily in technology but its relationship was so bad that the technology was never exploited to the company's advantage. I am sure this has happened in many other cases, less visible..

This points to the importance of what we can do in terms of relationship, because technology is often dependent on a time decision. You listen to all the wise counsel, call upon all the expertise available, and you make a decision about technology. But once you have made the decision you cannot change it every year. On other hand, relationship is something which has to be managed every day. You cannot say, we have managed relationships well and sit back.

This brings us to the point that managing relationships is ultimately managing performance as far as the manager is concerned. I am now talking, not necessarily about the chief executives who may have a lot to say in managing or changing technology, but about middle-level managers who can't change technology. Essential they are responsible for managing day-to-day relationships and that is the area I want to focus on in terms of what we can do and not what should happen.

The Stick and the Carrot

The people around us seem to be changing. I remember, thirty years ago, when I entered my first textile mill. The department head told me. "Look we maintain discipline here without touching a worker: we kick him out". That is the way discipline was enforced those days. The use of fear was very strong. Today, I don't think that anybody can say that he can sack anyone.. In fact, sacking a subordinate is a full-time job and the chances are fifty-fifty that he actually leaves on his own. Consequently, no manager in his senses would take up such a job. Fear has gone out of the window.

There is a generational change and we managers have to manage without resorting to fear, except in a few cases. If the chap is in casual employment or on probation, we use fear. But once he gets his confirmation letter, we know the use of fear has no meaning.

The next step is, if the stick doesn't work, try the carrot, give him some incentive. One of the easiest incentive systems is overtime and you all know what happens with over time. Once it gets in, people work only on overtime. As a worker told me, time is money. Sooner or later the consequences of such incentives catch up with us..

If both money and fear have gone out of the window – that is, if both the stick and the carrot are thrown out, what do we use? That is the real problem for us when we talk about managing performance. And my suggestion is that we can in combination I use the sense of identity, the second a sense of importance and the sense of development.

Sense of Identity

Wherever you see managers doing a dramatic job, check on the means they have used. Especially in big units in the organized sector, you will find that they have used fear or money as the motivators. What they have done is, they have created a sense identity. Take a company like Tisco, where the worker tends to identity himself with the company. During the Janata Party regime, George Fernandes and Biju Patnaik suggested that Tisco should be nationalized. The loudest protest came from Tisco workers. The 60,000 workers of Tisco don't own even one percent of the shares. So it was not the legal ownership, but the emotional ownership that was important and that is something that, functions very effectively.

I'd like to take up the examples of our defense forces. When we talk of motivations and performance in industry,, this is what we really mean: that if the chap who is at the workplace for eight hours and working for hardly four hours puts in an extra hour of work we are very happy and say that he is motivated. In the Army, when they talk about a soldier being motivated, what they mean is that he is ready to risk his life. Remember, when a commander asks a soldier to go and capture an enemy post, the soldier knows that the enemy is sitting there with a machine gun. Now, if every soldier does a cost benefit analysis -- what are my chances of capturing the post of getting a medal or a promotion and what on the other hand are my chances of catching a bullet and lying horizontal forever--, do you think that the army would be able to function? So, when they talk to soldiers on motivation, what they are saying is risk your life and that is just what the soldiers do. How they do it is worth looking at and this is where we see that an identity is created. The day a person enters a unit, he is given an identity through his uniform and through the colours of the battalion. Every regiment has its colour and the soldier is made to feel proud of those colours.

The Japanese Example

This method is one that has been used in armies, all armies, for a long time. The Japanese are the ones who have used it in management by giving the same uniform to every one, from chairman to the sweeper. This visual identity is very important. This is so even among religious sects. If you're a Rajneesh follower you wear a kind of uniform colour which identifies you. This way of creating an identity is very important in motivating a person.

This second way of creating this identity is to make people do physical work together. The easiest kind of physical activity, of course, is singing. In Japan, as soon as the siren sounds, everyone stands up and sings the company anthem. In India, we have problems even in singing the national anthem. I mean, if we need to have the national anthem, someone has to play a record of it. Everybody will stand up in silence as if they are paying their respects at the funeral of the national anthem. If you ask someone why don't you sing, he will say," with my voice, how can I sing?" But if you start an aarti of his god, he will sing. Why? Because the god is his. But the nation is still on probation after forty years, we are not yet confirmed, we are not sure it is ours.

In Japan, by singing the company anthem, a person is reminding himself: this is my company. After the anthem is over, it is one, two three, four on the public address system and everybody does physical exercises for three minutes. It is supposed to be a warming-up, but I would say the warming up is not physical, it is emotional. A sweeper is sweeping the chairman's room. The siren sounds. The chairman and the sweeper stand together, sing the company anthem and then do the physical exercises together. What happens to the sweeper? He says, this chairman is probably ten, twelve, fifteen – I dint know how many – levels above me. But he is part of my team. I have identity with him because he wears the same uniform, sings the same songs and we do the same exercises together.

Group Activity

This group physical activity is a great thing for creating identity. People get up, sit down, sing, kneel together.Hindu temples, the important ones, are all built in difficult places, on top of hills. Whether you take Triupathi, Sabarimala or Vaishnodevi, Badrinath or Kedarnath. What is the purpose? It is that people should climb together, they do physical work together. When they begin they don't feel part of the team. I have seen it happening in Badrinath, which people start the climb, but in different groups – they are Maharashtrian, they are Tamils, they are Telugus, they are Kannadigas, they are Keralites. By the time they go up, although they don't talk each other's language, certain feelings have developed.And if one doesn't come up,. youngsters in the group are sent down to help the old because they are part of the group. This is the purpose of walking two days together. Going to Pandarpur in Maharashtra, there is a system called 'dindi' i.e, a group of devotees walk together, in spite of all modern conveniences being available, they don't use any vehicle and they walk for several days from wherever they are to Pandarpur. This is considered very important because it creates identity among people who undertake physical exertion togethe. These days there are roads right up to Badrinath. People can get out of the bus and see Badrinath, if they want. What I say is, if God is to be so easily accessible, he would be in Mughal Sarai so that everybody can get to him and back again very easily. The very fact these inaccessible places were chosen means the purpose was to create group feeling.

Creating Energy

Physical work together is essential and this is another thing I've noticed in all the people who are liable to get performance. Tthey create a lot of energy and physical work. In fact, one of the things I noticed immediately about a sick unit is this lack of energy together. People ask me, how do you recognize a sick unit ? Do you study the balance sheet? I say no. In India, nobody believes in balance sheets. I go and look at the factory : I find pipes are leaking, drums are leaking, cement is getting spoilt in the open. I ask the worker, what is all this ? You know what he says? "Oh nobody is bothered. Even if I tell, my supervisor, nothing will happen. Even the manager cannot do anything. Everybody has very low energy.".

Sometimes you go to the railway or some other government office, you can see this happening. But it's not so everywhere. In some places. you find people moving energetically. In others, even the most urgent things are done casually.

But a lot of apparent energy and people moving about does not necessarily mean performance. The energy can be directed, non-directed or miss directed. If it is directed, energy results in performance. If it is non- directed, it creates confusion,duplication, with people running around doings things, with the same things being done again and again. Every time I have organized a conference I have seen this as one of the problems. You get a lot of energy, youngsters are very anxious to work, but people have tendency to duplicate. And you find at the end, that a lot of effort was really wasted. This can also happen in an organization.

Misdirected Energy

Then there is misdirection. As the organization grows. people don't work for the organization any more, they work for compartments within the organization. So you get compartments feuds: marketing vs. production, : production vs. purchasing, production vs finance, finance vs. everybody else. These are the feuds that go on in many organizations. I asked a normally morose chap the other day, "You look happy today. What happened?". He answered: "You know, the factory's boiler has burst. the production chaps are screwed up for the next two weeks." You see,as far as he was concerned, his enemy No. 1 was not the marketing of the competing company, it was the production unit of his own company. And this is where you find energy getting misdirected. When the marketing chap walks into production, the whisper goes round, "he has come for information. Don't gave him any information. Even if he asks what's the time, say that it depends." Tthis is the kind of thing which creates misdirected energy.

Whether or not this happens depends on the extent to which a manager is able to direct the energies or most of the energies available. There is no perfect manager and I have yet to see an organization in which at least some of the enemies are not non-directed or miss directed. And there is, therefore, no perfect organization. But, in a good organization, a very large percentage of the energy is directed towards the real goal.

Sense of Importance

Such direction is very important. It creates identity which in turn creates importance. The sense of importance is vital. You have all heard the statement, power corrupts and absolute power corrupts absolutely. I give you another statement to think about. Powerlessness corrodes and absolute powerlessness corrodes absolutely. In an organizations where people feel that whatever they see or find cannot be changed, they really can do nothing about it. Helplessness is one of the biggest adverse factors in motivation When a person feels that he has the ability to do things, he gets the motivation.

There are many organizations where there is no feeling of power, where the worker feels he can't do any thing. "I know something is wrong but can I do anything? I am too small. " And the chap who says I'm too small is not always worker or a supervisors.I have heard even managers, senior manager saying this. "At my level, I can do anything." This is where you see that performance gets affected adversely. Whenever people feel-- and this is an important feeling you can give to your subordinates –that if they find some thing wrong, you are there to fight it on their behalf, then you can get a lot of performance out of them. The energy gets directed.

Sense of Development

The final important factor contributing to performance is the feeling of development. I find particularly, that youngsters these days are very ambitious. Everybody wants to be an MD, or chairman, or both and they don't think there can be only one in a company. Many of them say, " if this company does not accommodate me. I'll go elsewhere". And this is where you get a lot of motivation to learn to develop. Not necessarily the motivation to develop is in order to help the company. The motivation is for self, "I want to develop and I can always find myself a job".

I have found this feeling to be strongest in Hindustan Lever where, every time they promote a director to chairman, two other directors leave. They make Tandon chairman, Basu and Chandy leave. They make Thomas chairman, Mathias and Varadarajan leave. Three years ago, they made Ganguly chairman and three persons, Banerjee, Bijawat and Chopra left. And those who leave, all become chairman or vice- chairman elsewhere. Now this I find is a highly motivating performance-creating factor down the line. This also happens when a manager is promoted to director and another manager leaves. I mean, it goes down the line. And the feeling is that, " if I develop myself I can develop my transfer value and get what I want when I want it. Of course, I want to remain in this company if I can become chairman here. But if I cannot become chairman here, I don't mind stepping out and becoming chairman elsewhere". This is the kind of feeling which is a feeling of development, that I am talking about.

Transfer Value

On the other hand, companies where people have the feeling that whatever they are or do, nobody is going to recognize them, have not developed a transfer value. The other day in the factory of a public sector fertilizer corporation, someone told me that for the job he was doing there the private sector would pay twice the amount he was getting. Why don't you join the private sector, was my question. The reply was: who will give me even half of what I am getting here? That's strange arithmetic, but it is true. Basically, what he is saying is that his contribution value is good: he is doing a good job where he is. He is worth twice what he is getting in terms of private sector payy levels. But when it comes to transfer value, when he goes out into the market for a job, then his value is low. Of course, he immediately blames circumstances, saying fertilizers is a very small industry and there are not very many units.

But here again, I can cite a very interesting case. BHEL, Trichy – not all of BHEL, just one single factory, has provided 23 persons at chairman / managing director or the next level, not only for their own organization, but for other organizations as well. Deenadayalu was executive director at Trichy, he became the CMD of Madras Refineries, having moved into a technology which had nothing to do with boiler technology.

This has happened because, somehow, BHEL Trichy has been consistently creating a very great transfer value. So this high transfer value is not a function of being in the private sector or the public sector. It is basically an atmosphere crated in the organization, where every person feels :I am developing, I am growing and I can go to an interview and demonstrate that I am of value, not only in producing boilers (because there are not very many companies producing boilers in India), but in producing any thing you want to make. "I am a manager: I can perform.. Now if one feels confident about this particularly ability, that is in itself a motivating factor and it develops performance.

So, as you can see, when fear and money are thrown out of the window, the three great performers that we can create are a sense of identity, a sense of importance and a sense of development.

Performance Appraisal

The last point I want to deal with here is to do with performance appraisal. I remember that at one time, when I was working in a multinational subsidiary, performance appraisal was considered the great modern thing to do. If you were a sophisticated organization, you must have a good performance appraisal system So lots of forms were designed. Initially it was a two-page form. Then it grew of four pages, six pages and then came back again to two. So it went on. Every three years, the company would get a new consultant who would devise a new form.

I have noticed that it is in very few companies that performance appraisal does any good. In most companies it has created problems. In government,, the performance appraisal has existed for a long item. At the time of the East India Company it was called C.R which meant Confidential Roll. The word roll was used because in those days, the paper could not be folded, it would crack, so it was rolled up and kept in the director's office of the company. Every year, another portion of a person's confidential roll was written up and sent to the office to be stuck to the roll and add its length.

That system still continuous today but it no longer has credibility., There are very, very few organizations where people feel that the performance appraisal has credibility.Confucius said 2000 years ago that government exists on strength of guns, rice and faith. The most important of the there is faith. Translated into modern management language, I would say that every modern management concept depends on three things – the ability to reward, the ability to punish and credibility. The most important is credibility. If this credibility is lost, then the performance appraisal system becomes pointless. I know of situations where in union negotiations managements have agreed that they will not use the performance appraisal system for any purpose whatsoever, whether for increments. or promotions or for anything else but, they say, "since we have the right to appraise, we are going to appraise". And the union says, "as long as you don't use i, we don't mind your doing it". If the performance appraisal.and appraisal system is brought to this stage, it has no real value. It is an exercise in futility. But I have also seen what this system can do, where it does work., If a performance system looks at performance, not necessary for performance appraisal but for evaluating ther performance, for comparison with others. If you get a D and someone else gets a B and someone else again gets an A, then, of course, everyone is upset.But if one were to say about your performance, "could we improver it next year?" Then obviously people would say "yes, provided ..."

Everyone performance is affected by two factors: One is the support provided by the organizations and the other is individual effort. Many may feel that their performance has not been up to the mark because the support provided by the organizations has been inadequate. The boss then says, "okay, I'll see what I can do about the support, but lets also see what yourself have to do because that's also a factor". This and guides the performance system and the system eventually becomes credible. Then the worker says, "If my boss is going to do something about the system support, then I am ready to do something to improve myself in such a way that performance is better next year."

This is the kind of feeling which, particularly when it is tied with the development of the individual, creates a sense of motivation which is the basis of managing performance. So I would say that, in addition to creating a sense of identity, a sense of importance and a sense of development, you must in your role relating to your subordinates, creates a performance improvement system. This need not be on printed forms it can be verbal, But basically, the boss and the subordinate must sit together once a month, once a quarter or once in six months whatever is appropriate, to discuss to what extent performance has lived up to expectation, where it is lacking and what can be done about it on both sides. If this kind of improvement system comes in, I am sure performance will be managed better.

Total Quality Management: A People Building Journey

U K Chaubey

In the stiff competition both global and domestic, Total Quality Management (TQM) has now become a buzz word in the industries world. Customers have been demanding goods and services of a high quality. The term Quality itself has not remained static in its sweep and meaning but has been behaving like a moving point. Therefore, organizations have been trying to understand the meaning of TQM and then applying it for better and better results. For quite some time Statistical Quality Control (SQC) was confined to the quality of finished goods. The result was that in some organizations while the finished product was expected to be of a high order, other services like the staff functions, the services and maintenance etc could have continued to be handled in a slovenly manner.

In this kind of situation it is natural that the organizations were not able to produce goods and services of a high quality over a period of time. Particularly in the United States of America in the 50s this subject was being discussed and debated in an intense manner. Dr D W Edwards Deming the Father of Modern Quality Movement (TQM) in the world, after studying the phenomenon of bad quality and after deep and long observation advised the industries and managers to view the subject of Quality in totality covering under its scope all the aspects of the functioning of an organization. However, the leaders of American industry did not bother much about the precepts being propounded by Dr Deming. More or less at the same time the Japanese were very keen to restructure their industries after the devastation of the Second World War.

On the advice of American government Dr Deming went to Japan where he lectured to the leaders of the industries and said that Quality should be viewed as a holistic concept covering the totality of the organization functioning. He further said that quality assurance cannot be achieved merely through inspections at the end of product process, because this involves double work and wastage of resources. He advised that the concept of quality should be built in the system itself so that quality assurance becomes the second nature of Workers, Supervisors and Managers. His observation was that 80% of the problems are caused by 20% of the causes. The causes are generally rooted in the system of production and management. The Industrialists and Scientists in Japan were much impressed by the exhortations of Dr Deming and they started implementing his advice in totality. Dr Deming was of the view that quality must come from Top Down i.e. the commitment of Chief Executive and top management is necessary because people should be at the centre of the movement.

New Management Philosophy

Dr Deming said that in order that quality movement is embraced by the rank and file, it is necessary that the following fourteen points must be accepted and implemented in totality.

1. **Create constancy of purpose for improvement of product and service.** Not only does Deming stress the need for a continuing emphasis on quality improvement, he also, more subtly, points out that quality, not profit, should be the primary purpose. Profit, for Deming, is a consequence, a by-product, of a management approach centered on quality.

2. **Adopt the new philosophy.** Here Deming reiterates the need for constancy of purpose while emphasizing how important it is for this purpose to be shared by everyone in the organization and inculcated like a philosophy, which it really is.
3. **Cease dependence on mass inspection.** Quality cannot be added on; it must be built in from the start. Mass inspection is completely off the mark. It assumes that quality can be achieved by identifying and then correcting errors. This means that workers are paid to make errors and are then paid again to correct them. This is not to say that workers like this any more than do managers. Deming notes that almost all workers want to do work of a high quality, work in which they can feel pride and a sense of accomplishment.
4. **End the practice of awarding business on price tag alone.** Deming does not advocate ignoring price when looking for suppliers. He only insists that price is a relatively minor factor, especially compared with the supplier's interest in and willingness to meet the customer's needs–that is the needs of the organization that purchases the supplies. (Those needs, of course, are driven in turn by the needs of the organization's clients and customers). The choice among suppliers should be based mostly on the quality of the materials they supply and on their willingness to work to improve that quality in the context of a long-term relationship.
5. **Improve constantly and forever the system of production and service.** This point restates management's never ending obligation to seek out ways to improve quality.
6. **Institute training.** Deming does not limit training to the use of statistical quality control and other tools for improving quality. He also means training in how to do the job. Many workers never get adequate training in doing the jobs for which they are responsible. In American industry, about 70% of all training dollars go for management education and development. Only 30% is spent on training for lower-level line employees, those who actually make products or deliver services. This imbalance

can not only lead to errors, it makes it more difficult for workers to figure out what management expects of the them. In Japan, the proportions of funds spent on training for workers and training for managers are approximately the reverse. In India also, perhaps the situation may be similar. To make TQM work, frontline employees must receive ongoing training.

7. **Institute leadership.** Being a leader is different from being a supervisor. Supervisors tell workers what to do and then watch to make sure they do it. They administer rewards and disciple as needed to ensure that employees comply with orders. In contrast, leaders assume that workers want to do the best job they can. At lower organizational level, the job of a leader is to assist workers by coaching and by arranging for training when needed. For top management, leadership means designing the system on the basis of TQM, applying strategic vision to build a TQM culture, and constantly and consistently modeling behavior that exemplifies the values that support such a culture.
8. **Drive out fear.** This is without a doubt one of the most important of Deming's points. In many organizations, people are afraid to speak up, to point out problems, or just to ask questions. Managers rule by fear, using either special favors or, more often, various punishments to make sure that workers do as they are told. People are sometimes fired for bringing a problem to the attention of management. A concern for quality requires that employees feel secure. High quality cannot be attained unless managers operate in a culture of openers, in which no one is afraid telling the truth, pointing out a problem, or trying to learn to do the job better may lead to the adverse consequences.
9. **Break down barriers between staff areas.** Traditional organizational structures encourage competition among units, departments, divisions, and so on. But this makes it difficult, if not impossible, to work together to achieve quality. People in different areas and departments must understand that they have the same overriding

goals, that they are in competition with other organizations, not with their colleagues and coworkers.

10. **Eliminate slogans, Exhortations, and targets for the work force.** In this point, Deming is criticizing those who think that quality can come from motivation, from getting people all worked up through motivational speakers and inspirational tracts. This approach actually makes things worse in the long run, because even if workers really want to do better they still don't know how, they don't have the tools they need to improve, and they are not supported by the organization's culture. Deming has said that slogans and targets put people in the position of having an idea of where they want to go but no map of how to get there.

These days some consultants give impassioned speeches and create a lot of histrionics. One examples of such a consultant has been mentioned in the book *Adversity Ouotient,* written by Dr Paul G. Stoltz and is mentioned below:

"Ultimate Power with Freddy Savage boasted the marquis in front of the Phoenix Convention Center. This was the big event. I was guided to my seat by a member of Freddy's perfectly groomed entourage. At that moment, the rock music pounding through a Superdomesized sound system softened noticeably. A Master of Ceremonies took over the microphone on stage.

As he went through his introduction, I scanned the room. I saw the full range–individuals who later introduced themselves as students, professionals, entrepreneurs, and the temporarily unemployed–good, earnest people–executives, salespeople, children, retirees, laborers, homemakers, investing their hard-earned money for one reason–to find something they had lost along the ways their motivation. They sought an escape from the pervasive sense of helplessness that surrounded them. They wanted to feel good again. They wanted to feel in control. "Finally it's here, "The big moment you've all been waiting for. The sultan of Success, The Professor of Personal Power, The Monster of Motivation.... Freddeeeeee Saaavage!" The Crowd roared.

There he was, larger than life. Freddy Savage. He bounded across the stage and grabbed the microphone. "Yes!" His voice boomed forth. "Yes!" The crowd roared back.

"Everybody up!" He demanded. All 2,000 people jumped to their feet. "Form groups of their feet. "Form groups of three now!" We formed groups of three. "Put one person in the middle. Go!" One person jumped in the middle. "Give that person a full body massage. Go!" I found myself and some guy in a suit rubbing from head to toe a community college secretary we'd never met. "Does it feel good?" Feddy asked. "It feels good," the three-hundred people responded.

"No, does it feeeeel gooooood?" Freddy challenged.

"Oooooh! It feeeeels gooood!" 666 people bellowed.

"Take a seat," Freddy directed. Everyone sat.

"You are in charge of your own destiny. You are in control. "He paused as he flashed his million-dollar smile at his adoring fans. "You can fly with the buffalo, you can swim with the eagles, you can roam with the sharks" (or something like that). And so it went for eleven hours straight. I watched as 2,000 people from all walks of life soaked up every word. The energy was palpable. I had never seen so many hard-working individuals so completely energized at the end of an eleven-hour day. They were pumped! But were they changed?"

11. **Eliminate numerical quotas.** Quotas encourage people to ignore quality. The goal is to meet or exceed the quota at any cost and regardless of quality. Even when quality meets specifications, quotas can have hidden costs. For example, one department may produce its quota, but the products, while technically meeting specifications, may not meet the needs of the uses the output of the first as one important part of a larger product. The result will be continuing conflicts as well as the added costs of rework so that the first department" output is fit for use by the second department, its internal customer. Goals must focus on quality issues, not merely on numbers produced.
12. **Remove barriers to pride of workmanship.** Eliminate the annual rating or merit systems. Deming assumes that people want to do a good job, not a poor one. They need help in overcoming

such barriers as the poor quality of the materials they receive to work with, the poor quality of their equipment, and inadequate job management designed and supported system of operation is needed that allows all employees to do their jobs well, not one that tries to coerce performance from them. In the Indian context both group assessment and individual assessment would have to be blended together.

13. **Institute a vigorous program of education and improvement.** Deming does not downplay the need for everyone to have a thorough grounding in the tools and techniques of quality control. These tools are the language of quality. But he also points out that people must learn new ways of working together as terms and new behaviors that support the new management philosophy–the TQM culture.
14. **Take action to accomplish the transformation.** Everyone in the organization must work together to implement a quality culture. Top management in particular must focus on a strategy and a plan and take actions to put the plan into effect. Workers cannot be expected to do it on their own irrespective of the training they receive in the use of quality control tools and techniques. Only management can begin the process of getting the entire organization–management as well as workers to take the actions that result in a TQM culture.

These fourteen points are the basic elements in the Deming's new philosophy of management and constitute an organic whole of a TQM culture. They have to be applied in totality and at the same time. Otherwise the result may be counterproductive.

Creating Quality Assurance Framework

Quality assurance involves the following three aspects.

(a) **Counting**–tools, techniques and training in their use for analyzing, understanding, and solving quality problems.

(b) **Customers**–quality for the customers as a driving force and central concern

(c) **Culture**–shared values and beliefs, expressed by leaders, that define and support quality.

In a few organizations TQM has been taken to merely an understanding and implementing the seven tools of TQM namely: (a) Control Charts (b) Pareto Charts (c) Fishbone Diagram (d) Run Chart (e) Histogram (f) Scatter Diagram and (g) Flow Chart. This is what generally leads to the failure of TQM movement because TQM is not at all confined to the tools. The tools are meant to help implementation of the concepts of TQM through involvement and commitment of people is not generated to its highest pitch, TQM cannot be brought in just by mechanical application of the tools.

Therefore it is necessary to understand what TQM really means. According to Japanese industrial standard 28101–1981 Quality control is a system of means to economically produce goods or services which satisfy customer requirements.

From customer angle quality is fitness for use.

Thus TQM can be defined as under:

TQM means that the organization's culture is defined by and supports the constant attainment of customer satisfaction through an integrated system of tools, techniques and training, This involves the continuous improvement of organizational processes resulting in high quality products and services. The application of tools leads to a proper understanding and application of the Deming's process namely Plan, Do, Check and Analyze (PDCA) leading to further improvements. Continuous application of tools generates self-efficacy, and self-confidence, and self-esteem results from doing and succeeding by recognizing that success was due to one's own action and not due to fare or chance. In order therefore that the quality is in-built in the organizational process it is necessary that the quality check points are embedded in the process of the working of the organization. These quality check points are:

QC-I at the customers end. In other words where the customers accept the goods or services provided by the organization with joy and confidence in a sustained manner it will be deemed that the organization has a TQM culture. Otherwise, whatever the organization may do, it cannot say that in fact it has implemented TQM. At this point the quality check can be done through customer survey and through other, responses from the customers which the organizations may be getting continuously.

QC-II at the finishing and dispatch line from where the goods and services are handed over to the customer. Generally the organizations have concentrated all their effort in quality improvement at this point. This leads to a lot of rejection and then extra effort is required to correct the imbalance. Therefore in addition to QC-II, QC-III is required.

QC-III is located at the site of product or in the totality of work activity. In some organizations this is termed as Process Control. This is assured through constant use of QC charts or through Statistical Process Control (SPC). This is also assured by putting concentrated effort on the 20% of causes which lead to 80% of the problems.

QC-IV In addition to the above point it is very necessary to check the quality of incoming materials from vendors and suppliers. Where the incoming material is not of a high order, high quality cannot be assured.

QC-V Good result at QC-IV can be assured only if the design for product of input material, i.e. raw-materials, spare parts etc is as per the specifications laid down by the organizations where these would be utilized. This is why in a large number of organizations there are specialists to handle the quality problems in the organizations of their vendors and suppliers. It would be seen from the above that while the work flows from suppliers to the customers clock-wise, flow of quality check points is anti-clock-wise starting from QC-I.

Quality can be assured if the model prepared by Dr Juran another American Quality expert is followed : Juran's road map to high quality involves :

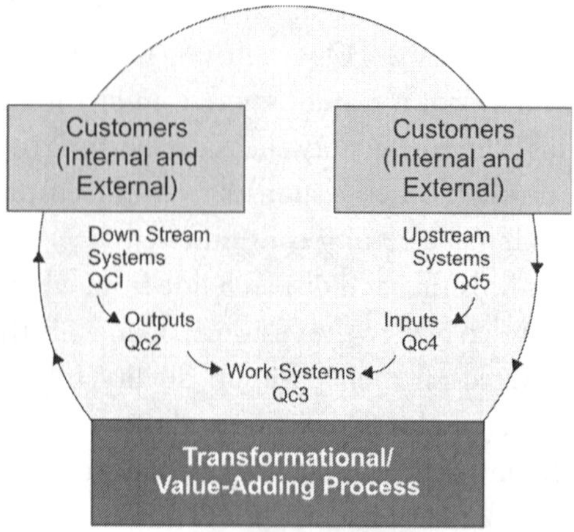

Step 1: Ask, "Who are our customers? Executives, Managers and Employees must first step back and ask who the customer is. They must make a list and then talk to people on the list to see whether they have identified the right people and to ask whether important customers have been left off. This will lead to the concept of both internal as well as external customer.

Step 2: Ask Customers, "What do you want and need?" Customers' needs and desires are listed and explored in detail. The list reviewed with other customers to see whether it is correct and complete.

Step 3: Ask, "What do these needs mean to us" The needs and desires that customers describe are translated into product and service terms that are meaningful to people within the organization. Again, a list is made. This list is reviewed with employees, modified as needed, translated, and checked for accuracy with customers.

Step 4: Ask, "What are the characteristics of a product/service that satisfies these needs?" Executives, managers, and employees throughout the organization must prepare the list of customer needs and identify the specific characteristics of products of services that meet them. Again, these product of service descriptions must be checked with customers.

Step 5: Ask, "How do we make this product?" Or ask, "How do we deliver this service?" Actual plans for making products or delivering services are developed in writing and in detail. Those who must carry out the plans are involved from the start. The who must carry out the plans are involved from the start. The plans are shared widely throughout the organization. The focus is always on the question, "How do we do it right the first time?"

Step 6: Put the plans into operation. After carrying out the plans, check back with customers to make sure that the products or services have actually satisfied customers' needs. An emphasis on measurement must be present throughout this sex-step process for building customers' needs into the system of organization functioning. What's more, the process is not a one-time-only event. It must be repeated again and again. These six steps can be applied in service organizations as well. In fact in service organizations, it may be relatively more convenient to do it, because in such organizations delighting the customers has to be done mainly through the application of knowledge, skills, attitude, innovation and disciplined behavior.

TQM Culture

In order that a TQM culture is embedded in the working of a organization, the following eight crucial elements of TQM culture must be followed scrupulously in a holistic manner:

Culture Element 1	Quality information must be used for improvement, not to judge or control people.
Culture Element 2	Authority must be equal to responsibility.
Culture Element 3	There must be rewards for results.
Culture Element 4	Cooperation, not competition, must be the basis for working together.
Culture Element 5	Employees must have secure jobs.
Culture Element 6	There must be a climate of fairness.
Culture Element 7	Compensation should be equitable.
Culture Element 8	Employees should have an ownership stake.

The above elements of TQM culture mentioned above are self explanatory and can be easily understood by the people of almost all the organizations.

The eight crucial elements of TQM culture mentioned above are basically applicable more or less to all the organizations. However, in fact there are very few organizations which have all the cultural elements mentioned above. These would have to be integrated with the basic management philosophy shown in the fourteen points of Deming mentioned earlier in this paper. This is why the cultural elements are so crucial because people in general would believe in a particular type of culture only if it is reflected through the activities of the top management. Where these cultural elements are propagated only through Lectures, Banners and others signs without being reflected in the activities of the management including supervisors etc., the employees in general respond by being indifferent or even alienated with the exhortations. This is so because culture is the cumulative perception of how the organization treats people and how people expect to treat one another. It is based on consistent and persistent management action as seen by employees, vendors and customers.

TQM culture can be created and sustained if the organizations have the following elements.

- Action that develop trust, such as sharing useful information and making good on commitments.
- Acting consistently, so that employees are not surprised or taken aback by unexpected management actions or decisions.
- Being scrupulously truthful and avoiding so called white lies and actions designed to manipulate others by giving a certain (false) impression.
- Demonstrating integrity by keeping confidences and observing basic ethical guidelines to show one's concern for others.
- Meeting with one's employees to discuss and define exactly what is expected of them.
- Making sure that people are treated equitably, that is, giving equivalent rewards for similar performance by different employees and avoiding actual or apparent special treatment for favorites.

- Giving employees meaningful influence over decisions about their own work, especially how to accomplish their work goals and what to do about work problems.
- Adhering to clear standards that are seen as just and reasonable, for example, not giving praise out of proportion to accomplishments or imposing penalties disproportionate to an offence.
- Demonstrating respect towards employees, showing by actions that one really cares about others and recognizes their strengths and contributions following due process, that is, procedures that are open to public scrutiny and that permit everyone to participate actively in their application

Leaders' Role

In this, the role of leader is really crucial, the leader has to be a designer, a steward and a teacher. He has to first design the system, process, and procedures which lead to a TQM culture. Then he has to lead various levels of employees into implementing this culture and then he has to be a teacher coaching the employees as to how do it progressively better. This is the kind of leadership which transforms organizations in which it is a joy to work transforms organizations in which it is a joy to work and where self fulfillment is generated through performance.

Reaction to Armed Robbery

James Tappin

A robbery may be a manager's worst nightmare. Fortunately, in most cases, the chances of it happening are remote. However some retail and other businesses are at a higher risk and therefore management must be aware of their responsibilities towards the safety and welfare of their staff.

Good training and a strong sense of security awareness at all levels will assist, with the aim always being to try to prevent an incient occurring. Although robbery accounts for a small proportion of retail and other business loss it is amongst the most common reason for serious violence against staff. Management must educate staff to understand that : *Your first priority is always to prevent harm to yourself, colleagues, or your customers'.*

Use the following advice as an insurance policy to minimise the risk of being assaulted. It had come about by pooling best practise from the police, retailers, other businesses and security companies. Use this information and you will feel confident that you are minimising the risk to yourself should you find yourself involved in a robbery.

What is robbery ?

The English Law Definition of robbery states that : 'A person is guilty of robbery if he/she steals and immediately before or at any time of so doing, in order to do so, uses force, or puts or seeks to put any person, in fear of being subjected to force'. Simply robbery is stealing your goods or money with threats, or actual violence being used to get you to co-operate. A robbery may attempt to steal your takings, till contents, goods, or your money/goods in transit. Their main aim is to get what they came for and escape as quickly as possible, not to assault you. A 'snatch' is generally quicker that a robbery and does not always have the open threat of violence to individuals. However, should you try and stop the thief you may run the same risk or threat of violence as a store or bank robbery.

The threat of robbery for retailers has increased over recent years because banks and building societies, traditional target, have spent a lot of money to fortify their premises. As a result the whole retail sector, including wholesalers, has become a softer target for the criminal fraternity. By designing out theft opportunities, using security products to deter and detect, and following tried and tested safe operating procedures, you can greatly reduce the risk.

- An attack is likely if: Security is non existent, staff are inefficient, it is easily committed and there is little chance of being caught.
- An attacker is encouraged if he/she: Is likely to be seen, is unlikely to be seen, is unlikely to be identified, noticed few persons available and sees good escape routes.
- Your routines will be noticed. Ensure there are safe routines and that they agree with your insurers requirements.
- If you are uncertain about any situation, secure the premises and call the police.

Actions During the Robbery

Having done everything to prevent a robbery from happening, all that really matters if it does happen is your safety and that if it does happen is your safety and that of your staff and customers. Robbers are desperate people looking for the opportunity to steal your cash of goods. Once they have committed themselves to steal, the generally will not stop at assaulting you, if you give them cause to do so. Robberies can be quick, with many lasting no longer than 90 seconds. A robber's main aim is to get what he wants with no obstruction and leave without being caught. They will be nervous and 'psyched up' and may have taken drugs, so don't do anything to surprise or obstruct them.

- If you are fortunate enough to spot a robber's intentions before they start the robbery, then this is the only time you should use a door lock, remote alarm or activate a fast rising screen.
- If faced with an armed robber, co-operate.
- Give them the money or merchandise they want.
- Control your emotions, be cool and clam.
- Do exactly as you are told, do not talk or argue, let the robber do the talking, because all the time they are talking, they are less likely to attack you.
- Do not bluff or tell lies as this will aggravate the robber.
- Make no sudden movements or noises.
- Do not surprise them or let others surprise them; warn the robbers of the presence of other staff or customers who might panic them into an assault.
- If a customer tries to get involved shout a command telling them to stop. Do not turn your back on the robber.
- Let the robber see your hands at all times.
- Let the robber see your hands at all times.
- Do not have a go because you are likely to come off worst. Although it is tempting, do not use a hidden weapon to attack a robber.
- Don't activate any hand held or silent/panic alarms while robber is with you as it may cause them to assault you out of anger. Wait until after they have left.
- If a robber puts their weapon down do not attempt to touch it.

- If you are not involved with the robbery, keep away. If out of sight, keep out of sight. Activate a remote alarm or telephone the police if you have access to a phone. Try to take a note of what is going on and a mental description of the robber(s). don't try to leave by an emergency or other exit, it may be alarmed.

Although the importance of co-operating and not resisting the robber in any way is emphasised, there are exceptions to the rule. If you have no alternatives but to defend yourself because you are being held, and not to do so may put you at further risk, do so quickly, 'Bash and Dash'. Do not stop to make more than one attack, get away fast. Shout for help and continue to make as much noise as you can while you run. Fighting is your last resort, once committed you have no alternatives but to hit and run to avoid further injury. If you are forced to leave your premises, co-operate with your assailant, because the best place to resist is usually outside where you may be able to run, fight or shout for help.

Post robbery Procedures

After a robbery do not go chasing after the robber and risk being attacked. Stay inside the premises. Try to notice which directions the robber(s) take and if by vehicle try to get a description and registration number. Carry out these actions :

- Lock the doors, call the police and give immediately important information.
- If necessary tell the police you need an ambulance and conduct any first aid requirements.
- Preserve the scene of the crime. Be mindful of everything the robber may have touched, so even if you are going to lock a door, make sure you do not touch any part of it you may think the robber has touched.
- Do not move or touch anything, including CCTV tapes, until the police arrive.
- Help any customers that are in the premises and ask them to stay as witnesses. You cannot force them to stay, so if they really

need to leave, ask them for their name, address and telephone number where the police may contact them.

- Call the premises' owner or your emergency contact.
- While waiting for the police write down everything you can remember of the incident, so that you can give them a clear indication of what happened.
- Be accurate and include the exact time, place, people involved, description of the robber(s), their direction and means of escape.
- If two or more are present during the incident prepare your notes separately. Putting these together later will provide a far more comprehensive picture than if you completed one statement together.
- If you have been assaulted, depending on the extent of your injuries, you may be required to attend hospital or see a local police surgeon.
- Once the robbery details have been finalised, do not discuss them with anyone who does not have the need to know, especially the amount of money or goods involved. Publicity can create the wrong effect and may set the scene for a repeat robbery.

Post Incident measures and support

After a violent attack or threat to staff, short and long term negative psychological and physical effects can occur. A violent incident is always an unpredictable and frightening experience. Even if medical help is not necessary, it should be appreciated that staff involved are likely to suffer from emotional stress and trauma. If this is not acknowledge and dealt with, both personal and work problems may occur. Other staff, including those who were not on the premises at the time of the attack, may also suffer feelings of guilt because they were not there or fear that if may happen to them.

Violence in a robbery and the fear of it can affect anyone. It can lead to low staff morale, high absenteeism, high staff turnover, compensation claims for injury and higher insurance premiums.

Apart from actual physical harm, a robbery can cause stress brought on by shock. Victims can suffer symptoms such as: fear, anxiety, depression, sleeplessness, feelings of victimisation, lack of confidence, mood swings and emotional changes. All of these add up to impaired work performance.

A victim may handle the situation calmly at the time of the incident but may experience a range of disturbing and negative emotions afterwards. They may feel: guilt over what they did to provoke the situation, fear about being vulnerable to repeat attack, anger and feelings of victimisation over why it happened to them and anxiety and lack of confidence in continuing to deal with the public and do their job. Managers and members of staff should look out for all these signs and take action to support the person(s) involved.

After an incident, review your security measures and procedures and institute a staff retraining exercise.

Summary

The moment an incident occurs the priority must be the safety of all those involved. The time spent in the incident is a time of survival and the word SURVIVAL can be used as a mnemonic, a memory aid, to assist in guiding persons through the situations.

Size up the situation: Consider yourself, your comrades, and your adversaries.

Undue haste makes waste: Use time to your advantage.

Remember where you are: Take stock of the situation, memories details.

Vanquish fear and panic: Stay calm, keep assessing.

Improvise: Make use of time and equipment.

Value living: Value your own and others lives.

Act to suit the situations: Do as you are told and do as taught.

Learn basic skills: Basic training and continuation training.

Self Development

Renu Mattoo

Develop yourself before you think of developing others. With all the discussion on developing subordinates, we tend to forget that before we can think of their progress, we must take a look at ourselves, and locate areas in our own personality and skills that need attention. In fact, if a manager does not want to, or is not interested to enhance his own skills, he cannot develop those of his subordinates. If you do not feel committed to personal growth, an dare less than enthusiastic about your development, you will lose the zest of living, and the joy of achieving.

In the E-era, continuous and fast learning is critical: Continuous self-development has always been a valid requirement. Today, however, this development must come faster than ever, because we live in an era of quick an ever-increasing information and change. With new knowledge coming our way at break-neck from myriad media, learning is never complete, nor updated. You take a nap, and wake up to find your environment has changed beyond recognition! So, speed of self-development is critical. Fast self –development requires efficient and effective strategies. Many people believe that development is a natural process, and that no special effort need be made for self-advancement. They may be right, but not quite, because the road to self-betterment has many barriers, most of them erected by the traveller himself. Some of these self imposed impediments are disinterest, laziness, the arrogance of I know-it-all", and the discomfort of change etc. These barriers are best tackled by a willingness to change, by welcoming and anticipating change, and seeking opportunities for self enrichment.

The first step to self-development is self-appraisal. You need to take a good, objective and intimate look at yourself. An ordered, effective way of doing that is by using the SWOT method. Identify first only your strengths. These are the knowledge, skills, positive behaviours, and attitudes you posses. Do not be modest. Write these down on paper. Look at this paper every day, and keep adding as you discover more strengths. As you note them down, you will be pleasantly surprised to see that you are good at many things. As your list increases in length, your self-confidence will get a boost. Your strengths are asset that you can use currently and in future to take decisions and to solve problems. After a week of listing only your strengths, now also and simultaneously, start to note your weaknesses, those areas that you are not strong in. This list will include all the knowledge and skills that you should have to be the best in your job, but either do not have at all or not enough. The list should also contain your behavioural weaknesses, and negative attitudinal traits.

While both strengths and weaknesses are internal to you, we turn to the external environment to identify opportunities and threats. Opportunities are all those favourable realities and situations around you that you can use for your advancement. The keener your eye to locate opportunities and the more developed your strengths, the greater the possibility of using opportunities for self-enrichment. Make a list of all opportunities in your immediate, middle distance and remote environment. Use the time dimension to see into the future for favourable situations. Given the shrinkage of both time and space, even the remote and far future are not really so. They will be within touching distance even as you think about them.

Now, consider the threats ion your environment. These are also realities, but those that could stall your attempts at growth and development. While some threats are patently clear, others lurk in the shadows. You need night vision-deep insight, and anticipation of what trends could create which negative state-to identify and locate these.

Now, what do you do with these four lists? You enhance and use your strengths; find ways to overcome your weaknesses; do not let opportunities slip by, but stay alert to them, and use as many as you can to advance yourself; and you use your strengths to reduce the severity of threats. Excellence, in other words, is an option, a choice for you.

To achieve excellence

1. Listen and Learn

Learn by reading, watching educative TV programmes, discussing with experts, and mainly by listening. Seek knowledge and develop new abilities, not only in your particular area of specialisation, but also in related areas.

2. Question and Clarify

Ask others to tell you what you are good at, and where you lack, invite thoughts on what you should be doing, how you can do better.

3. Risk Ridicule and Failure

Learn to take the risks of ridicule and even the failure of efforts as you try to develop your skills and knowledge. Do also know that there are three types of risks: One: Those not taken at all. Two: Reckless and rash ones. Three: Calculated risks. Take the last.

4. Plan and Practice

Make your own plans for advancement in your career. Do not wait for others to do that for you. No one can be as interested in your growth as you yourself. Practice your learning. There is no better way to develop any skill.

5. Develop a Winning Attitude

(a) Learn to love your job, and be enthusiastic about your responsibilities

(b) Use your strengths to shape your destiny by determining your environment.

Eight percent of employees like only twenty percent aspects of their job. This means that most people dislike major aspects of their job tasks. To be successful, however, it is essential that you like what you do, that you not only enjoy your work, but also value it greatly. Many people, however, believe that liking or disliking a job has a lost to do with the job itself, the kind of people one works with, the environment one works in, the chances of promotion and growth, etc. Success, they say, is dependent on extraneous factors.

The truth, however, is that we all have more power, greater energies, and more strength than we realise. Only the weak believe that circumstances control their destiny. The strong create their own environment. They are in control of circumstances, and take full responsibility for their situation.

You have the power to manage your environment, and take from it all that you need. If you do not do so, you will be left out in the cold. If you depend on others for help, you may have to wait forever, for no one else – neither family, friends, bosses, nor colleagues – have the time, inclination, and skills to help you achieve success. Ultimately, it is what you do, and with what attitude you do it, that matters. So, how do you ensure your success? Here are some ways for you to consider.

6. Ensuring Success on the Job

- Move away from negative though patterns:

  [a] Why should I work any smarter, or harder, when there are no complaints about my performance? My boss and others are quite okay with my current output.

  [b] I want to acquire more skills, and perform better, but what can I do? My boss does not nominate me to any training pro-

grammes. He piles me with so much work that I have no time even to read the newspaper.

[c] I have no choice but to work harder, better, as that will please my boss and he will take care of me when the time comes for announcing increments, promotions and perks.

- Take personnel control of your life as you steer yourself towards your goal of self-development. A man reinvests in his own business not because someone tells him to do so, but because he wants to you will not be driven by an externally controlled motivation, but by an inner-determined inspiration. Your script will now read; I am going to develop myself because / want to, and I am capable of doing it. You are no more the couch that the railway engine pulls and pushes on the track to get moving. You are the engine, driven by an inner energy !! You have the choice.
- Decide what you want to do and how. Along with a change in attitude, you will need to first decide your job goals, and then develop a concrete, well-ordered, not haphazard, plan of action. It must sure what steps you will take, by when, and how. This plan must then be executed in a determined and proper manner.
- First, Picture your ideal job: Describe your fantasy: What would you rather be doing with what type of boss, colleagues, subordinates, in what kind of physical work environment. This is the profile of your current dream and goal. Once you know what you want to achieve, you can map the route to the destination. Write down in as much details as possible the various aspects of this dream job.
- Break the big picture into little snapshots. To develop a route, you need to identify landmarks on the way. You need to find places you can stop at, rest a while, refresh yourself, and then move on. These little images within the big picture are the various aspects of your dream job. They are the stepping stones, the rungs on the ladder to achieving the dream, and later, will help you move from one position to the next.
- Next, compare your dream job with what you currently have.

You are Assistant Manager in Administration, but want to be Head of Public Relations. You have a wimpy, weak Boss, but want a decisive, powerful one. You have a comer desk in a room full or noisy typists and typewriters, but you want a comer room with a word processor.

- Take charge. Be self-driven. Ask yourself what it is that YOU (not others) can do in order to change the picture. Note the alternatives open and available to you. Those that appears 'un-achievable' are so only because YOU believe they are impossible. Consider, for example, the first step in the direction of your goal. Ask "Cant I ask for a much lower position in PR? But, first, for them even to think of me as a possible candidate, I must acquire a relevant qualification."
- Treat your company as a client, and yourself as a supplier or contractor. This means looking after your company as you would look after your own business if you had one, and looking after your own interest, if you were a supplier. You would meet the demands of your client (your company to his satisfaction, and reinvest in various aspects of your business (your self) for further and further growth. This is the best way to ensure that you will be regular in following your plant.
- Take steps to improve your work atmosphere, by interacting with people around you in a more friendly, responsible, and positive way. Stop constantly complaining about your job, your boss, and your colleagues, Change your attitude. This is an essential step to enhancing your personal situation at work. Learn to smile, greet, make small talk, and offer to help others. Even if you have not got along very well with others in the past, as you initiate these friendly moves, many positive outcomes will emerge. Most importantly, your seniors will begin to have a better opinion of your abilities to work well with people. Though this will surprise some, the sincerity of your approach will soon be clear. People will soon recognise your changed attitude, and they will relate to you themselves in a positive, friendly manner. As you feel the warmth

of friendship, you will find your environment less stressful.

- Work towards getting the support of your seniors. Identify what your particular boss considers valuable traits. Does he like people to be casual and friendly, or serious and task – oriented? Should they be creative or logical an detail – oriented? Does he like 'yes' men, or those who can take an independent, but right stand? Since success depends in fair measures on support from the top, check which traits you need to develop in order to get this support. You do not have to be a sycophant that is the role of the weak and the inefficient. You do have to find ways to gain his support and respect, by becoming likeable, useful, and an effective achiever.
- Find ways to become more visible- pleasantly. Exhibit yourself positively. Write articles for trade journals, the house magazine, an for internal circulation. Involve yourself in company and local club activities, and become a member of professional bodies. Don't only become a member be an active one.
- Find yourself a mentor. Seek preferably someone a few rungs higher than you, power full, and himself well positioned. Seek his advice on what is the best way to position yourself in your kind of industry. Don't flaunt your closeness to him. In fact, I don't get too close to him, but admire an respect him from within touching distance.
- Promote yourself: Now, look for occasions to tell those who matter – your boss and other influential people in the company that you have the ability to contribute a lot more and that you want to be make yourself more valuable to the company. Though the performance review meeting is a good formal occasion, you do not have to wait for it to initiate dialogue with your boss. Pick a moment when your relationship with him is at its strongest, and say:" I am happy here, and with what I am doing. I want to make myself more valuable to the company. I believe I can do a lot more. What would you like me to do so that the value of my contribution increases?" Sometimes asking directly for a

promotion works, but not many situations allow for a direct: "I think I am ready for a promotion". Ask instead for what you can do to accomplish more, and achieve higher output.

- Develop your job skills: Seek actively to join training programme, and attend seminars. Let your boss know that you are interested in enhancing your skills, and that the benefits of such enrichment will go not only to you personally, but also the company. Apart from leading to your goals, this shows your motivation level.
- Offer new, constructive ideas to improve the performance of the whole department: If you are very good only in discharging your current, limited responsibilities, you may become so indispensable that your boss will never think of taking you away to another position. Even as you continue to perform well in your specified duties, let your boss know that you have lot more potential by offering constructive suggestions about improving your own output and that of the department. Develop new ideas. Think thee out well, so that they have unambiguous merit, and are clearly worth trying out. Taking the initiatives in this respect is a good way of presenting evidence of how well you could perform in other areas.
- Seek opportunities to help and support your boss and colleagues. The best way of demonstrating your worth an positive-ness is by volunteering to help others, including your boss. Look for opportunities – when your boss is working late or when a colleagues is struck with a stubborn problem. Not only does this foster better relations, it shows initiatives. Offer to add more to your tasks. It gives your boss a change to test your additional abilities,. Your offer may not always be taken up, you may see the opportunity but not have the time, but do not give up. Continue to look around for the next opportunity.
- Maintain a task and achievement dairy" Get into the habit of entering in a diary your daily/weekly tasks to be completed. In particular, enter in it (in different ink or in capital letters) any special achievements. This will help you keep track of your ac-

complishments. Let your boss see you use this diary. Also, when your boss gives you special instructions, note them down quickly in his presence. When you go to tell him that you have completed the task, again in his presence, refer to the diary. This tells him that you are maintaining a record of your achievements. One beneficial fallout of this habit is that a boss who habitually denies or alters instructions whimsically, or insists. I told you yesterday' when he did not, is more careful when dealing with you. Sometimes a boss may dispute the value of your achievements. The diary will provide hard evidence. A few days in advance of the annual performance review, find ways to let him know what you have accomplished.

- Look confident: Dress today ass if you were already tomorrow's position. Smile pleasantly, but not too widely. Stand and site straight. Walk briskly. Look people in the eye, but do not stare or glare at them. Speak clearly, and strongly. Know your facts. Plan and organise your life, stay focussed.

All of the above appears a tall order. But as you take one step at a time, the goal will get gradually closer to realisation. There is no reason why you cannot do what you want to. You have unique strengths and opportunities waiting to be used. Just do it!

About IISSM

The International Institute of Security and Safety Management (IISSM) is a non-profit educational society registered under the Indian Societies Act. It is devoted to promoting professionalism among security and loss prevention practitioners and creating all-round security awareness and consciousness amongst personnel in the related management cadre. IISSM is the Asia's oldest society in the field of security and loss prevention, which is continuously engaged for the last 21 years in disseminating latest developments and techniques in the area of security and loss prevention. It offers consultancy services and runs customised and thematic courses covering all aspects of industrial security, safety, fire prevention, loss prevention and allied subjects. It acts as a catalyst to bring professionals together for experience-sharing and updating professional knowledge through numerous training courses, seminars and workshops. It has an elaborate Professional Certification Programme for consultants, security and safety practitioners and bestows fellowship on highly deserving professionals.

Every year since 1991, IISSM has been organising international seminars, at times accompanied by exhibitions, attracting a large number of security and loss prevention professionals from India and abroad. Faculties in these seminars comprise well-known experts drawn from all over the world. Participants come from private sector industries, public sector undertakings, private security agencies, systems integrators, security equipment manufacturers, academic institutions, financial institutions, banking industry and the government departments. Countries so far represented in IISSM training programmes include Australia, Bangladesh, Belgium, Canada, Denmark, France, Germany, Hong Kong, Special Administrative Region, Indonesia, Israel, Kuwait, Malaysia, Mauritius, Mozambique, Nepal, Reunion Island, Saudi Arabia, Singapore, South Africa, Taiwan, Province of China, Thailand, Turkey, UK, USA, Zambia, Zimbabwe and India.

IISSM recently entered into an MoU with International Institute of Risk and Safety Management (IIRSM), UK, for accreditation of training centres, trainers and courses as also to run focused courses on Loss Prevention with IIRSM as a knowledge partner. A proposal to offer duel membership (IISSM & IIRSM) to each member is in advanced stages of consideration.

IISSM also proposes to conduct PG Diploma, Degree and MBA level courses (Level 1, 2 and 3) in collaboration with Indira Gandhi National Open University (IGNOU).

Suggested Readings

Norman Abrams *Anti-Terrorism and Criminal Enforcement (American Casebooks) West,* Third Edition (10 June 2008)

Victor V Ramraj, Michael Hor, Kent Roach, George Williams *Global Anti-Terrorism Law and Policy,* Second Edition; Cambridge University Press; (31 January 2012)

Sandra Rollings-Magnusson *Anti-Terrorism: Security and Insecurity After 9/11*; Fernwood Publishing Co. Ltd. (1 September 2009)

Marcus Mann *Anti-Terrorism Risk Assessments: Effective Profiles, Predictions & Prevention*; Pearson Publications (January 2005)

Randall K. Nichols, Panos C. Lekkas *Wireless Security: Models, Threats, and Solutions;* McGraw-Hill Professional (13 December 2001)

Wenke Lee, Cliff Wang, David Dagon *Botnet Detection: Countering the Largest Security Threat (Advances in Information Security)* Springer (25 November 2010)

Kathleen M Sweet *Transportation and Cargo Security: Threats and Solutions;* Prentice Hall (19 August 2005)

Mark Egan, Tim Mather *The Executive Guide to Information Security: Threats, Challenges, and Solutions,* First Edition; Addison-Wesley Profes-

sional (10 December 2004)
Patsy Hall Sargent, Mary Faye Ward *Security First Bank: A Banking Customer Simulation South,* Fifth Edition; Western Educational Publication (24 February 2006)
R E Anderson *Bank security;* Butterworth 1981
CW Laws, Larry Averitt, Southern Methodist University, Southwestern Graduate School of Banking, *Bank security: devices and controls for detection and prevention of robbery;* S.M.U. 1973
Byron Acohido, Jon Swartz *Zero Day Threat: The Shocking Truth of How Banks and Credit Bureaus Help Cyber Crooks Steal Your Money and Identity;* Union Square Press (1 April 2008)
Benton E Gup *Bank Fraud: Exposing the Hidden Threat to Financial Institutions;* Probus Professional Pub (March 1990)
Brian J Cudahy *Cash, Tokens, & Transfers: A History of Urban Mass Transit in North America,* First Edition; Fordham University Press (1 January 1990)
A Robert Abboud, William G Schopf , Geoffrey N Smith *Money in the Bank: How Safe Is It?,* First Edition; Irwin Professional Pub (January 1988)
Walter Updegrave *How to Keep Your Savings Safe: Protecting the Money You Can't Afford to Lose Crown Business*; Upd Sub Edition (18 January 1994)
Jonathan Spall *Investing in Gold: The Essential Safe Haven Investment for Every Portfolio,* First Edition; McGraw-Hill (20 November 2008)
Thomas D Tarman, Edward L Witzke *Implementing Security for ATM Networks,* First Edition; Artech House (1 December 2001)
Mike Sexton *Broadband Networking ATM, ADH and SONET (Artech House Telecommunications Library);* Artech House Publishers (31 August 1997)
Nicholas Hames Protecting Financial Institutions from ATM Fraud. An article from: Canadian Manager [HTML] [Digital] Canadian Institute of Management
Srikanta Ghosh *Indian Banking: Crime and Security in Indian Banks;* South Asia Books (April 1992)
Aurora Ferrari, Inderbir Singh Dhingra *India's Investment Climate: Voices*

of Indian Business; World Bank Publications (26 November 2008)

Vasant C Joshi, Vinay V Joshi *Managing Indian Banks: The Challenges Ahead;* Second Edition, (Response Books); Sage Publications Pvt. Ltd (May 2002)

Darrell Duffie *How Big Banks Fail and What to Do About It;* Princeton University Press (October 18, 2010)

W Goosen, A Pampallis, Amelia van der Merwe *Banking in the New Millenium;* Juta Academic (1 January 1999)

Retail financial services: *The challenge of virtual banking in the new millenium: Financial Services Industry Practice and Price Waterhouse;* World Technology Centre *(1996)*

Mads Andenas, Joseph Jude Norton, Joseph Gold, Ruth Gold *International Monetary and Financial Law upon Entering the New Millenium: A Tribute to Sir Joseph and Ruth Gold (Sir Joseph Gold Memorial Series)* British Inst of Intl & Comparative (May 2003)

George Macesich *Issues in Money and Banking;* Praeger Publishers (30 June 2000)

Christopher A Chung High-tech training tools. (bomb threat simulator computer program): An article from: **Security Management** [HTML] [Digital] American Society for Industrial Security (July 28, 2005)

Ellahi M Ishteeaque *Security in airports: Design, conditions and measures to combat air piracy, sabotage, bomb threats and acts of unlawful interference;* Arab Security Studies & Training Center (1982)

Patrick Kane CPP *Practical Security Training;* Butterworth-Heinemann (8 November 1999)

Stephen E. Brock, Jonathan Sandoval, Sharon Lewis *Preparing for Crises in the Schools;* Second Edition– A Manual for Building School Crisis Response Teams, Wiley (16 January 2001)

Robert Cooper *Corporate Treasury and Cash Management*; Palgrave Macmillan (21 February 2004)

Peter S Rose, Sylvia C Hudgins, Peter Rose, Sylvia Hudgins *Bank Management and Financial Services Standard & Poor's Educational Version of Market Insight Ethics in Finance Powerweb;* McGraw-Hill/Irwin Sixth Edition (5 March 2004)

Michele Allman-Ward, James Sagner *Essentials of Managing Corporate Cash;* Wiley (21 February 2003)

Marie Dolfe, Anna Koritz *European Cash Management; A Guide to Best Practice* Wiley (7 December 1999)

Col Apurva Kumar Bardalai *Changing Security Scenario: Implications for UN Peace Making Knowledge;* World International (1 December, 2006)

Volker C Franke *Security in a Changing World, Case Studies in U S National Security Management;* Praeger (30 March 2002)

Seumas Miller *Terrorism and Counter Terrorism Ethics and Liberal Democracy;* Wiley-Blackwell (24 June 2008)

Audrey Kurth Cronin, James M Ludes *Attacking Terrorism Elements of a Grand Strategy;* Georgetown University Press (February 2004)

G Chatterjee *Effective Interrogation Naxalism-Police-Intelligence;* Manas Publications (30 January 2011)

Richard Bejtlich *Extrusion Detection Security Monitoring for Internal Intrusions;* Addison -Wesley Professional (18 November 2005)

P S Agarwal *Naxalism: Causes and Cure;* Manas Publications (30 April 2010)

R K Mishra *Operation Naxalism;* Yking Books (5 May 2011)

Stephen Dycus, Arthur L Berney, William C Banks, Peter Raven-Hansen *National Security Law*, Fifth Edition; Aspen Publishers (17 August 2011)

Brian J Cudahy *Cash, Tokens, & Transfers: A History of Urban Mass Transit in North America;* Fordham University Press (January 1, 1990)

John F Chown *A History of Money: From AD 800;* Routledge (1 February 1997)

Marc Flandreau, Owen Leeming (Translator) *The Glitter of Gold: France, Bimetallism, and the Emergence of the International Gold Standard, 1848-1873;* Oxford University Press, USA (6 May 2004)

Martin T Biegelman Fraud, Joel T Bartow *Prevention in Banking Industry – Scope for convergence*

Executive Roadmap to Fraud *Prevention and Internal Controls: Creating a Culture of Compliance*; First Edition, Wiley (20 January 2006)

Joseph T Wells *Principles of Fraud Examination;* Third Edition, Wiley

(28 December 2010)

Joseph T Wells *Corporate Fraud Handbook: Prevention and Detection*; 3 Edition, Wiley (3 May 2011)

Martin T Biegelman *Identity Theft Handbook: Detection, Prevention, and Security;* First Edition, Wiley (9 February 2009)

David Coderre *Computer Aided Fraud Prevention and Detection;* First Edition, A Step by Step Guide Wiley (23 March 2009)

David A Montague (Author) *Essentials of Online payment Security and Fraud Prevention (Essentials Series)*; First Edition, Wiley (November 9, 2010)

Zabihollah Rezaee, Richard Riley *Financial Statement Fraud: Prevention and Detection;* Second Edition, Wiley (28 September 2009)

Daniel M Fox *The Convergence of Science and Governance: Research, Health Policy;* First Edition, and American States University of California Press (17 February 2010)

William J Baumol, Richard R Nelson, Edward N Wolff *Convergence of Productivity: Cross-National Studies and Historical Evidence;* Oxford University Press, USA (30 June 1994)

Susan J Drucker, Gary Gumpert *Regulating Convergence;* First Edition Peter Lang Publishing (8 September 2010)

Stella M Nkomo, Myron D Fottler, R Bruce McAfee *Human Resource Management Applications;* Seventh Edition, South-Western College Publication (September 29, 2010)

Stella M Nkomo, Myron D Fottler, R Bruce McAfee *Human Resource Management Applications;* Cases, Exercises, Incidents, and Skill Builders South-Western College Pub, Sixth Edition (17 April 2007)

Ashly Pinnington, Rob Macklin, Tom Campbell *Human Resource Management;* Ethics and Employment Oxford University Press, USA (29 March 2007)

David Lacey *Managing the Human Factor in Information Security;* First Edition, Wiley (17 March 2009)

Robert L Mathis, John H Jackson *Human Resource Management;* Twelfth Edition, South-Western College Pubication (11 September 2007)

Bill Ballad, Tricia Ballad, Erin Banks *Access Control, Authentication, and*

Public Key Infrastructure (Information Systems Security & Assurance) Jones & Bartlett Learning (10 September 2010)

Charles Cresson Wood, Information Shield *Information Security Policies Made Easy;* Version 10 Information Shield (1 February 2008)

Leif Ekstrom *The Bank Secrecy Act: Information Sharing and Security Efforts;* Nova Science Pubication Inc (15 June 2010)

Marjie T Britz *Computer Forensics and Cyber Crime;* Second Edition, Prentice Hall (17 October 2008)

Felicia Donovan, Kristyn Bernier *Cyber Crime Fighters: Tales from the Trenches Que;* First Edition (14 December 2008)

K Jaishankar *Cyber Criminology: Exploring Internet Crimes and Criminal Behavior;* First Edition, CRC Press (22 February 2011)

Edward Amoroso *Cyber Security* Silicon (27 September 2006)

Jody R Westby *International Guide to Cyber Security;* American Bar Association (12 January 2005)

Franklin D Kramer, Stuart H Starr, Larry Wentz *Cyberpower and National Security*; First Edition, Potomac Books Inc. (30 April 2009)

Robert D Austin *Measuring and Managing Performance in Organizations* Dorset House (June 1996)

Herman Aguinis *Performance Management;* Second Edition, Prentice Hall (27 January 2008)

Aubrey C Daniels, James E Daniels *Performance Management Changing Behavior that Drives Organizational Effectiveness,* Fourth Edition; Performance Management Publications (July 2004)

Robert Bacal *Performance Management;* McGraw-Hill (30 November 1998)

Gary Cokins *Performance Management: First Edition, Integrating Strategy Execution, Methodologies, Risk and Analytics;* Wiley (6 April 2009)

Bob Paladino *Five Key Principles of Corporate Performance Management;* Wiley (22 January 2007)

Angela Costabile, Barbara A Spears *The Impact of Technology on Relationships in Educational Settings Routledge;* (19 March 2012)

Anne Bruce, James S Pepitone *Motivating Employees;* McGraw-Hill (1 (October 1998)

Barry Silverstein *Best Practices, Motivating Employees: Bringing Out the Best in Your People;* Harper Paperbacks (3 April 2007)

Barbara Glanz *Handle With CARE: Motivating and Retaining Employees* McGraw-Hill (19 June 2002)

John Adair *Effective Motivation: How to Get Extraordinary Results from Everyone* (Effective Series) Macmillan UK (1 May 2002)

William F Baker, Michael O'Malley Ph D *Leading with Kindness: How Good People Consistently Get Superior Results;* AMACOM (13 August 2008)

Morten Hansen *Collaboration: How Leaders Avoid the Traps, Create Unity, and Reap Big Results;* Harvard Business School Press (11 May 2009)

Jack Wiley , Brenda Kowske *Respect: Delivering Results by Giving Employees What They Really Want;* Pfeiffer (18 October 2011)

Lee Colan *Engaging the Hearts and Minds of All Your Employees: How to Ignite Passionate Performance for Better Business Results;* McGraw-Hill (August 15, 2008)

Aleks Srbinoski *Motivation Now: Productivity and Persuasion Secrets for Modern Day Excellence and Effectiveness (Success Secrets Series),* First Edition Fulfilling Happiness (26 August 2011)

Roger Matthews *Armed Robbery;* Willan (1 April 2002)

Robin Geiss, Anna Petrig *Piracy and Armed Robbery at Sea: The Legal Framework for Counter-Piracy Operations in Somalia and the Gulf of Aden* Oxford University Press, USA (15 April 2011)

Terry Smith *The Art of Armed Robbery: The True Story of Britain's Most Infamous Armed Robber;* John Blake (1 July 2005)

John Marshall MacDonald *Armed Robbery: Offenders and their Victims* Charles C Thomas Pub Ltd (June 1975)

Harold S Long *Successful Armed Robbery Loompanics Unlimited;* (February 1990)

Louis William Rogers *Self Development and the Way to Power*; Nabu Press (22 February 2010)

David B Peterson, Mary Dee Hicks *Development First: Strategies for Self-Development Personnel Decisions Intl*; First Edition (June 1995)

Steve Pavlina *Personal Development for Smart People: The Conscious Pursuit* *of Personal Growth;* Hay House (15 October 2009)

Karl Moore *The Secret Art of Self-Development: 16 little-known rules for eternal happiness & freedom* [Kindle Edition]

Joseph J Luciani *The Power of Self-Coaching The Five Essential Steps to Creating the Life You Want,* First Edition; Wiley(4 August 2004)

Louise Richardson *What Terrorists Want: Understanding the Enemy, Containing the Threat;* Random House Trade Paperbacks (13 November 2007)

Bruce Hoffman *Inside Terrorism;* Revised & Enlarged Edition, Columbia University Press (30 May 2006)

Jennifer L Merolla, Elizabeth J Zechmeister *Democracy at Risk: How Terrorist Threats Affect the Public;* First Edition, University of Chicago Press(1 October 2009)

Roger Scruton *The West and the Rest:* Globalization and the Terrorist Threat Intercollegiate Studies Institute (September 2002)

Michael Arena, Bruce Arrigo *The Terrorist Identity: Explaining the Terrorist Threat;* NYU Press (1 November 2006)

Kim Cragin *The Dynamic Terrorist Threat;* An Assessment of Group Motivations and Capabilities in a Changing World Rand Publishing (23 April 2004)

George B Tremmel *Counterfeit Currency of the Confederate States of America McFarland & Company;* (4 February 2003)

George B Tremmel *A Guide Book of Counterfeit Confederate Currency;* First Edition, Whitman Publishing (2007)

John Cooley *Currency Wars: How Forged Money is the New Weapon of Mass Destruction;* Skyhorse Publishing (1 May 2008)

Stephen Mihm *A Nation of Counterfeiters: Capitalists, Con Men, and the Making of the United States;* Harvard University Press (1 May 2009)

Klaus W. Bender *Moneymakers the Secret World of Banknote Printing* Wiley-VCH (16 May 2006)

Kelly T Tian, Bill Keep *Customer Fraud and Business Responses Let the Marketer Beware;* Praeger (30 December 2001)

W Steve Albrecht, Chad O Albrecht, Conan C Albrecht, Mark F Zimbelman *Fraud Examination;* Fourth Edition; South-Western College Pub

(2 February 2011)

Tommie W Singleton, Aaron J Singleton *Fraud Auditing and Forensic Accounting;* Fourth Edition, Wiley (7 September 2010)

Gerald L Kovacich CFE CPP CISSP *Fighting Fraud How to Establish and Manage an Anti-Fraud Program;* Butterworth-Heinemann (10 September 2007)

David Coderre *Computer Aided Fraud Prevention and Detection;* First Edition, Wiley (23 March 2009)

David L Goetsch, Stanley Davis *Quality Management for Organizational Excellence;* Sixth Edition (9 January 2009)

James R Evans *Total Quality: Management, Organization and Strategy;* Forth Edition, South-Western College Pub (1 November 2004)

Dale H Besterfield, Carol Besterfield-Michna, Glen Besterfield, Mary Besterfield-Sacre *Total Quality Management;* Third Edition, Prentice Hall; (28 October 2002)

Stephen George, Arnold Weimerskirch *Total Quality Management: Strategies and Techniques Proven at Today's Most Successful Companies;* Second Edition, Wiley (February 1998)

Paul F Wilson, Larry D Dell, Gaylord F Anderson *Root Cause Analysis, A Tool for Total Quality Management(H0701),* First Edition; Amer Society for Quality (September 1993)

Joseph A. Dobson *Training Guard and Protection Dogs;* Pocket Books (April 1984)

Michael Volkin The Ultimate Basic Training Guidebook: *Tips, Tricks, and Tactics for Surviving Boot Camp Savas Beatie;* Secomd Edition (April 2007)

Sgt Michael Volkin Ultimate Interactive Basic Training Workbook: *What You Must Know to Survive and Thrive in Boot Camp* Savas Beatie (September 2007)

Nicholas Van Wormer The Ultimate Air Force Basic Training Guidebook: *Tips, Tricks, and Tactics for Surviving Boot Camp;* Savas Beatie (November 2010)

About The Author

An internationally acclaimed trainer in the field of Security and Loss Prevention Management and Investigation, **Ravindra Kishore Sinha** founded the Security and Intelligence Services (India) Limited, popularly known as SIS, in 1974. A graduate of Political Science and Law, Sinha started his career as a journalist specializing in crime and political reporting. He is recognized as one of the most successful investigative journalist of his time. He also covered India-Pakistan war of 1971 in the Khulna-Khustia-Isardih sector. Having witnessed the student movement of Bihar, led by Loknayak Jai Prakash Narayan (1974-1975), he wrote a well-researched book titled *Janandolan*. Sinha's jest for learning took him far and wide. As a private security professional, he visited almost all states of the United States of America, Europe and China.

His professional expertise and excellent training skills helped him hold many professional offices like the Regional Vice President of

World Safety Organisation for South Asia (1989-1991); President, National Institute of Security Professional of India (1990-1995); Area Governor of Association of Security Organisation of India (1988-2001); Chapter Chairman, ASIS, for India Sub Continent Chapter (1990-2000), Executive Chairman and founder President and Director General of International Institute of Security and Safety Management and Founder Chairman of the Central Association for the Private Security Industry of India and Security Skills Council of India. Under his leadership, IISSM has in the past two decades become a truly representative body of security and fire services users, providers, manufacturers and consultants.

During the NDA Government (1999-2004), Sinha was the Security Advisor to the Ministery of HRD, Science & Technology and Ocean Development, Government of India, looking after security concerns of seven ministries and more than 50 sensitive national level research laboratories. He has also been instrumental in the making of the Private Security Agencies Regulation Act (which was enacted in 2005) in the early 1990s when S B Chavan was the Minister for Home Affairs.

A man of many hues, Sinha is the Founder Chairman of Indian Public School, one of the best boarding schools of Dehradun-Mussorie Valley.

He is also Chairman of Rituraj Resorts Limited besides being actively associated with several social and charitable organisations.

Sinha was in the news recently for first ever PE Fund investment in Security Industry when US second largest PE Fund DESCO picked up 14 per cent stakes in SIS. Sinha also became the owner of the largest Security Services Provider with SIS buying Chubb Security Guarding Company of Australia, a 100-year old market leader with a total annual sales of over Rs 2000 crore (US$ 500 million).